DUBLIN
as a
WORK *of* ART

for Martine

DUBLIN
as a
WORK *of* ART

COLM LINCOLN

photographs
ALAN O'CONNOR

THE O'BRIEN PRESS
DUBLIN

FIRST PUBLISHED 1992 BY THE O'BRIEN PRESS LTD.
20 VICTORIA ROAD, DUBLIN 6, IRELAND.

BRITISH LIBRARY CATALOGUING-IN-PUBLICATION DATA
LINCOLN, COLM,
DUBLIN AS A WORK OF ART
I. TITLE
720.941835
ISBN0-86278-313-5

10   9   8   7   6   5   4   3   2   1

THE O'BRIEN PRESS RECEIVES ASSISTANCE FROM THE ARTS COUNCIL /
AN CHOMHAIRLE EALAÍON.

TYPESETTING, LAYOUT AND DESIGN: THE O'BRIEN PRESS
COVER DESIGN: ALAN O'CONNOR AND MICHAEL O'BRIEN
SEPARATIONS: THE CITY OFFICE, DUBLIN
PRINTING: BUTLER AND TANNER LTD., SOMERSET, ENGLAND

FRONT COVER PHOTOGRAPH: THE CUSTOM HOUSE
BACK COVER: DETAIL OF THE DOME AT THE FOUR COURTS
INSIDE FLAP: STREET SCENE, KILDARE STREET
PAGE 1: GRAFTON STREET
PAGE 2: DETAIL, CHAPEL, ROTUNDA HOSPITAL

CONTENTS

Author: Colm Lincoln

Photographer: Alan O'Connor

Foreword

The city is both natural object and a thing to be cultivated;
individual and group; something lived and something dreamed;
it is the human invention par excellence

CLAUDE LÉVI-STRAUSS

When asked some years ago to write a Dublin guide I thought that it would be a relatively easy task or, at least, straightforward. However, as I soon discovered, there is nothing at all straightforward about a guide, for rarely have history or architecture evolved in a neat topographical order. Indeed architecture, which is what guides traditionally deal with, only tells part of the story, for a city is more than the sum of its buildings or of its individual inhabitants. What interested me was that each of the individual buildings and spaces has its own distinct history while, at the same time, they come together to create something larger; an urban picture which, however stubbornly it may resist a schematic ordering, still has an independent logic and validity of its own. I wanted to get to grips with the wider picture as well as its more significant details and, if possible, to see what together they might reveal about the priorities – or lack of them – of the people who gave us today's Dublin. The quest may not always have been successful but as Milan Kundera once said, 'to be a writer does not mean to preach a truth, it means to *discover* a truth'. In much the same spirit I have attempted to discover Dublin, for what we see and the urban culture that it represents, is one of the great truths of Irish life, though one that is not always acknowledged.

In an early short story Samuel Beckett recalls looking at a picture in the National Gallery – or at least trying to – for the painting, 'owing to the glittering vitrine behind which the canvas cowers, can only be apprehended in sections'. The way we approach any work of art makes a difference to it and none more so than a city. A guide, of its nature, can only apprehend elements of the total picture but, within that constraint, I have attempted to structure this work so that the individual descriptions can be considered independently and yet read together. If, in the case of Beckett's canvas, 'patience ... and a retentive memory' allowed him 'to elicit a total statement approximating to the intention of the painter', presumption and a reliance on the research of others have allowed me to construct this topographical odyssey so that, taken together, its three chapters might approximate to a visual narrative of how Dublin came to be what it is today. The area of exploration is defined by the city's two principal axes – the quays running west to east and the O'Connell Street-Grafton Street axis running north to south – for it is these, I believe, which account for Dublin's urban form and demonstrate its importance as a showcase for some of the finest buildings in Europe. Other areas of the city are no less interesting in what they may tell us but they are not dealt with here, if for no other reason than there has to be some limit to my publisher's patience.

Apart from my publisher there are others on whose patience I have presumed and on whose work I have greatly relied, as is evident from my references. I would like to acknowledge a particular debt to Maurice Craig's delightful masterpiece, *Dublin 1660-1860*, Frank McDonald's innumerable articles in the *Irish Times* and Edward McParland's various works (most notably on the Wide Streets Commissioners and James Gandon) whose erudition I could never hope to match. I would also like to thank Michael Cronin, Helena Doddy, Colm Gallagher, Brian Kennedy, Edward McParland and Tyrella Nash for their help and encouragement, and the staff of the Irish Architectural Archive and of the Berkeley Library at Trinity College for their assistance and cooperation.

It is with great pleasure that I acknowledge the magnificent contribution of the National Library and its director, Pat Donlon. If the library has proven to be a rich treasure trove which I have raided happily over the years, it must be said that its staff have always shown great kindness and, indeed, enthusiasm in aiding and abetting both myself and countless other readers in their nefarious researches. In the case of this book the library not alone provided much of the research material but, most evident of all, the great majority of the photographs. These were specially commissioned from Alan O'Connor, as part of the library's policy of building up a contemporary photographic collection which can be used by researchers in years to come. All of the illustrations, apart from those mentioned below, come from what is now the Alan O'Connor Collection. Their quality tells of the enthusiasm and ability which Alan brought to the project.

I would like to thank the following for permission to use photographs from their collections: Dublin Corporation (and, in particular, the city archivist, Mary Clarke) for material from the Wide Streets Commissioners pp.20, 131, 132, 215; the British Library p.64; the Irish Architectural Archive pp. 2 and 71 (David Davison), 32, 80, 81, 156; the National Library of Ireland for prints from the *Irish Builder* pp. 23, 68, 125, and the Lawrence Collection p.67.

A special acknowledgement is due to Nicolas, Guillaume and Niamh, for having put up with their father's book for so long. Above all, I must thank my wife Martine for it is she who bore the brunt of my involvement and yet continued to provide encouragement; and encouragement was needed in persevering with a project that at times seemed perilously close to never achieving fruition. It is to her – and in fond memory of our years in Dublin – that I dedicate this book.

The Bank of Ireland, College Green.

INTRODUCTION

Dublin as a Work of Art may seem provocative as a title. To some degree I hope it is, for, despite all the evident devastation, Dublin deserves to be looked at afresh. There is more to the city than many of us may imagine. Moreover, the fact remains that Dublin was at one time a showpiece capital, laid out and developed on premises that were largely aesthetic and, despite the vagaries of fortune, the grand ambition of those years has fixed the pattern of the city that we know and see.

The title also makes reference to Donald J. Olsen's *The City as a Work of Art*,[1] for though the nature of this exploration is entirely different, it is my belief that Dublin is certainly as fruitful a field of study as were the cities of Olsen's choice: London, Paris and Vienna. However, in the nineteenth century when those cities attempted to turn themselves into monuments, Dublin was in decline – the exception to the rule, a case apart in the urban history of western Europe. Whereas London, Paris and Vienna are now cities of world renown, whose monumental imagery has taken on a reality of its own – where we can effortlessly bring to mind that litany of sights that must be seen – Dublin exists in quite a different category. Indeed, despite the peregrinations of Mr Bloom, it is not the place as such which occupies the imagination for, if Dublin features, it features as a half-remembered backdrop where others of more significance have passed through.

If Dublin exists as a city of the imagination it exists as a literary image and, most crucially, as an image bequeathed by those who have left. The sorry sagas of some of the departed luminaries have not necessarily been to the city's credit. Shaw complained that he was unable to identify any 'seed of culture' that was essentially native; O'Casey felt that to remain 'would become embarrassing to me' as all Dublin's streets 'led into the same square where everyone met, where hands were shaken, shoulders clapped and drinks taken to everyone's health.' One man's poison may, of course, be another man's meat. That very intimacy which O'Casey complained of is a quality which appeals to others. Shaw, it should be said, loved his city sufficiently to leave a generous bequest to the National Gallery in Merrion Square. But the point I wish to make is that the Dublin at issue here is not just the city which has been bequeathed to literature, but a bricks-and-mortar Dublin which is just as intriguing.

Yet, however intriguing it may be, it must be admitted that there are few Dubliners – or indeed, other Irish people – who would think of the city's brick and mortar as a work of art. Indeed, one fictionalised emigrant (on returning to a city which he found 'pretty awful ... Everything has gotten old and grey and dirty – apart from what was new, vulgar and shoddily flash') was stung into

At Christchurch Cathedral.

remembering that 'people born blind who recover their sight in later years often become depressed by the sheer ugliness of the world.' Like the hero of Michael O'Loughlin's short story, many of us on returning to Dublin can be depressed by 'its wretchedness, its wrecked buildings and blasted centre.'[2]

However, the feeling is 'pretty awful', not just because it is unpleasant to encounter poverty and dereliction, but because there is a sense of personal loss. This is perhaps only to be expected, for, as has been suggested by the architectural theorist Aldo Rossi, 'the city itself is the collective memory of its people, and like memory it is associated with objects and places. The city is the *locus* of the collective memory.'[3] Indeed, 'there is *something in the nature of urban artifacts that renders them very similar – and not only metaphorically – to a work of art.* They are material constructions, but not withstanding the material, something different: although they are conditioned, they also condition.'[4] Saying much the same, just over a half-century ago, Lewis Mumford claimed about the city that, 'with language itself, it remains man's greatest work of art'.[5] For all the importance of theatre and literature, music and cinema, it is the built environment which has the most profound and inescapable effect on us.

However, if as Rossi suggests, the relationship between the city and its citizens evolves, it is not so much an evolution as a deterioration that has been evident in Dublin and, in particular, a deterioration in the very idea of the city

Exchange Street, named for its proximity to the former Royal Exchange.

and our image of it. For all its importance, Irish people seem to find it hard to accept that the urban environment – and Dublin in particular – is a crucial part of the country's cultural heritage. A standard work on the cultural history of modern Ireland by Terence Brown gives scarcely a dozen lines to architecture and planning.[6] Richard Kearney's challenging exploration of narratives in modern Irish culture uses all the weaponry of contemporary European thought to argue the case for cultural diversity against the idea of a single all-absorbing national culture; yet, despite the breadth of the exploration and his belief in the importance of the interaction between Ireland and the broader world, the built environment (which gives ample example of such interaction) does not feature at all.[7]

If Dublin features in contemporary writing, it almost invariably features as 'a broken, spent, desolate place'.[8] Perhaps Dublin can find some consolation in the realisation that cities as such have rarely enjoyed a good press. If we have learnt from Virgil that a man's high deed is to found a city, we have also learnt from countless others of its rapid fall from grace. Lamentations on the evils of city life are nothing new, 'from Juvenal to Cobbet, from Saint Augustine to Jefferson, poets and moralists, publicists and philosophers have subjected the

The Wapshot Chronical play in the Attic, Burgh Quay.

city to righteous abuse. ... Yet with rare exceptions, such as Ireland before the Viking invasions, the civilisations of the past have regarded cities as neither shameful nor inevitable, but as deliberate creations, worth making sacrifices to build, maintain and embellish.'[9] The quote comes from Olsen who, in what is perhaps his only reference to Ireland, may have tumbled on something which partly accounts for Irish attitudes to urban culture, namely some half-remembered notions concerning a pre-urban past.

Irish ideology owes much to historiography and in particular to the nineteenth-century view of history as an unfolding epic, a progress from barbarity to civilisation or, in the Irish variant, from centuries of foreign oppression to the rediscovery of an idealised Gaelic Ireland. Whatever about the very real merits of Gaelic civilisation, the preoccupations of many who professed to be its advocates have been professedly rural, with little time for urban culture or the foreignness with which they associated it. (Curiously they took no heed of the fact that for most of its history, Dublin has had a significant Irish-speaking population.)[10] Dublin, in this unfortunate recreation of Irish history, was hardly Irish at all; a foreign stronghold founded by the Vikings, consolidated by the Normans and transformed into an Augustan capital – to use Louis MacNeice's term – by the Anglo-Irish. That anywhere else in Ireland was as likely to share a similar racial mix seems to have been beside the point.

The reality of course has been more mundane. Ireland like anywhere else needs a capital, but the idea that it was somehow less Irish, not meriting pride or embellishment, had insidiously taken root in the prevailing orthodoxy for much of this century. Worse, those very elements which give Dublin a genuine claim to international importance – namely the remaining Georgian city – would, until recent years, have failed the litmus test of political respectability. Irrespective of any indifferences to urban values in general, the destruction of the Georgian city could be (and on occasion was) presented in a positive light, as representing the eradication of an alien colonial culture. The irony, of course, is that the society which gave eighteenth-century Dublin some of the grandest public buildings of any capital in Europe did so, in part, because of its pride in having forced the government in London to hand over legislative independence in internal matters to the Parliament in Dublin.

For whatever reason, the urban culture through which eighteenth-century society boasted its Irishness had gone by the time this century had got underway, to be replaced by the idea that the urban world was not fully Irish at all. Indeed, unlike other capitals which give a lead to civic society, Dublin in this century has seen a reversal of roles, for, while the political and administrative structures for running the country are based in the capital, they have often seemed little concerned with it. Perhaps the long and demoralising decades of

Skateboarding on the podium of the Berkeley Library, Trinity College.

nineteenth-century decay had taken their toll: if the ideologues of the new Ireland dreamt of a future based on rural values they are in part to be excused, for the appalling poverty which characterised Dublin life in the early twentieth century was not an inspiring prospect. Indeed, the poverty still remains, though many of those who peopled O'Casey's tenements are now a diaspora marginalised in housing estates on the city's fringes.

And yet Dublin has known better; its history is the history of cities and urban life in Ireland and its achievements are the achievements of a multifaceted culture. You can see this achievement in the Georgian streets and stunning public buildings of a society who believed that to be Irish was to be both urban and international. You can see it in the great churches which were built after Catholic emancipation as proud and cultured testimonials to the survival of a persecuted faith. And this century too has had its achievements, though buildings such as Busáras have at times – like so many great twentieth-century buildings elsewhere – shown scant regard for their setting.

If, for some, it is the failures that are all too evident, it must be recognised that the greatest failure has been an intellectual one, for, while politics in the narrow sense has held an honoured place in the Irish revolutionary agenda, there has not been any real development of the idea of how the city might be a liberating and invigorating force in Irish life. Those who concerned themselves

Along the quays.

with planning – such as the 'garden suburb' advocates in the years before the First World War – carried no real weight in the newly independent Ireland and what influence they had only seemed to undermine the very idea of the city. Then and since, Dublin has been much influenced by the views of the leading lights in Anglo-American planning, the result being a manifest disregard for what has been happening elsewhere in Europe and a glaring a-historicism. As for the architects, during the forties, fifties and sixties, not only were they not interested in the history of architecture, but those nurtured in the modern movement were philosophically opposed to the very idea of its importance. The reappraisal of the modern movement has at last led to a revival of interest in history and many architects and planners are now showing a new awareness of the historical process of which they are inextricably part.

However, not only do the planners and architects need to know where they have got to and why, but so do we all. As the schoolmaster in Brian Friel's play *Translations* reminds us, 'it is not the literal past, the "facts" of history, that shape us, but images of the past'; and he went on to say, 'we must never cease renewing those images; because once we do, we fossilise.' [11] This book makes a tentative attempt at exploring how we constructed some of those images. If the result is personal and fractured, I nonetheless hope that it may encourage others to renew their contact with Dublin, as an understanding of this great city is intrinsic to any understanding of Irish culture. If it is the case, as Dermot Bolger has so rightly said, that 'a city by its nature is comprised of migrants and the children and grandchildren of migrants,' then 'Dublin – like the country it is capital of – has a blessedly bastardised population.'[12] We should all therefore consider this capital as our birthright and find in it an eloquent expression of our Irishness.

The Quays

THE QUAYS

'Soft morning, city! Lsp! I am leafy speafing'
The Liffey greeting Dublin in

FINNEGANS WAKE

Despite the renown of Dublin's remaining Georgian streets and squares – and the importance of many of its individual public buildings – it is the quays which are the city's most important landmark, flanking the Liffey on the final stage of its journey to the Irish Sea. It was the river and its quays which determined the development of the city, beginning, in the early tenth century, with a Viking earthen bank at Wood Quay. From there the medieval city expanded along a ridge of high ground, protected by the Liffey to the north and the valley of the Poddle to the south. While the Liffey was joined by a number of tributaries as it stole sluggishly seaward, it was the Poddle which was the most significant, not least because it was from the sheltered black pool or *dubh linn* where the Poddle met the Liffey that the city got its English name.

Above: Original elevation for numbers 1-3, Inns' Quay by Patrick Byrne.
Previous page: Along the quays at Bachelor's Walk – bargains still to be found.

The city's Irish name, Baile Atha Cliath, comes from a different source – the Ford of the Hurdles, the *áth cliath*, which was located just a short distance upstream from Wood Quay. This was the crossing place for the great road from the north and remained so until the city's first bridge was built on the site of the present Father Mathew Bridge (more commonly known as Church Street Bridge). It was built by King John around 1215 and may have replaced an earlier structure, the Droichet Dubhgall. When it was swept away by a flood in 1385, the Dominicans replaced the original Norman structure with a toll bridge which survived until 1802, when it too fell victim to a lightning flood (the river was only finally tamed when hydro-electric works were built at Poulaphouca and Leixlip in the early 1950s).

For almost four hundred years, the Bridge of Dublin was the only bridge connecting the walled city with the suburb of Oxmantown, north of the river. However, in a spurt of accelerated development between 1670 and 1684, four new bridges were built: Bloody Bridge (now Rory O'Moore) in 1670, Essex Bridge (now Grattan) in 1678, Ormond Bridge (now gone) and Arran Bridge (now Liam Mellowes) in 1684. At the same time the quays began their bold advance seaward. A Ballast Board was created in 1707 to formulate plans for dredging a proper channel and, four years later, work began on the strand wall which became known as the North Wall. By the 1730s a river and seawall stretched from Bachelor's Walk as far as today's East Link toll bridge (though much of the area behind it was to remain subject to tidal flooding for generations) and, to the south, an equally extensive stretch of former estuary was walled in by Sir John Rogerson. The Liffey, with its long line of quays, has been central to the development of Dublin. It was to the quays that maritime trade came and the battle over its displacement – as bridge construction shoved port activity relentlessly further downstream – resulted in some of the city's important characteristics: a sequence of cross-river axes and a long and distinctive river front punctuated by a display of great monumental architecture. For an understanding of how this relationship evolved, where better to begin than Capel Street Bridge.

Dublin as seen from Grattan Bridge

Grattan Bridge (previously called Essex Bridge, but known colloquially as Capel Street Bridge). The existence of this seemingly inauspicious structure is crucial to the development of the city as it decisively pushed beyond its medieval confines in the late seventeenth century. This is the period associated with the return of Charles II to the throne and, in the case of Dublin, with the arrival of a new viceroy, James, Duke of Ormond. He landed at Dublin Bay in the summer of 1602, to be joyously welcomed to the refrain of '*Thugamar féin an samhradh linn'* (we brought the summer with us).[1] Ormond was a cosmopolitan figure, who returned from the splendour of continental Europe to an impoverished capital of less than 9,000 inhabitants. By 1700 the population had grown to an estimated 70,000 as the city experienced a period of unprecedented growth. If Ormond has been credited as being the inspiration for much of what took place – in particular with the encouragement of open quays along the Liffey – it was Dublin Corporation, along with some notable private developers, who actually initiated the most crucial developments. The Corporation made the first move when they decided in 1664 to transform the former common at St Stephen's Green into a residential square chiefly for the reputation, advantage, ornament and pleasure of the city'.[2] A year later they divided up Oxmantown Green, on the north west of the Liffey, into lots for development, presenting seven acres to the Duke of Ormond in the hope that he might build a residence there; but he never did. Finally, along the Liffey, where the area between high and low water marks belonged to the municipality, they also began to lease out major stretches of ground for development.

What turned out to be the most contentious development was a private initiative connected with the building of Essex Bridge. The lowest crossing point on the Liffey was still 'the Bridge of Dublin' (at what is now Church Street), and the land which lay below it, across from the medieval city, had once belonged to St Mary's Abbey. Before being dissolved by Henry VIII, this was the wealthiest abbey in the country. In 1674 a group of developers, led by Sir Humphrey Jervis, bought up a portion of the former abbey, directly across the river from Dublin Castle (the abbey property had passed through a number of hands by this stage). A year later, in Easter 1675, the stretch of ground along the nearby river edge (now Ormond Quay and Bachelor's Walk) was leased to a junior clerk in the Corporation, Jonathan Armory, for a period of 299 years at an annual rent of fifty shillings sterling plus 'a couple of fatt [sic] capons, or five shillings sterling, in lieu thereof, every Christmas to the Lord Mayor'.[3] Jervis, who was one of the two city sheriffs, seems to have financed the Armory purchase and was probably able to use his official position in favour of the grant. Whatever the exact arrangement, Armory disappeared from the scene a year after the grant was issued and his beneficial interest in the property was taken over by none other than Humphrey Jervis.

The fact that Jervis was developing land on the far side of the river from the medieval city was in itself uncontentious; what was contentious was his proposal to link his new development directly to the old city by building a bridge. In one stroke the Corporation's distant development at Oxmantown was upstaged, not to mention its impact on property owners with wharfage and warehousing upstream of the new bridge. Sir Humphrey's opponents alleged

The old Custom House and Essex (Capel Street) Bridge, 1706.

that he promised the Viceroy, Lord Essex, that he would name the new bridge in his honour and decorate it with the Essex arms if the viceroy supported his scheme; doubtless he did. In any event, Essex directed that part of the proceeds of the Dublin customs should be set aside to fund its construction and when, after various tribulations, the bridge was completed in 1678, it was called after Essex, and the principal street leading to it became Capel Street – Capel being the Essex family name. Essex Bridge transformed the city, for it created something entirely new, a north-south axis running along Capel Street and crossing the river, from where a jumble of narrow lanes led uphill to Dublin Castle. A new suburb based on a rectilinear pattern of streets was developed along the Capel Street axis, which successfully vied with the Corporation's own developments in both St Stephen's Green and Oxmantown Green. Despite the protracted in-fighting, Sir Humphrey was eventually to triumph – though jailed in 1685 – for he was twice elected Lord Mayor (1681 and 1682), was knighted and, to crown his success, succeeded in having the official venue of the city markets moved north of the river onto his development where it became the Ormond Market (it survived until about 1890 and its place is now occupied by Ormond Square). He died in 1708.

The original stone bridge, Essex Bridge (1678), was quite narrow and the traffic conditions leading to it became so chaotic that the Lord Mayor had to issue traffic regulations. These apparently were 'attended with such good effects' that it was decided in 1748 'to make the regulation more extensive' and require 'all drivers of public carriages to keep the gutters, or the middle of the streets through which they pass, on their left' (the general requirement to drive on the left was introduced only in the 1840s).[4] As the principal bridge in the city

– at least until Sackville Bridge (O'Connell Bridge) was built in the 1790s – Essex Bridge was chosen as a location for an equestrian statue of the monarch. Given its narrowness, a special island-like structure was built on the bridge's upstream side, where the statue of George I (by John Van Nost, the elder) was unveiled on 1 August 1722. It was removed after the bridge collapsed due to flooding in 1751.

To ensure that the piers of the new Essex Bridge would not be washed away as before, the designer George Semple used cofferdams to get down to the rock foundation. The new structure (1753-55) was modelled on London's Westminster Bridge (1739-48) which had become one of the great engineering references of the period. Based on this experience, Semple published one of the first Irish textbooks on civil engineering, *A Treatise on Building in Water* (1776). Semple also envisaged a new street which was to terminate in a colonnaded square in front of Dublin Castle and it was there that he proposed to relocate Van Nost's statue of George I. As the plan for the square came to nought the statue was never properly relocated. William Makepeace Thackeray spotted it years later 'peering over a paling' in the Mansion House grounds. In the 1920s it was put up for sale and, unloved and unwanted, it was eventually sold (minus one leg) to the Barber Institute of Fine Art in Birmingham in 1937.[5] The bridge itself was remodelled and renamed in honour of Henry Grattan in 1874.

The Wide Streets Commissioners. If the Corporation's initiative at Oxmantown Green was upstaged by Sir Humphrey Jervis with the building of Essex Bridge, it was to have a sequel, some eighty years later, when the Corporation's attempt to improve the link between the bridge and the Castle was upstaged by Parliament. The first known attempts at street widening were made during the reign of Charles I when the Earl of Strafford proposed widening the approach to Dublin Castle by removing portions of the buildings on Cork Hill (the street which runs round two sides of today's City Hall). This scheme got nowhere and it wasn't until 1710 that the next effort was made, when Queen Anne agreed that £3,000 could be made available for much the same project. These improvements seem to have been relatively minor, and up until the opening of Parliament Street, traffic coming from north of the river (across Capel Street Bridge) had to make its way to the Castle along the narrow Crane Lane or else by Upper Exchange Street. Once on Cork Hill, the traffic wound its way up to the entrance of the Castle and either entered or continued westward along Castle Street to get to High Street and Christchurch. (Until Lord Edward Street was opened in the late nineteenth century, Castle Street was the main artery linking Dame Street and Cork Hill with Christchurch and the rest of the old city.)

Parliament Street. Despite its name the initiative to open Parliament Street came not from Parliament but from the merchant oligarchy who ran the Corporation. Stimulated by the improvements being made by their counterparts in

London, Dublin Corporation commissioned George Semple in 1751 to recon-
struct Essex Bridge which had collapsed due to flooding. Semple went to
London not only to examine the recently completed Westminster Bridge but also
to 'find out the methods which were at that time in agitation, for opening up
streets in London and Westminster'.[6] The result therefore was not just a new
bridge but also a plan for a street which would cut through the tangle of
medieval lanes and terminate in a colonnaded square in front of the castle.[7] The
Corporation lobbied Parliament for the necessary legislation and it was in
response to this that the Irish House of Commons approved the famous plan of
1758 'for making a wide and convenient way, street or passage from Essex
Bridge to the Castle of Dublin'.[8] It took a further Act of Parliament in 1760 to
put the project on its feet and so, in 1762, the new fifty-one-foot wide Parliament
Street came into being.

The commissioners were given powers of compulsory purchase, the right to
assess property valuations (which were adjudged by special juries) and the duty
to compensate persons displaced by the clearance. However, while the owners
were compensated, the actual inhabitants being displaced did not fare so well.
In the case of Parliament Street, the commissioners' agent discovered that
though 'the money adjudged to their landlords had been paid' some of the
tenants 'who were lodgers or roomkeepers only ... conceived that they had a
right to continue'; worse, they intended to take out injunctions so that they could
at least stay on for another six months. 'Knowing well the prodigious delay such
suits would produce', the agent had as many workmen and labourers as he
could get 'unroof the several houses of those who were to file those bills; and ...
by eight o'clock in the morning the slates were totally stripped off, and several
of the inhabitants, men, women, and children, had run directly from their beds
into the streets; some of them, in their fright, conceiving (it being then wartime)
that the city had been taken by storm ... but I heard no more of the matter, save
that, for some time, it afforded excellent sport to the city'.[9] So much for the
unfortunate tenants.

While Parliament supported the opening up of the new street, it had no time
for such ambitious ideas as a colonnaded square in front of the Castle or, indeed,
for the suggestion by some merchants that a site be provided for an exchange
or for an extension to the Custom House, then located just downstream from
Essex Bridge. There were various reasons for this, not least being the fact that
the Corporation and Parliament represented different interests, the Corporation
being a merchant oligarchy with business interests in the old city, whereas
Parliament represented a landowning aristocracy whose townhouses were now
to be found in the developing downstream suburbs. But it was not just a
question of location that tempered Parliament's response, for, at this early stage,

the Wide Streets Commissioners were not at all concerned about the sort of ambitious town planning considerations with which they were to transform Dublin in later years – this new enthusiasm came only when their membership changed radically in the 1780s. Indeed, in the case of Parliament Street (where the legislation required that building leases be sold to ensure rebuilding of the cleared areas on either side of the new street) the commissioners restricted their aesthetic interest to simply regulating the building line and height of the new blocks, though there was a vague requirement that 'some posts or pillars to be before the doors'.[10]

Read's of Parliament Street. From the 1620s to the 1790s the old Custom House was located outside the city walls, on a site just downstream from Grattan Bridge (Essex/Capel Street Bridge). Before the opening of Essex Gate (1675) traffic between the Custom House and the city had therefore to make its way up the narrow Crane Lane to Cork Hill. As such, Crane Lane was a major thoroughfare and Read's Cutlers relocated there in 1750 – the shop had originally opened on Blind Quay (Lower Exchange Street) in 1670. When Parliament Street was created in the early 1760s, one of the first shops to open there was Read's, which the family did by simply changing the entrance of their shop so that the previous front in Crane Lane now became the rear. There is a framed licence from 1793 in the Parliament Street shop which permits the firm to sell swords and halberds. They also made knives, scissors, surgeons' scalpels and a variety of other blades, such as the world's smallest pair of working scissors – suitable, apparently, for cutting 'a house fly's whiskers'! – as well as the world's largest penknife with 576 blades. The last of the Reads to work there sold the premises in 1989, but fortunately the new owners continue the cutlery tradition and retain the glass-fronted display cabinets and other period fittings in what is now Dublin's oldest shop.[11]

The City Hall. If the great north axis which Sir Humphrey Jervis brought about with the opening of Essex Bridge in 1678 was completed by the opening of Parliament Street in 1762, it was to achieve its apogee with the building of this great monument in the 1770s. By then the city had spread decisively down the Liffey – with new aristocratic suburbs rivalling each other on either bank – and consequently the siting of the building was a matter of great debate. Indeed, not only was the building's architecture radically new for Ireland in the 1770s, its location – on a key site just within the confines of the old city – was equally surprising, given the direction in which Dublin was developing at that time. From the early 1760s, the merchants, conscious of the need for an exchange to meet the city's expanding commerce, but equally conscious of the Wide Streets Commissioners' lack of enthusiasm for such a project (especially if it was to be within the old city), appealed directly to the political executive in Dublin Castle for its support. Their lobbying was successful, for when the Wide Streets Commissioners (whose only interest in the old city was in improving access to the Castle) applied for more funds for this purpose in 1764, the Chief Secretary suggested that the two projects should be combined and an exchange built 'in that part of the new street in which it would be a termination of the view from Capel Street, Essex Bridge and Parliament Street'.[12] The commissioners were still not cooperative, giving a high estimate of the costs and pointing out that they had no powers which would allow them to actually erect a new building. It was only after further pressure from the Castle executive, from Dublin Corporation and eventually Parliament itself that the site was handed over to the Exchange Trustees for £4,000 in May 1768. Parliament granted an initial £13,500 to the project and the rest of the money was to come from subscriptions and lotteries. (When completed in 1779 the total bill came to £58,000.)

The merchants wanted a building that would be second to none and an open competition was announced in July 1768. The closing date was extended by a month to encourage English entries, for it was felt that these would be the most likely source of designs in the latest neoclassical fashion. The result was a success for Irish architecture, but not for Irish architects, for though the Royal Exchange was the first public building in Dublin to embrace neoclassicism, the winning architect was Thomas Cooley (1740-84), who was an Englishman, as were the other award winners, James Gandon and Thomas Sandby (Cooley was to spend the rest of his career in Ireland, as was Gandon, from 1781). Despite the consolation prizes awarded to three Irish entrants – Thomas Ivory, Thomas Jarratt, and Sproale and Myers – the outcome was a disappointment for Irish architects and only 'confirmed an already existing sense of inferiority which lasted until at least 1800'.[13] This lack of local self-confidence was new, for in the late seventeenth and early eighteenth centuries, major new buildings in Ireland were designed, as a rule, by Irish architects or at least by architects resident in Ireland. Dublin gained, however, from this new influx of talent and especially so in the case of the exchange.

Cooley's completed building succeeds magnificently, not only in the quality of the work and its plan but also in the way in which it addressed the city in which the merchants were interested. Its principal front looked north towards the late seventeenth-century suburb developed by Sir Humphrey Jervis and his associates on the far side of the Liffey; the other looked west, towards the medieval city. In locating it where they did, the Dublin merchant oligarchy were in a sense attempting to turn the development of the city full circle, turning their backs on the expanding aristocratic suburbs in the east in favour of a site which was firmly located in their sphere of interest. (Unfortunately, the park created on the eastern side of the City Hall in 1987, from land left over from street widening, distorts this original emphasis in the building's design.) Yet, despite its magnificence, the Royal Exchange was not to mark a shift in the city's development back towards its medieval core, for, like the flow of the Liffey, the city continued to drift inexorably seaward.

Both porticos indicate the interior arrangement of the building with its two axes meeting under a Pantheon-like dome. This great domed rotunda, ringed with giant fluted columns, is the principal feature of the exchange for it was there that the merchants met to transact their business. The rotunda now houses a number of notable statues: Charles Lucas by Edward Smyth, Henry Grattan by Sir Francis Chantrey, and Daniel O'Connell, Thomas Davis and Thomas Drummond by John Hogan. Simon Vierpyl was responsible for the exceptional quality of the ornamental carving in the building and his earlier work for Lord Charlemont at the Casino in Marino may account for the similarity of the motifs in both buildings. Since 1852 the exchange has served as the City Hall (the Council Chamber is located in what was originally the coffee room). In the muniment room are stored municipal archives dating back to the twelfth century, including the papers and maps belonging to the Wide Streets Commissioners, the commissioners no doubt have turned many times in their graves at the thought of their powers being transferred to Dublin Corporation. This occurred under the Dublin Improvement Act of 1849, and these powers are still exercised today by the Roads and Traffic Department of Dublin Corporation.

The old Custom House. The Clarence Hotel, just downstream from Capel Street Bridge, stands roughly on the site of the old Custom House. Originally the customs had been collected at the crane on Wood Quay at the foot of Winetavern Street, but around 1620 it was decided to build a Custom House and quay on a site just outside the city walls. By the mid-seventeenth century the wharf had been extended and a new Custom House built which was in turn replaced by a Custom House designed by Thomas Burgh (1670-1730) architect of the enormous Royal Barracks – now Collins Barracks – and of the Library at Trinity College. Burgh's Custom House was about 200-feet long and was dignified by a pedimented breakfront, which stepped out slightly from the rest of the building above a ground-level arcade. By the 1770s the building had fallen into bad repair and the case was made that a replacement should be built further downstream, given that the river was invariably congested at this site with as many as eight ships deep at the quay, not to mention the plight of the ships who could not get sufficient draught to make the journey upstream.

Developers who had property downstream of the bridge had a strong interest in having the Custom House relocated seawards as this would allow for the possibility of opening a bridge and a new cross-river axis. If a bridge had been crucial to the development of the Jervis estate in the late seventeenth century, it was to be equally crucial for the Gardiner estate a century later. One of the first blows in the campaign for a new easterly bridge was struck by a parliamentary committee which was set up in 1749 to examine the cause of traffic congestion on Capel Street Bridge. The two-member committee decided that the problem was due to the lack of a new easterly bridge, a view that was hardly surprising given that one of the two members was Charles Gardiner, the son of the great Luke Gardiner who was responsible for developing what is now O'Connell Street. However, the Corporation waged a successful campaign against this and later proposals, with both the Revenue Commissioners and the Wide Streets Commissioners being sympathetic to the Corporation's case. The Revenue Commissioners were particularly crucial to the outcome as a new bridge could only be built if they agreed to relocate the Custom House further downstream.

However, the pendulum was to swing finally in a downstream direction in the early 1780s with the appointment of new revenue commissioners, for in their ranks now was the extremely influential John Beresford who was an enthusiastic supporter of easterly development. Nonetheless, it wasn't until James Agar, another commissioner who was heir to property in the Ellis Quay area (upstream from Capel Street Bridge), was placated by the promise of the Four Courts for Inns' Quay that the project finally went ahead. Parliament, which had previously rejected proposals for a new bridge, now backed the scheme and the reconstituted Wide Streets Commissioners were at last granted £15,000 in March 1782 'to open a convenient communication between the northern and southern sides of the city, to the east of Essex Bridge' (Capel Street Bridge). Appropriately enough, both the new Custom House and the Four Courts (both by Gandon) can be seen from Capel Street Bridge.

Burgh's old Custom House was converted into a barracks after the departure of the Revenue Commissioners in the 1790s. During the 1798 rebellion the Dumbarton Fencibles who were stationed there 'administered pitch-caps and flogging at the triangles to the disaffected'. The seizure of the barracks formed part of Robert Emmet's planned rebellion in 1803. Amongst other ideas that Emmet had was, 'if money had been got, to purchase Rafferty's cheese-shop, opposite to it, to make a depot and assembly, and to mine under and blow up part of the Custom House, and attack them in confusion'.[14] Unfortunately, for Emmet, the plan came to nought and, as for the Custom House, it either collapsed or was demolished not long after. Any remaining houses which backed on to the river disappeared with the construction of Wellington Quay in 1812. As for the Poddle, all that can be seen of where it meets with the Liffey is a grating in the quay wall, placed there by the authorities during the time of the Fenians so that the culvert through which it flows would pose no threat to the security of Dublin Castle.

The quays and urban renewal. Back in the 1970s, long before urban renewal became an issue of popular concern, the British *Architectural Review*, in a special supplement on the future of Dublin, declared that the success of any move to restore the city 'may fairly be measured by whether or not it brings to the quays a return to prosperity and coherence'. According to the *Review*,

> it is the quays which give topographical coherence to Dublin. They are the frontispiece to the city and the nation: grand, yet human in scale, varied yet orderly, they present a picture of a satisfactory city community: it is as though two ranks of people were lined up, mildly varying in their gifts, appearance and fortunes, but happily agreed on basic values ... these riverside buildings are the essential Dublin. Individually unremarkable as works of architecture, collectively they are superb, and form a perfect foil to the special buildings, such as the Four Courts and the Custom House. If they are allowed to disintegrate, to be replaced by unsympathetic new buildings, the most memorable aspect of the city will be lost ... two large and special buildings, both on the north side, act like bookends to the long terraces; the Custom House (plus Liberty Hall, its insensitive tall neighbour) at the seaward end, the Four Courts at the other, its dome nobly articulating a bend in the river.[15]

From Capel Street Bridge, as mentioned, both bookends can be seen, as well as a third neoclassical masterpiece, the City Hall, which sits on rising ground at the southern end of Parliament Street. While the large and special buildings can still be seen, the context in which they sit is changing dramatically, largely due to the impact of the Urban Renewal Scheme which began in 1986. Virtually the whole length of the quays has been declared a 'designated area' to which tax incentives apply, with the most important site (with the most beneficial tax incentives) being at the Custom House Docks. As a result, as you look downstream the new Financial Services Centre now rises behind the dome of the Custom House.

However, in retrospect, it may not be urban renewal but the road widening projects pursued by the road planners in the closing decades of this century which may have the most important impact on the quays, for, if Dublin faced the Liffey thanks to the intervention of the Duke of Ormond (unlike most seventeenth-century European cities which turned their backs to the river) the quayside widths were certainly not drawn up with twentieth-century traffic in mind. In the case of the Armory lease (1675), which became Ormond Quay and Bachelor's Walk, there was a 60-foot roadway stipulation, and in the Ellis lease

(1682) – Arran and Ellis quays – a much narrower provision of 36 feet. Few of the ordinary riverside buildings which the *Architectural Review* found superb back in the 1970s were to withstand the quay-widening envisaged by the Corporation road planners.

In the early 1980s the impending mutilation was methodically plotted out. Ellis Quay and Arran Quay were to be widened to provide an overall width of 50 feet; likewise Usher's Quay, Ormond Quay Lower, Crampton Quay and Wellington Quay were to be enlarged to provide an overall width of 60 feet; Bachelor's Walk and Essex Quay were to be 'only marginally affected' with just 'the façade lines' of Bachelor's Walk at risk (though with 'only' the façades gone one wonders what was to be left); Usher's Island was to achieve a new width of 64 feet and, in the case of Wood Quay, no widening was required as the buildings there had already been demolished to make room for the Corporation's own Civic Offices.[16] Considering the dereliction which resulted from this quay widening policy it was singularly inappropriate that the City Council should have seriously considered renaming stretches of the devastated quay in honour of notable Dublin writers such as James Joyce and Sean O'Casey; it was certainly a dubious compliment in the case of Joyce, for the Corporation's plans included the obliteration of 15 Usher's Island, the setting of his famous story 'The Dead'.

From Heuston Station to the Ha'penny Bridge

Heuston Station. The station stands at the western end of the city quays, at a point where the city appears to meet the countryside or, at least, the Phoenix Park. The station was built as the terminus and headquarters of the Great Southern and Western Railway Company in the 1840s; the charming Renaissance palazzo which faces towards the city was designed by Sancton Woods and the iron and glass passenger sheds behind by Sir John MacNeill. The station was called Kingsbridge after the nearby cast-iron bridge (1828, by George Papworth) which was named in commemoration of George IV's visit to Dublin in 1821. Both have since been renamed to commemorate Captain Seán Heuston, a former railway employee who was executed for his part in the 1916 rebellion. The concrete bridge above Heuston Bridge (1979), is named after a former Alderman, Frank Sherwin.

Dr Steevens' Hospital. Immediately to the south of the station stands the headquarters of the Eastern Health Board, the former Dr Steevens' Hospital. It was hidden from view for years by an ugly late nineteenth-century nurses' home which happily was removed as part of the restoration programme under the direction of Arthur Gibney (completed 1992). As the original entrance on Steevens' Lane could no longer be used (largely due to traffic), it was simply

Kingsbridge, now Heuston, station.

replicated on the northern front with a new limestone doorcase and fenestration in the Queen Anne style. The magnificent rococo ceiling in the entrance hall was rescued from the Johnstown Kennedy house, Co. Dublin.

The hospital, founded in 1717 with a bequest from Dr Richard Steevens, took twelve years to build under the direction of the doctor's sister, Madam Grizel Steevens. It was designed by Thomas Burgh in what was then a rather archaic seventeenth-century style, its square plan evidently influenced by the building's better-known neighbour, the Royal Hospital Kilmainham (1679). The chief treasure of Dr Steevens' was the library, bequeathed by Dr Edward Worth (1678-1733), the son of John Worth, Dean of St Patrick's. Edward, who was allegedly described by Dean Swift as 'a lazy, modish son of melancholy spleen', was educated at Oxford and studied medicine at Leyden, Utrecht and Trinity. His collection of four-and-a-half thousand volumes was kept in the original boardroom (this interior has been attributed to Burgh's successor, Sir Edward Lovett Pearce).

Victoria Quay. Downstream from Heuston Bridge is Victoria Quay, now little more than a speedway for the traffic escaping west past Guinness's wall. This was the last up-river quay to be in active use. Until 1961 barrels of export stout were ferried downstream from here to the Guinness ships on Custom House Quay. As the name suggests, the quay is a nineteenth-century creation. Previously, travellers heading west met a great limestone gateway (1812, by Francis Johnston) at the foot of Watling Street. This gate – called the Richmond Guard Tower – marked an approach to the Royal Hospital in Kilmainham. It was removed in the 1840s at the expense of the railway company and, in its new location, became the western entrance to the Royal Hospital.

Collins Barracks. The barracks sits back from the river to the north of Wolfe Tone Quay. It was begun in 1706 on the site where the Corporation had hoped that the Duke of Ormond would build a residence. The architect was Thomas Burgh who had been appointed Surveyor General in 1700. Apart from the Royal Hospital Kilmainham, it is the earliest major public building in Dublin and the only surviving early eighteenth-century building standing on the Liffey. It was Burgh's first and largest commission, housing four regiments of foot and four of horse. The barracks, which has been greatly enlarged over the years, was handed over to the National Army in 1922 and renamed in honour of Michael Collins.

Sarsfield Quay. Under the terms of the Urban Renewal Scheme which began in 1986, virtually the entire length of the quays was declared to be a designated area to which tax incentives for rebuilding applied. Initially, all the new development was office-based and it was only when it became evident that there was a serious oversupply of office space that a number of developers began to switch to residential schemes, taking heed of the commercial success of a McInerney development at Sarsfield Quay, which was completed in 1991 by architects Burke-Kennedy-Doyle and Partners. (Sadly, this sits on the site of a handsome early nineteenth-century unified terrace which had been allowed to fall into such a state of disrepair that it had to be demolished.) The McInerney scheme was the first residential development to be built on the city quays for several decades (apart from corporation housing at City Quay, 1975-79) and, hopefully, marks a shift in direction in the housing history of the inner city.

Rory O'Moore Bridge. Though officially called after a leader of the 1641 rebellion, most Dubliners call it Watling Street Bridge, after the street leading to it from south of the river. When a wooden bridge was first erected on the site in 1670, it was obviously a threat to the ferry 'which had previously plied in the same locality'. As a result 'a number of apprentices assembled riotously for the purpose of destroying the new erection'.[17] In the ensuing riot twenty of the apprentices were arrested but, as the military were taking them to the Bridewell, an attempt was made to rescue them and four were killed. This incident gave rise to the name Bloody Bridge. In 1704 a new bridge called Barrack Bridge was built on the site and in 1863 this was in turn replaced by the present metal structure which was named after Queen Victoria, renamed as Emancipation Bridge in 1929 (the centenary of Catholic emancipation) and later again renamed after Sir Rory O'Moore. Looking west from the bridge you can see the 205-foot Wellington Monument in the distance. This great obelisk, designed by Sir Robert Smirke, was intended as a testimonial to the great duke, though, given the length of time it took to complete (1817-61), one may wonder about its testamentary value.

Usher's Island. The name comes from John Ussher who, in 1597, leased from the Corporation the island formed by a small tributary of the Liffey called the Camac. The Camac split into two at the northern end of Watling Street, one stream flowing into the Liffey at what is now Rory O'Moore Bridge – where there was a watermill – while the other stream flowed parallel to the Liffey as far as an inlet called Usher's Pill (which is shown, unnamed, in Speed's map of 1610). With the opening of Bridgefoot Street and the erection of a bridge in 1683 (now Liam Mellowes Bridge), this long stretch of ground was reclaimed, and though no longer an island, the old name remained.

15 Usher's Island. Sadly, this is now one of the last surviving Georgian houses on the quay; it was at one time the home of James Joyce's great aunts, Mrs Julia Lyons and Mrs Ellen Callanan, and Ellen's daughter, Mary Ellen. Members of the Joyce family, as they became old enough, went each Christmas to number 15 where Joyce's father carved the goose and made the after-dinner speech. As happens all the time with Joyce, this autobiographical material found its way into his work and number 15 is the setting for the richly laden Christmas table of 'The Dead'. After completing *Dubliners*, which portrayed much that was unattractive about his native city, Joyce seems to have felt that he had not been quite fair to its tradition of generous hospitality and, spurred on by hunger and homesickness (in December 1906 he was living in Rome) and the thought of the great Christmas celebrations at Usher's Island, he decided to add 'The Dead' as the final and most important story in the book.

Ellis Quay. The quay gets its name from Sir John and Sir William Ellis, through whom the Agar-Ellises, Viscounts Clifden, acquired a valuable lease-hold interest on Arran Quay and other stretches on the north bank of the Liffey running westward towards the Phoenix Park. As with the Amory grant (which covered what is now Ormond Quay, Bachelor's Walk and Eden Quay) the Ellis grant stipulated that there should be open quays 'for the advantage, ornament and beauty of the city'. However, whereas the Amory grant stipulates a 60-foot wide quayside, the Ellis grant was for a 36-foot-wide strip. Certainly Sir John or Sir William could have had little idea of the havoc this difference in quay widths would lead to in later years, for it has been the Corporation's policy to widen the quays to 60 feet to speed up the procession of juggernauts travelling to the port.

Liam Mellowes Bridge. Better known as Queen Street Bridge, it only acquired its present name in 1942 when it was renamed to commemorate Liam Mellowes who was executed in Mountjoy Gaol in December 1922. A bridge was first built on the site in 1683. It was rebuilt in 1764, apparently to the design of General Charles Vallency, who was an engineer in the Ordnance Survey. It was then called Queen's Bridge after Queen Charlotte, wife of George III, and in the 1920s was renamed after Queen Maeve. It is now the oldest bridge on the Liffey and, with its three arches, its niches and handsome balustrade, it is perhaps the finest.

Bridgefoot Street. This street, which runs south from Liam Mellowes Bridge, has been partially widened to dual-carriageway proportions as a result of being on the outer loop of the inner tangent (a roadway system to the west of the central business district, intended to divert traffic from the centre of the city – its 'merits' have been the subject of much dispute). Earlier this century, the street was the location of one of the city's 'hot-walls' (hot, because the furnace of a bakery was on the other side) where the poor and unemployed stood to warm their backs in the cold winter months. Unfortunately, poverty and unemployment are still endemic in the area. The church at the top of the hill is St Catherine's and was designed by John Smyth in the 1760s. It has a powerful granite façade but, as so often happened, the tower and intended spire were not completed. It was outside St Catherine's that Robert Emmet was hanged on 20 September 1803.

Usher's Quay. This takes its name from the Ussher family, in this case because of its proximity to their house which appears to have been situated near the rear of what is now the Brazen Head Hotel. It was in the Ussher house that the first printed version of the New Testament in Irish was made in 1602; as the title page proudly stated: 'The New Testament of our Lord and Saviour Jesus Christ, faithfully translated from the Greek into the Irish by William O'Donnell. Printed in Dublin in the house of Master William Ussher, at the foot of the Bridge, by John Franche, 1602'.[18] Another famous member of the family was James Ussher (1581-1656) who, in 1607, was appointed to the chair of 'theological controversies' at Trinity College, the title of his professorship indicating only too well the religious atmosphere of the period. He is now remembered for having devised a system of chronology which placed the date of creation at 4004 BC.

The municipal flats here are called after Oliver Bond (1760-1798) one of the leaders of the United Irishmen, who is buried in St Michan's church. These pitched-roof flats (1933) are an early example of the work of Herbert Simms, the Corporation's first housing architect. Later schemes, such as the four-storey flats at Chancery Place (1935), east of the Four Courts, were more avant garde.

The most exotic petrol station in the land!

Further downstream there is what has been described as 'the most exotic petrol station in the land' (1985-86) by Louis Burke. The canopies over the pumps were, apparently, inspired by the dome of the Four Courts![19]

Arran Quay. Some years ago, in a book by Micheál MacLiammóir, we were told that 'to look along the Liffey' was still, 'despite the intrusion of a few functional cubes, like seeing an eighteenth-century aquatint come to life.'[20] The possibility of appreciating such a view is less and less, given that the few Georgian buildings that remain continue to be demolished. A terrace of five such houses on Arran Quay (owned by Linders of Smithfield) was illegally demolished as recently as January 1989 though the terrace (which was not in a dilapidated condition) formed an integral part of the setting of St Paul's church. It was followed not long after by the demolition of a further quayside terrace east of St Paul's, including the remains of the former penal chapel which was situated at what was the rear of numbers 11 and 12 (number 12 was Edmund Burke's birthplace). They have since been replaced by a disappointing office complex by the Ambrose F. Kelly architectural partnership for the developer Dunloe House and P. J. Walls.

St Paul's Church (1835-42, by Patrick Byrne). This is among the city's most memorable churches. Its portico and graceful bell-tower stand confidently on the quayside, punctuating the Liffey's progress downstream and setting the scene for that other great architectural tour-de-force, the Four Courts. St Paul's was one of the first churches to be built after the granting of Catholic emancipation (1829) and was certainly the most conspicuous, calmly commanding its setting in a way which infuriated those who had objected to emancipation. Nonetheless, it is a very simple building. The interior consists of an oblong nave with an apse illuminated by concealed top lighting. The finely carved altar is by Sir Thomas Farrell. Behind the altar there is a large painting, flanked by two Doric pillars, which is a copy of Rubens's 'Conversion of St Paul'.

Fr Mathew Bridge. Better known as Church Street Bridge, this bridge was renamed in 1938 to commemorate the centenary of Fr Mathew's own signing of the pledge of total abstinence from alcohol, which he did with the words 'Here goes in the name of God'. The present bridge dates from 1816-17, and was probably designed by George Knowles, resident engineer to the Royal Canal Company. It is very similar to the next downstream bridge, O'Donovan Rossa Bridge; both bridges were built around the same date as replacements for older bridges which were demolished by a great flood in 1802. The bridges are linked by an open balustrade along Inns' Quay and were designed so as to harmonise with the Four Courts.

Fr Mathew Bridge is a successor to the original Bridge of Dublin which was built by King John *c.* 1215, a little to the east of the supposed site of the Ford of the Hurdles which gave the name Ath Cliath to the Gaelic settlement there. King John's bridge was swept away in 1385 and the Dominicans replaced it by Friars' Bridge (a toll bridge) which in turn was swept away by floods in 1802. Until 1683 this was the only bridge connecting the medieval walled city with the suburb of Oxmantown, north of the river.

The Brazen Head. Immediately south of Fr Mathew Bridge there is yet another depressing example of what road-widening policies can lead to. To create a filter lane for traffic coming on to the quays from Bridge Street, Burke's pub on the corner was demolished along with the covered entrance which gave the seventeenth-century Brazen Head an air of mystery and antiquity. The castellated wall which replaced the original street frontage in the late 1980s only adds insult to injury and in no way suggests that the building beyond is in fact the oldest tavern in the city. It was established around 1666, but is said to have been built on the site of a much older inn. Henry Grattan, Wolfe Tone, Robert Emmet, Daniel O'Connell – all patronised the Brazen Head and it was a regular meeting place of the United Irishmen, some of whose leaders were arrested there in 1798. Oliver Bond, who gave his name to the nearby municipal flats, lived at number 9, Bridge Street (now demolished).

Inns' Quay. The quay takes its name from the King's Inns which, along with

Dublin's oldest pub, The Brazen Head.

some private houses, occupied a site on the quay since its foundation in 1561. Before that, there had been a Dominican foundation there, the Abbey of St Saviour, but this was suppressed by Henry VIII. By the mid-eighteenth century, the buildings occupied by the King's Inns were in a very poor condition, the only part of the former monastery which remained in their possession being 'the mouldering Chambers of Judges' with some of it 'in the occupancy of clerks in the public offices, or abandoned by them to the sojournment of prostitutes and thieves'.[21] Parliament was well aware that the security of titles to estates depended on the proper maintenance of the parliamentary and judicial records that were housed in these appalling conditions and, in 1756, finally galvanised themselves to petition the King for funds to build a new records office.

The King gave his approval but, due to various delays, it was only in October 1776 that the first stone was laid. The architect was Thomas Cooley who appears to have envisaged a building on an E-shaped plan, having a shallow central block flanked by long wings stretching towards the quay. However, it was not clear if the building was intended solely as a records office or whether the King's Inns and courts were to be relocated there as well. (The courts were then housed beside Christchurch Cathedral.) The decision as to what exactly should be located at Inns' Quay was tied up with the dispute over the building of a new Custom House, and Welbore Ellis and Lord Clifden – two very influential opponents of a downstream Custom House – conceded only when it was clear that the courts were coming their way (their property interests lay upstream from Arran Quay). By the time the issue was finally settled in 1784 Cooley had died leaving the way clear for Gandon.

The Four Courts (1786-1802). Gandon's plan subsumed Cooley's earlier work by extending the central block to the quayside and by linking it to the flanking ranges by arcaded screens. The addition of the great drum and dome transformed the earlier plan entirely for, instead of a building which stepped back from the river, Gandon's Four Courts powerfully rises above the other quayside buildings, its brooding drum visible for miles downstream. Behind the portico, which Gandon wanted to project out over the footpath, an apsed porch leads, via a vestibule, to a great rotunda beneath a double dome. From here the four courts (King's Bench, Chancery, Exchequer and Common Pleas) radiated towards the corners of the central block; a fifth court, the Rolls Court, lay further along the main axis. The building, along with the Law Library and the Public Record Office, was severely damaged during the Civil War. In the restoration the rotunda was retained, though the site of the Rolls Court, along with much else, was replanned on new lines. The exterior was accurately restored save for the two side ranges which were shortened by one bay and no longer project beyond the arcades as Gandon intended.

The Four Courts and numbers 1-3, Inns' Quay.

As in all Gandon's buildings there is excellent sculptural work by Edward Smyth. On the pediment, Moses is flanked by Justice and Mercy, with Wisdom and Authority seated on the corners. This sculptural emphasis is repeated on a lesser note in the adjoining arcades where the elegant triumphal arches are crowned by magnificent trophies of arms, echoing the soaring architectural theme of the central block. However, there is an ironic acknowledgement of sorts of the Crown's unwitting role in the building's destruction (for it was that connection which was at the kernel of the dispute that became the Civil War) in that the arms now sit emasculated over their triumphal arches, their crowns removed and replaced instead by an incongruous set of balls.

The Civil War. If the thirty-two-county republic which Pádraig Pearse had so solemnly proclaimed under the portico of the General Post Office in 1916 existed only as an ideal, the Irish Free State which was so tortuously negotiated during the truce in the Anglo-Irish war had all the signs of becoming a tangible reality by 1922. However, in name it would not be a republic and the King would be recognised as head of the Commonwealth. This continuing link with the Crown (especially the contentious Oath of Allegiance to be sworn by members of the Irish Parliament) was anathema to those who opposed the Treaty. As the drift towards Civil War became inevitable it was yet another of the city's great classical monuments which was to provide the backdrop to the drama.

On 14 April 1922 the Four Courts was seized by an anti-Treaty group of the old IRA – or 'Irregulars' as they were called by the Provisional Government – confirming a deteriorating trend in which government troops and Irregulars manoeuvred for possession of positions of strategic importance. It seemed only a matter of time before serious fighting would break out. The spark was ignited on 26 June when a raiding party from the Four Courts captured the Deputy Chief-of-Staff of the pro-Treaty army (in retaliation for the capture of the leader of an earlier raiding party who had been 'acquiring' transport from a nearby garage). This was a challenge which the Provisional Government could not ignore and the attack on Gandon's masterpiece began on the morning of Wednesday, 28 June 1922, using artillery provided by the British (provided, in their case, because they believed that the leader of the Four Courts garrison was responsible for the recent assassination in London of Field Marshal Sir Henry Wilson). It ended three days later when flames made the building untenable and the garrison surrendered. Before doing so they mined the building and so destroyed the country's greatest archive of legal and historical documents which dated back to the twelfth century.

1-3 Inns' Quay (between Chancery Place and Charles Street). The Wide Streets Commissioners, despite a major downturn in their activity after the Act of Union, were still attempting to control standards well into the nineteenth

O'Donovan Rossa Bridge.

century. In 1825 they paid Patrick Byrne £5 13s 9d for two sets of elevations. One was for a four-storey terrace of three houses, the upper stories in red brick and the ground level in rusticated stone work with windows set into arches. The alternative design, which was rejected, incorporated shops at ground level.[22] However, it was a variant of the rejected design that was built. On 5 May 1826 the commissioners, under the Chairmanship of John Claudius Beresford (son of John Beresford of Custom House fame) approved a proposal by Denis Kehoe for two four-storey houses with shop windows at ground level. They also directed that an elevation by Charles Hopes for an adjoining house should be modified to conform with Kehoe's elevation.[23] The completed terrace of three four-storey houses can still be seen, though some of the façades have been altered.

O'Donovan Rossa Bridge. Better known as Winetavern Street Bridge, this was built in 1813-16, most probably to a design by J. Savage who was the superintendent of mason-work to the Royal Canal Company. The previous bridge (Ormond Bridge, 1682) which was swept away in the flood of 1802, had been situated slightly further downstream. O'Donovan Rossa Bridge (or Richmond Bridge, as it was previously called) has six carved keystone heads; those on the upstream side are Peace, Hibernia and Commerce and those facing downstream are Plenty, the Liffey and Industry.

Adam and Eve's, Merchants' Quay. The years following emancipation saw a wave of Catholic church building in the city, and Patrick Byrne (1783-1864), the architect of St Paul's on Arran Quay, 'was to ride high on this tide'. Over the next thirty-five years he designed numerous churches, both in the city as well as in the new suburbs which were developing beyond the canals. While the Catholic community knew what it wanted – confident and self-assured buildings on the principal streets from which they had been so long banished – finances were limited and so, 'restraint in style and resources was to dictate the form and structure of Byrne's earlier ecclesiastical work'.[24] Byrne's first commission was the Franciscan Church of the Immaculate Conception which replaced an old Mass House off Rosemary Lane (a lane running from Cook Street to the quay past the church's western entrance). The Mass House was located at the rear of a tavern called Adam and Eve's, hence the name by which the church is still known. The nave and transepts are part of the work begun under Byrne in 1830 but the ambulatory, the apse behind the altar and other enlargements, such as the aisles and chapels, are later additions. The scale of the church is not very evident from Merchants' Quay, though the Franciscan property is now quite extensive and includes a Georgian house with some of the most lavish decoration in the city. The one blot on the Franciscan landscape is St Anthony's Hall, a crude 1960s building.

Adam and Eve's Church, Merchants' Quay.

Wood Quay. Thirty years ago Wood Quay was virtually indistinguishable from the other quays which lined the Liffey: a terrace of tall houses and shops with, however, a remarkable pub on the corner with Winetavern Street – the Irish House (1870 – mid-1960s). The outside walls of the pub were almost entirely covered with plasterwork, depicting all sorts of patriotic folklore, from Henry Grattan's 'Last address to the Irish Parliament' to 'Erin weeping on a stringless harp'. Erin can weep indeed, for the Irish House and everything else has been obliterated to be replaced by a windswept site and two threatening blockhouses. These are the uncompleted Civic Offices; two further squat towers, to be built lower down on the site, are part of the architect's plan. In terms of scale, location and money, this is the most ambitious and grandiose building project which the Corporation undertook in this century, but whatever high hopes the project may have sought to express, it was seen by most Dubliners as a symbol of the obduracy and bloody-mindness of the city administration.

The plans for centralised municipal offices on the site date back to 1956 when the Corporation approved Wood Quay as the most appropriate location for such a development. Jones and Kelly, then consultant architects to the Corporation, designed a massive building which appeared to take its reference from the Fascist architecture of the 1930s – perhaps appropriately, given the lurking totalitarianism of the city's motto, *'Obedientia civium urbis felicitas'* (the obedience of the citizens is the happiness of the city). The RIAI (Royal Institute of the Architects of Ireland) argued that there should be a full-scale architectural competition and, in a partial response, the Corporation decided to hold a competition for developers. There were forty-five entries and from these, six were shortlisted and asked to submit detailed architectural and financial proposals. The winning scheme, selected at the end of 1989, was by Stephenson Gibney and Associates in conjunction with the Green Property Company.

As far as the architecture went it was very much a Sam Stephenson affair. Anthony Gibney, though a partner of Stephenson's at the time, had entered a rival design through the firm of Building Design Associates. Whereas Gibney's other submission was broken down into a loose assembly of buildings relating to the surrounding buildings and the quayside, Stephenson's design concentrated the bulk of the offices into four monolithic towers (originally cruciform in plan) which were arranged informally on the site, with views of Christchurch between them. It was the towers which were at the crux of the subsequent controversies, for they required deep foundations and Wood Quay – as was evident from excavations in High Street – was certainly layered with archaeological material which, if properly excavated, would provide invaluable data on the origins of the city. (Wood Quay gets its name from the wooden quays which were pushed out from the shores of the Liffey from *c.*1200.)

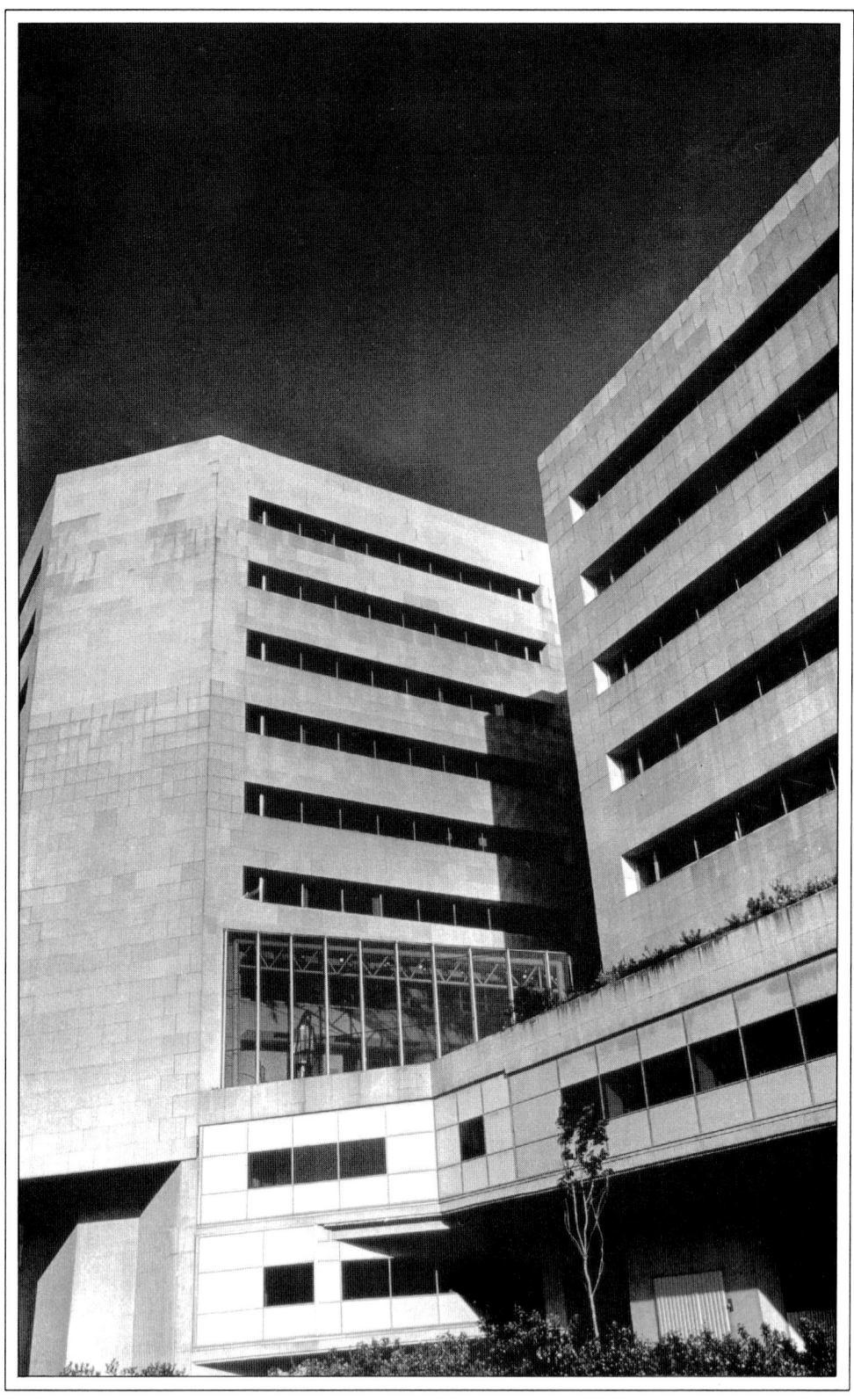

A flattering view of the Civic Offices.

The Corporation granted itself planning permission for the development on Christmas Eve 1970 and immediately there were objections from the National Monuments Advisory Council, who were concerned about the archaeological deposits, and from a host of others who were worried about the cost and the burden it would place on the rate-payers. The Minister for Local Government confirmed the Corporation's decision in July 1972 and, undeterred by the recent collapse of the Green Property Company, the Corporation raised its own loans and in June 1973 placed a contract for clearance of the site. Then in November 1973, the Government, to the astonishment of the city authorities, decided that the project 'should cease, pending consultation and further investigation' because of 'the significant location of the site in relation to Christchurch Cathedral, its archaeological importance and its value as an open space'. The solution proposed by the Corporation, as involving the least delay and disruption, was to relocate the four office blocks on the eastern side of the site (where they would incorporate a section of the recently unearthed city walls) and leave a 'clear and unobstructed view' of Christchurch from the quays. This solution, condemned by An Taisce at the time as 'the worst possible compromise', was approved by the Minister for Local Government in February 1974 and site works recommenced in September. An agreement was reached with the National Museum, who had started desultory excavations at Wood Quay in 1970, on a schedule for the archaeological dig which was to be completed in phases by March 1977.

In October 1977 a contract for the first phase of the project (it had now been phased due to financial constraints) was placed with the building contractors John Paul Ltd. By this stage Sam Stephenson's original proposals had been virtually redesigned or 'refined' to 'a very simple prismatic form'. In the words of the architect: 'the hard edges were cut off, the roof was chamfered and the fenestration recessed. By the time the redesign was finished, the blocks were almost solid and the glazing was hardly noticeable.'[25]

However, it was not the architecture but the more immediate threat of bulldozers running amuck on large sections of the yet unexcavated site that caught the public imagination. The National Museum had abandoned its excavation work in July 1976 and this led to charges of 'collusion' with the Corporation. More funds were provided by the Government to resume the dig but the recently established Friends of Medieval Dublin were not convinced of the Corporation's conversion to the archaeological cause and, less than two months after the contractor had moved into the site, they obtained the first of several injunctions to prevent the demolition of archaeological deposits without the prior consent of the Commissioners of Public Works. From the Corporation's point of view worse was to come, for on 30 June 1978 Mr Justice Hamilton declared much of the site to be a national monument. The site itself was occupied by a group of preservationists that June, in a move which won wide public support.

Later that September some 20,000 people marched to protest against the destruction at Wood Quay. The size of the protest should not have surprised the Corporation for, by now, Wood Quay had become the rallying cry for thousands of Dubliners who wanted to voice their frustration over the seemingly mindless destruction with which their local administration was credited, fairly or otherwise. As the *Irish Times* reported it at the time, the city of Dublin had found a cause. Indeed, the newly elected City Council had a majority in favour of saving the archaeological remains – if necessary by relocating the Civic Offices – but the die was cast, for the building contract ruled the possibility out and the Government, who had already spent a considerable sum on the excavations, were in no mood to pick up the additional price tag. Despite further appeals from the Council of Europe and other bodies, not to mind a petition signed by over 200,000 citizens, the archaeological excavations at last ended on 22 March 1981.

What are we to make of phase one of the project which was finally completed in 1986? The architect, with some justification, claims that judgement should be suspended until the entire complex is complete, i.e., the two further towers nearer the quayside, the underground Viking museum and Council Chamber. Certainly two lower towers would help by bringing the scale of the structure down to the quayside (now widened to virtual motorway dimensions). However, even if completed, the fundamental problem will always remain, namely that these squat towers are far too big for their surroundings. Unlike the dome of Gandon's Four Courts, which takes careful account of its location, these offices ignore everything outside the site's perimeter. Being shoved to one side to reveal Christchurch only further highlights the horrendous clash between the Civic Offices' horizontal window slits and the thick verticals in the cathedral's structure, apart altogether from a comparison with the more delicate proportions of any remaining Georgian buildings on the quays.

Christchurch has now been exposed in a way that it was never intended to be. While it is a largely Victorian creation (having been extensively 'restored' in the 1870s), its importance should in no way be diminished by that fact. Indeed, the architect George Edmund Street made it the great monument that it is by transforming Christchurch and spinning it out as an ecclesiastical citadel along the crest of the hill, linking the cathedral to a new Synod Hall by a delightful version of the Bridge of Sighs. Street succeeded in giving Christchurch an authentic medieval impression, not by clearing away the buildings on the river side, but by capitalising on them, as they clustered at the foot of the cathedral, and using them to accentuate its apparent height. Now that the intervening

*Christchurch Cathedral; an amalgam of medieval ambition
and nineteenth-century restoration.*

buildings have been taken away, and the massively scaled Civic Offices built directly alongside, the cathedral no longer conjures up the intended effect of a medieval citadel but stands forlorn and diminished, cut-off from everything on which it depended.

For the passing pedestrian, it certainly is a depressing experience to stand before the Civic Offices, wondering whether they are just an unfortunate aberration or whether they are indeed a monument to something worse – an administration cut off from the city which it is meant to serve. The scheme deserves to be completed, but the form that it will take will hopefully confirm that the partial solution that was so brutally built there in the 1970s was indeed an aberration; the Corporation has shown in other areas that it can build developments which are exciting and friendly, and alive with the promise of what a city should be all about as we enter the next millennium.

Fishamble Street. Few buildings in Dublin predate the eighteenth century, and all that serves to remind us now of earlier centuries is the occasional street pattern or name and, of course, the results of archaeological digs such as those associated with the building of the Civic Offices.[26] These excavations have indicated that there was probably a pool and a small boarded quay near where Fishamble Street originally met Wood Quay (one of the most constant factors throughout the Viking and early medieval period was that the quayside was gradually pushed forward towards the central channel of the Liffey). This would have been the site of the 'Fysshe Slypp' where Dublin fishermen landed their catch. From there they hauled them up to be sold at the shambles or stalls, from which Fishamble Street takes its name. The charge for the use of a medieval stall was ½d a day, while a women selling simply from a basket paid ¼d a week. The hygiene controls of the period prescribed a 4d. fine for those who threw offal under their stalls or who failed to wash the boards on which fish were displayed.[27] The seafood for sale included oysters and salmon as well as fresh and salted herrings.

Lower Exchange Street. This was previously known as Blind Quay but the name was changed in the eighteenth century as the street had a unsavoury reputation. In the medieval period it was the first in a line of quays which ran upstream from Isolde's tower (at number 17) towards the city's only bridge (near the Four Courts). The graphic map-picture of the medieval city that was published by John Speed in 1611, mistakenly showed a fortified wall running along the quays, for they were, by that stage, open to the river. They were, however, protected by towers – Prickett's tower on Merchants Quay, Fyann's Castle at the foot of Fishamble Street, Fitzsymon's tower a little further east and Isolde's tower at what is now the bend in Lower Exchange Street. Isolde's tower, which projected slightly into the river, was the most important; it was a round

Traffic on Essex Quay (with detail from 'Báite', by Betty Maguire, in the foreground).

structure with nine-feet thick walls which rose thirty feet above the channel.[28] From there the town wall ran in a south-easterly direction to Dame's Gate (where Dame Street now meets the City Hall).

Essex Quay. That section of Essex Quay running parallel to Lower Exchange Street has been demolished and it is now difficult to envisage that it was once lined with late seventeenth-century gabled houses. However popular the skeletal longship ('Báite', 1989, by Betty Maguire) which now fills this forlorn spot, it is a poor substitute for the fact that the space exists not for its own sake but as part of the detritus left over from the street-widening. Both the quayside and Lower Exchange Street have been brutally mutilated in the process. Apart from the street – if one can still call it that – there is the damage done to Saints Michael & John (1811-15), for it is no longer evident that the church was deliberately located in a narrow street hidden from the main thoroughfare. To expose it crudely to the disinterested traffic on the quays is to deprive the building of its history and to deny the memory that we owe to the community who built their church in that cramped location in the years before Catholic emancipation.

Sunlight Chambers. At the corner of Essex Quay and Parliament Street there is a delightful building (1901) by the Liverpool architect Edward Ould. It was built as the Irish head office of Lever Brothers, the makers of Sunlight soap. The building sports two terracotta friezes which illustrate the story of soap and hygiene. The *Irish Builder*, however, was not impressed and the fact that the architect was not Irish did not help. Soon after the building was completed in February 1901 the journal disparagingly remarked that 'there appears to be a consensus of opinion that the ugliest building in Dublin is not a hundred miles from Grattan Bridge'. However, a defence of at least the mural work was offered by Count Plunkett in a lecture in 1908 when he confessed to admiring 'the courage of those who brought art of character into our city'.[29] Posterity seems to have sided with Count Plunkett and the building is now listed for preservation.

The Ormond Hotel (Ormond Quay Upper). It was against the backdrop of this genteelly respectable hotel that the reality of the Civic War was brought home to Dubliners on 7 December 1922 when gunmen fired on two men, killing one – Seán Hales TD – and wounding the other – Pádraig O'Máille, the Deputy Speaker of the Dáil. It was a gruesome benchmark in the Civil War, showing that the republican opponents of the Treaty meant what they had said when they threatened the members of the Dáil and Senate of the newly established Free State with death and destruction of their property. The Cabinet met that evening and decided 'as a solemn warning' that four republican prisoners were to be taken out and shot in reprisal the following morning. Kevin O'Higgins, as Minister of Justice, signed the death warrants, though the group included Rory O'Connor who had been best man at his wedding less than a year before. It was the new Government's first official reprisal, but once the first step was taken more followed, until a total of seventy-seven prisoners had been shot in retaliation for attacks committed by the republicans. Apart from those executed, there were also some 11,000-12,000 locked up for varying periods in government prisons.

Ormond Quay Upper. Close to Capel Street Bridge, at 3A Upper Ormond Quay, the Urban Renewal Scheme has given rise to one of the most pleasing 'infill' buildings of recent years – Grattan Bridge House. As the base of the building indicates, this was originally a church – a Presbyterian church of the mid-1840s with two spiky towers punctuating the skyline. It was demolished in the early 1950s and, like so many other derelict sites, became a carpark. In 1986 the site, which belonged to the Corporation, was one of the first to be sold under the Urban Renewal Scheme to an investment company who, together with the National Building Agency, commissioned Grafton Architects to design an office block. Apart from retaining the little that remained of the old church (the ground floor exterior), the architects took heed of the neighbouring buildings, in particular of the adjoining Bank of Ireland (it dates from the period of Dublin's reconstruction in the 1920s).

Ormond Quay Lower. Miraculously, this stretch of quayside still retains a mix

Sunlight Chambers from Grattan Bridge House.

Watts Bros. Gun Shop, Ormond Quay Upper.

of older houses which give an idea of how the quays used to look, though here, as elsewhere, there are plans for street widening. Running in parallel, but hidden behind the quayside buildings, is Great Strand Street. If nothing else, the name indicates that this was the northern edge of the Liffey before Sir Humphrey Jervis constructed Ormond Quay in the 1670s. The street had a brief flash of notoriety in the 1930s when it was the scene of a minor drama called the Great Strand Street Siege. During Lent 1933 Cardinal McRory denounced communists, saying that 'there is no room for them or their blasphemies among the children of St Patrick'. On Monday, 27 March a mob of several hundred, singing 'God Bless Our Pope' and 'Hail Glorious St Patrick', attacked Connolly House (number 64 Strand Street) where a meeting was being held under the auspices of the Revolutionary Workers Group on the theme 'The Danger of War'. If there was any danger it was to the 'revolutionary workers' who, luckily, managed to escape with nothing worse than the public burning of their literature before the police dispersed the mob.[30] In itself, the attack – which was repeated the following night – was of no great significance, though it was indicative of a widespread obsession with the threat of communism. This was taboo, largely because it was atheistic; most Irish people were unconcerned about the idea of a class war, still less with any notions about the dialectic.

Bachelor's Walk. Though Bachelor's Walk must have served as a pleasant promenade when it was initially extended downstream from Ormond Quay in the 1670s, its name comes not from any bachelors who may have walked there but, more prosaically, from a property owner called Bachelor. In more recent times CIE (Córas Iompair Eireann), in conjunction with a British property company, Arlington Securities, bought up much of the property between Bachelor's Walk and Abbey Street as a location for a shopping centre with a bus station on top (this was an alternative site after the original plans for a similar scheme at Temple Bar were overturned by the Government). Some of the surviving Georgian houses on Bachelor's Walk, with superb wood-panelled interiors, were demolished as late as 1991[31] – the year in which the city fêted its role as European City of Culture. A downturn in the property market and CIE's failure to secure government support for the bus station, resulted in Arlington Properties reassessing this massively scaled proposal and, instead, they have embarked on a number of smaller scale proposals – including the retention of the few remaining eighteenth-century properties – which may see the survival of Bachelor's Walk, one of the most striking images of the city as one looks westwards from O'Connell Bridge.

It was at Bachelor's Walk (alongside the Ha'penny Bridge) that a group of young and inexperienced soldiers fired on a hostile crowd on Sunday, 16 July 1914, as the troops returned to the Royal (now Collins) Barracks having unsuc-

*An antique shop on Bachelor's Walk, with a reflection of the
Central Bank's roofline rising over the quays.*

Bachelor's Walk.

cessfully attempted to impede the loading of arms by the Irish Volunteers at Howth earlier that day. In the confusion, several volleys were fired, leaving three dead and almost forty wounded, including women and children. If the early months of 1914 were marked by an atmosphere of increasing militancy over impending Home Rule, this incident served as yet another nail in the coffin of constitutional nationalism.

The Ha'penny Bridge. Liffey Bridge (formerly Wellington Bridge or the Metal Bridge but best known as the Ha'penny Bridge), was built in 1816 to replace a former ferry. A toll of a ha'penny was charged which many felt was exploitative. There were several plans to replace it by a road bridge and in 1912 it became the focus of a controversy when it was suggested that it be replaced by a gallery to house Sir Hugh Lane's gift of impressionist paintings, a gift which was conditional on the Corporation providing a suitable home for the collection. St Stephen's Green was ruled out by Lord Ardilaun – after all, he had paid for it to be landscaped and made accessible to the public – and the residents of Merrion Square were equally opposed to the idea of losing their private park, a reaction which was supported by George Moore who could only think 'with horror of its quiet gentilities invaded by endless streams of gaping visitors'. Sir Hugh Lane also disliked the site, but this was due to poor attendance at the

The Ha'penny Bridge.

neighbouring National Gallery. However, the idea of a gallery spanning the Liffey, like the Ponte Vecchio in Florence, was to prove irresistible to Lane and plans were commissioned from Sir Edwin Lutyens. His design consisted of two main galleries, one on either quay, connected by a minor gallery surmounted by a colonnaded footbridge. It was an inspired artistic choice but, unfortunately, one that was doomed to failure for this was a time of heightened nationalist sensibility and Lutyens, despite having an Irish mother, was not considered sufficiently Irish. Though the Corporation had voted yes to the site, there was much disquiet over the diversion of municipal funds to such a project especially as, in the words of William Martin Murphy, 'the mass of the people of Dublin don't care a thraneen whether Sir. H. Lane's "conditional" pictures are left here or taken away'[32]. The sorry saga ended with the pictures being taken away for, exasperated by the Corporation's refusal to bow to his demands, Sir Hugh had them removed to the National Gallery in London, where they were to become the subject of extended controversy between the British and Irish governments following Lane's death on board the *Lusitania*. At least the Ha'penny Bridge was reprieved and, divested of its advertising hoardings, it regained its original elegance. With the Nelson Pillar gone, it has now become an unofficial emblem of the city.

What's in a name? This chapter concludes as it began at Capel Street Bridge which, as is so often the case, has quite a different official name. George Semple's elegant Essex Bridge was widened and flattened in 1874 and, in its new guise, was renamed in honour of Henry Grattan, the patriot leader who won legislative freedom for the Irish Parliament in 1782. His name was immortalised by nineteenth-century historians who saw in 'Grattan's Parliament' a golden age whose promise seemed all the more poignant when compared with the sordid story of its downfall in the years leading to the Act of Union. The bridge's renaming marked one of the first steps in a campaign to nationalise the city's street names. Prior to the growth of the Home Rule movement in the 1880s 'the titles of the Dublin Streets' were an illustration of 'the continuous loyalty of its Corporation to the English connection ... being almost a complete index to the Lord Lieutenants'.[33] Henceforth, they became a rollcall of the great and famous in Irish nationalist history. Later in this century most of the Liffey bridges were again renamed, any remaining colonial nomenclature being jettisoned in favour of titles which were felt to be more symbolically appropriate to a newly independent state.

More recently, in 1991, some Dublin councillors proposed that the city quays be renamed after eminent Dublin writers to commemorate the city's ephemeral role as European City of Culture, the argument being that 'existing quay names, such as Essex, Wellington, Victoria and Sir John Rogerson were not particularly

Badge seller at the Ha'penny Bridge.

suggestive of Dublin'. Apparently oblivious of changes elsewhere in Europe – where cities such as St Petersburg were returning to the use of their original names – it was claimed that few Irish people 'would have any great interest in the old imperial legacy of Wellington or Essex' (indeed, it was jocosely claimed that it was unlikely that Burgh Quay was 'named after Chris de Burgh').[34] The London *Times* took up the issue on an even more ridiculous level, seeing it as the perfidious result of Irish ambivalence 'about their British roots'! This, of course, was to miss the point altogether for, irrespective of their Britishness or Irishness, these names are part and parcel of Dublin's roots. More pertinent – and wounding – was the *Times* comment that 'the desecration of Georgian Dublin ... including the failure to protect ... the quays' meant that 'to a conservationist, Dublin is now the City of European Philistinism'.[35] For a city which has been the birthplace of so many great writers it would certainly have been an unfortunate memorial not only to tolerate the continued destruction of the physical city which the writers knew – and maybe cherished – but to deny the very names by which they would have remembered it. For, to obliterate the names is to obliterate the language by which Dubliners and writers alike know their city; it is to deny Dublin its personality and dispossess it of its history. Brin Friel's play *Translations* describes how a whole people can be exiled by merely changing the names of their places. 'We must learn where we live,' the old hedge schoolmaster says near the end of the play. If the people the school master spoke to were obliged to accept place names which denied them their history and their culture, such an act would be no less tragic in the case of Dublin. Given the evident perishability of the built environment, it may be but a name which remains to recall the world of our forebears and to remind us of the fragility and mutability of so much that we take for granted; as such, these unbidden prompts play a vital role as part of our everyday culture.

Gardiner's Dublin

GARDINER'S DUBLIN

'Dublin – second city in His Majesty's dominions;
Esteemed the fifth for magnitude in Europe;
Possessed of one of the finest public avenues of any city.'

ENCYCLOPEDIA BRITANNICA , 1797

An introduction to modern Dublin: a short history of O'Connell Street

O'Connell Street is where Dublin officially begins. It is, as the buses inform us, the mysterious *An lár*, the centre from which the city takes its measure. And yet, despite its great buildings and the generous proportions which make it the inevitable location for such spectacles as the St Patrick's Day Parade, O'Connell Street reflects only too well those uncertainties that are all so characteristic of Dublin itself. If its spine is punctuated by monuments to the great and unremembered, its pavements are marked by more accurate totems of contemporary Dublin – the bus stops crowded with young Dubliners commuting from the

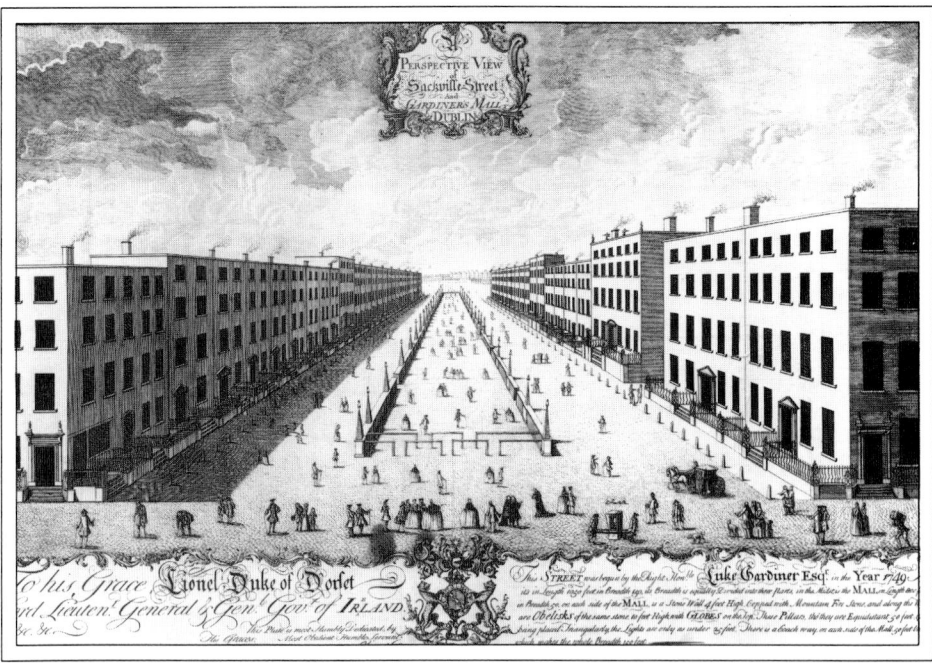

Above: Perspective view of Sackville Street and Gardiner's Mall, now O'Connell Street.
Previous page: Creations in stucco by Robert West in number 20, Lower Dominick Street.

distant suburbs. If its principal claim to architectural glory is the General Post Office (GPO), this is a monument which ironically reminds us not of the street's classical origins but of its role as the hijacked theatre for some of the great dramas in the emergence of nationalist Ireland. Indeed, for many Dubliners it is not for its history that the street will be remembered but for its cinemas and such irreverances as 'the floosie in the jacuzzi', a piece of sculptural ambition (officially known as 'The Millennium Fountain') which Dubliners have happily renamed and summarily brought down to size. This is a cautionary tale which serves to remind us that inflated ambition is a dangerous commodity, especially in a city where the reality has often fallen short of any grandiose intent. And yet, despite all the contradictions – or, indeed, because of them – O'Connell Street's claim to pre-eminence stands unchallenged, for here is one of the rare cases where a grandiose design was realised, giving Dublin its first great boulevard and a street which has been to the forefront, not just in terms of the city's urban development but as the location for some of the most important events in modern Irish history.

O'Connell Street owes its origins to the ambition of a self-made man, out to make his mark and money through assiduous property development. Indeed, the ascendancy-dominated society which gave Dublin some of its most distinguished architecture was, for all its aristocratic pretensions, relatively open to the self-made man: those having talent and ambition could elbow their way into the ranks of the eighteenth-century oligarchy provided that they conformed to the established church and, above all, to the social and political structures with which it was associated. The famous Earl of Clare, notorious for his vehement opposition to political rights for Catholics, was the son of a convert, and yet became Lord Chancellor. William Connolly, the reputed son of a Donegal innkeeper, became Speaker of the House of Commons and wealthy enough to build Castletown House. Joseph Leeson, the grandson of a brewer and property speculator, skipped up the aristocratic pecking order, becoming Baron Russborough in 1756, a viscount in 1760 and Earl of Miltown in 1763.

Luke Gardiner, the man responsible for O'Connell Street, was another of these self-made men, rising from obscurity through his evident administrative and financial ability. By 1725 he had become Deputy Vice-Treasurer and Receiver-General, with responsibility for remitting state revenues both within the country and overseas when Irish troops were sent abroad. In effect he became a most successful private banker which, combined with a further lucrative government post – Surveyor Generalship of Customs (in 1745) – secured his fortune, much of which was invested in property development. Between 1722 and 1729 he bought up much of the former St Mary's Abbey property on the north of the Liffey (including parts of it which were already developed) in a series of acquisitions that was to make his family the largest land-owning family on the north bank of the Liffey. He was also responsible for at least two major building initiatives, one being the laying out of Henrietta Street in the 1720s and the other, the development of Upper O'Connell Street in the late 1740s.[1]

While this second development lay on the fringes of the city, it was certainly not a green fields site. There was already a street in existence called Drogheda Street (it ran along the eastern side of what is now Upper O'Connell Street) but it was much narrower and evidently did not impress Luke Gardiner. He had the existing houses demolished and he pulled back the street line on the western side to give his new street a total width of 150 feet. It was renamed Sackville Street in honour of a Lord Lieutenant, though the handsome promenade which was built along the middle was called Gardiner's Mall.

Parades or walks such as Gardiner's Mall played an important role in eighteenth-century urban life, being the informally agreed location where 'polite society' went to stroll on fine days; generally in the early afternoon and, in the summer, in the evenings as well.[2] 'Parading', as it was called, marked a certain evolution in social relations, for distinctions in rank were ostensibly laid aside and everyone from Lord Lieutenant to impoverished clergymen could partake: everyone, that is, who was a recognisable member of 'polite society', for those who were not would have been snubbed into place had they dared to cross the great divide.

Malls also had important architectural and financial implications for, as Luke Gardiner realised, if Sackville Street could be turned into a fashionable parade, the value of his property would be greatly enhanced. His street of new houses provided an elegant backdrop and the mall itself was created by enclosing a long parading area within low stone walls: these were decorated with rows of stone obelisks supporting lanterns. The mall's clearly defined limits made abundantly clear the distinction between those who paraded and those who did not. 'Polite society' was delighted and, presumably, so too was Luke Gardiner, for if the area had previously lain on the fringes of the fashionable suburbs, it was now the focus of aristocratic life north of the Liffey.

In architectural terms the overall result was less a street than an elongated residential square, for the newly widened Sackville Street stretched southwards only as far as Henry Street; between here and the river there remained a densely built-up area, intersected by narrow streets and lanes. What we see today, of course, bears no resemblance to an elongated square, nor is it very fashionable and certainly in no way residential. Instead, there is a thoroughfare which runs straight to the river. It is possible that this is what Luke Gardiner always had in mind, for it certainly would have enhanced the value of his estate to have the most fashionable and easterly cross-city axis running through his property.

Sackville Street showing Nelson Pillar and the GPO (Lawrence Collection).

Indeed, if he had only envisaged his mall as the centrepiece of an elongated square it is odd that he did not seize the chance of coming to an arrangement with the Rotunda Hospital (the lease for the hospital site was acquired only in 1748) so that this fashionable charitable development could have acted as a focal point at the northern end of the mall. Instead, he opened Cavendish Row, which suggests that Sackville Street and its mall were conceived of as being ultimately part of a cross-city axis.

The extension of Sackville Street to the river would have meant little without a bridge and it was the decision to build a bridge was crucial in determining the development, not only of the Gardiner property but also of the rest of the city. For most of the eighteenth century, Essex Bridge (Grattan Bridge/Capel Street Bridge) was the lowest crossing point on the river and the possibility of opening a new bridge further downstream was seen as a major threat by the merchants and property owners who had commercial interests in the old city. The corollary, of course, was that downstream developers such as Gardiner had everything to gain from the exercise. It wasn't until the 1780s that the Gardiner grand plan was realised. This change in fortune owed much to John Beresford, an

Entrance to Gilbeys of Sackville (O'Connell) Street, the Irish Builder, *1 July 1867.*

enthusiastic supporter of easterly development, and an extremely influential member of both the Revenue Commissioners and the Wide Streets Commissioners. The Revenue Commissioners were particularly crucial to the outcome, as a new bridge could only be built if they agreed to relocate the Custom House further downstream. The decisive vote seems to have rested with James Agar – a revenue commissioner who was heir to upstream property – for it was only when he was placated by the promise of the Four Courts for Inns' Quay that the project finally went ahead. Parliament, which had previously rejected proposals for a new bridge, now backed the scheme and a reconstituted Wide Streets Commissioners were granted £15,000 in March 1782 'to open a convenient communication between the northern and southern sides of the city, to the east of Essex Bridge'.

That Sackville Street was at the pivot of the grand design became clear in May 1782 when the Wide Streets Commissioners decided to create a new street (North Frederick Street) which would enable it to link up with Dorset Street and the road to the north. In December 1785 the commissioners decided that the warren of streets between Sackville Street and the Liffey should go and that Sackville Street should be continued to the river along the same generous proportions as the original street laid out by Luke Gardiner. The new bridge was built in the early 1790s and Westmoreland Street, which leads to the Parliament in College Green, was well under way by 1800.[3]

The extension of Sackville Street to the river changed the mall's character completely. Whereas previously it had been an elongated square lined with private residences, it now became a great boulevard where shops were an integral part of the architecture. James Gandon prepared plans for blocks of houses incorporating ground-floor shops behind a unified palatial façade; and though these were not used, it is evident that the Wide Streets Commissioners were looking for original and sophisticated designs based on contemporary shopping streets in Paris.

Sackville Street was the first 'boulevard' street on these islands. John Nash's Regent Street in London, which is often credited with anticipating other street developments, was created much later, 1817-23; and even in Paris, the great avenues date largely from the time of Napoleon III and Baron Haussmann. Instead of being a prestigious residential address, Sackville Street now became a prestigious commercial area with, by 1805, some thirty to forty businesses and three hotels. If the residents objected to the arrival of 'persons in trade', there was always the possibility of moving to nearby Mountjoy Square and the adjoining streets which the second Luke Gardiner (grandson of the first) was in the process of developing before his death in the 1798 rebellion. Certainly, the Act of Union (1800) acted as a spur to the exodus of aristocratic residents but

A woman and her rosary beads – O' Connell Street.

there were perhaps other reasons as well. A guide book of 1821 described how 'for want of sewers, the filth and water were received in pits called cesspools, dug before the doors and covered in.' Despite an Act of 1807 which empowered the Paving Board to make sewers, the cesspool system 'continued in Sackville Street ... long after 1810, and many now remember the horrid sight and smell which periodically offended the inhabitants ... when the stygian pools were

The interior of the Rotunda Hospital Chapel.

opened and emptied'.[4] Hygiene was far from being an eighteenth-century preoccupation, though the idea did eventually catch on and, towards the end of the period, began to play an increasing role in the choice of residential location.

O'Connell Street still remains Dublin's principal thoroughfare but, ironically, by the time this great eighteenth-century set-piece was completed, the Parliament to which it led had voted itself out of existence and so, instead of commemorating the achievements of that ascendancy world, O'Connell Street is now remembered for its part in some of the great dramas in the emergence of Catholic nationalist Ireland. Its change of name is eloquent in itself for, if Sackville the man is now an unremembered Lord Lieutenant, O'Connell was certainly the most important representative of the up-and-coming Catholic middle-classes who upstaged the old order. Indeed, by 1829 – the year of the Catholic Relief Act which O'Connell had pioneered – Dublin had become a Catholic city with Catholics making up some 70 percent of the population and, in 1841 – a year after O'Connell's equally important Irish Municipal Reform Act – the 'Liberator' became the city's first Catholic Lord Mayor since the time of James II; the street has unofficially borne its modern name since the erection of the O'Connell Monument in 1882. It was also in O'Connell Street that Jim Larkin made his dramatic address to Dublin workers during the bitter lock-out of 1913 and it was in O'Connell Street that a small group of determined nationalists took over the GPO in Easter 1916 and declared an Irish republic. Indeed, it is due to this rebellion – and the later civil war – that so much of the eighteenth-century streetscape was destroyed. Though rebuilt in a classical style during the 1920s, O'Connell street no longer brings to mind the Ireland of Grattan's Parliament and its chief monuments commemorate instead the rich and varied sources of the nationalist tradition and their role in the birth of modern Ireland.

O'Connell Street and beyond

The Parnell Monument. (Completed 1911, by the Dublin-born American, Augustus St Gaudens). The early years of the new state were not noted for their liberalism and, between books being censored and divorce being banned, the omens for the newly independent Ireland were not encouraging. Story has it that W. B. Yeats consoled some distraught liberals by reminding them that the portents in the city's main thoroughfare were, nonetheless, encouraging. At one end stood O'Connell, of whom it was libellously said that you couldn't throw a stone over an orphanage wall without striking one of his illegitimate offspring (popular heroes must evidently be potent in all respects); near the GPO stood Admiral Lord Nelson, unkindly known as 'the one-handed adulterer' and at the street's northern extremity was the tragic lover Parnell, asserting from his plinth that no man has the right to fix the boundary to the march of a nation, while

The Parnell Monument (detail) by Augustus St Gaudens.

pointing at the nearby maternity hospital. In his autobiography *Twice Around the Black Church*, Austin Clarke tells of a fanciful Maynooth student who fears that some subconscious memory of ancient priapic cults had been reawakened by the Parnell obelisk. The evidence came from a priest in the Pro-Cathedral who interrogated a young Dubliner about his amatory adventures in a hallway: 'What did you say she held?' 'Me Parnell, Father.' 'Your what?'[5]

Charles Stewart Parnell (1846-91), deserves, however, to be remembered for more than his liaison with Katherine O'Shea (it was in any event an eminently respectable, indeed one could say an eminently Victorian relationship). He was the colossus that straddles any account of Irish history from the 1880s until the Great War. Though a landlord and a Protestant (Protestants were presumed to be Unionists) he took control of the Irish Nationalist Party in 1879 and, with an unscrupulous mastery of parliamentary procedure at Westminster, succeeded in bringing Home Rule to the forefront of political life as never before. At the same time he was actively involved in the Land War of 1879-92 which was to eventually result in the abolition of landlordism and the creation of a system of peasant proprietorship. This incredible ability, of combining the explosive force of agrarian radicalism with a mastery of parliamentary tactics, was certainly not appreciated by his opponents and in 1887 the London *Times* published an infamous series of articles called 'Parnellism and Crime' which accused Parnell of complicity in murder and other outrages. However, in 1890, after crucial letters in the *Times* case were shown to be a forgery, British public opinion turned in favour of Parnell and he reached the summit of his career. His downfall was to come just as dramatically only months later when he was cited in a divorce scandal linking him with Katherine O'Shea, an unhappily married woman with whom he had been living for years. The political fall-out was catastrophic and, in an attempt to maintain the crucial support of the British Liberal Party, Parnell's party deposed him. Parnell reacted fiercely, but died shortly afterwards in October 1891 (only five months after marrying the former Mrs O'Shea), leaving behind him, not only a divided party but a bitter if distorted legend – that of the lonely hero betrayed by English guile and Irish clerical interference, a legend which was to echo through Irish literature and politics for generations to come.

The Rotunda Hospital. 'The Dublin Lying-in Hospital' (to give it its proper title) was the first maternity hospital in these islands. It owes its existence to a philanthropist, Bartholomew Mosse (1712-59) who opened the hospital at his own initiative in 1745. He was the first master and was responsible for shifting the hospital to this site which he acquired in August 1748 (it had previously been located in South George's Street). The site was then at the very edge of the city, sloping upwards towards some barley fields and the open countryside. Mosse

A view of the Rotunda from the Gate Theatre.

decided to turn this into a source of funds for his new building by immediately laying out a pleasure garden on the lines of the popular Vauxhall Gardens in London. The garden opened to the public in September 1749 and was an immediate success (admission was a shilling).

In July 1751 work began on the actual hospital. The architect Richard Castle was a friend of Mosse's and, it seems, provided him with a plan based on that of Leinster House free of charge. The site architect was John Ensor. With its palatial façade, it is evident that Mosse intended his hospital to be among the city's principal buildings (though its impact has been marred by unsympathetic additions on the western side) for an important objective would have been to attract maximum interest amongst the fashionable and monied circles on whom the hospital depended for funds. The income from the gardens was supplemented from various sources: profits from lotteries, appeals for assistance to the Crown and Parliament, and receipts from charity sermons.

Charity sermons were a popular form of entertainment in the eighteenth century and the chapel where the sermons were preached was placed at the centre of the hospital's design, above the main entrance at first floor level. As in the great town-houses of its patrons, visitors made an 'aristocratic' progress through a sequence of elaborate public rooms, before ascending to the building's principal reception room, in this case the chapel. While these rooms 'of parade' – as they were described in the Hospital minutes – are elegantly proportioned and, in the case of the staircase hall, can boast of plasterwork by Robert West, they are soberness itself compared to the splendours of the chapel. Here, in a brilliant virtuoso display, the master stuccodore, Barthelemij (or Bartholomew) Cramillion inaugurated the German rococo style in Ireland.

In the chapel, Mosse made every effort to give emblematic expression to those Protestant values which inspired him. The Italian painter Giovanni Battista Capriani was asked to provide five paintings 'entirely free from any superstitious or Popish representation' and, though these never materialised, the empty spaces in which they were to sit now serve as a foil to the exuberance of the surrounding plasterwork; this was initially painted in white and gold but was later redone in semi-realistic colours. The allegory underpinning the decoration comes from a verse much cited by contemporary Protestant divines: 'And now abideth Faith, Hope, Charity, these three; but the greatest of these is Charity' (1 Corinthians, 13.3). In each side of the covered ceiling there is an alcove in which sit figures depicting the virtues: Faith represented by a blindfolded female holding a cross and bible; Hope with her head held upright holding an anchor and Charity nourishing an infant. Charity, and her attendant children occupy a privileged position in the decor, for just beneath them the Lamb of God sits enthroned above the Venetian window, flanked by kneeling angels and framed by a backdrop of flowing drapery. Cherubs and angels abound, the angels holding scrolls with Biblical citations, while the cherubs disport themselves among the vines and flowers. To maximise accommodation, a balcony supported by Corinthian columns was built around three sides of the chapel. A similar preoccupation led to various re-arrangements of the pews beneath, though happily the original mahogany was always reused. A good tear-jerking sermon could raise £1,000 in a morning.

If eighteenth-century Protestantism laid great emphasis on charity as the most important of the Christian virtues it was a virtue which, nonetheless, was exercised with fine discrimination, and much ingenuity went into distinguishing the 'deserving' from the 'undeserving' poor. Potential benefactors were assured that only women 'with proper certificates of their poverty and character have been admitted'. Catholic women were not excluded, though if there was to be any hope of converting them into grateful Protestants it was essential that they be accommodated. If Mosse's Protestantism was typical of the age, he was still by any standards a forward-looking, imaginative and generous man. At a time when abandoned children died by their thousands in the Dublin Foundling Hospital, he initiated a scheme for a school where poor children born in his Lying-in Hospital would be taught by 'able Protestant masters in the most useful trades and manufactures'. Sadly, this never got off the ground, for Mosse died less than two years after the opening of the Rotunda, leaving an impoverished widow with two children.[6]

The Rotunda. The hospital acquired its better-known name, 'The Rotunda', from the round shape of the principal building in a new series of rooms. These were initially commissioned so that those visiting the gardens would have somewhere to walk on wet days. While the Rotunda – by John Ensor – originally had a most undistinguished exterior, the interior was considered to be 'one of the noblest and most magnificent circular rooms in the British dominions'. From its opening in 1767 it was a success and hosted many memorable events – the famous Volunteer Convention of 1783, the first public appearances of John Field and the University Discourses of Cardinal Newman. In 1784 this entertainment complex was extended northwards to plans by Frederick Trench (a governor of the hospital and member of the Wide Streets Commissioners) with the working drawings and the eastern elevation by Richard Johnston (elder brother of Francis). The exterior wall of the Round Room was raised and decorated with sculpted panels and a Coade-stone frieze. To join it to the street, James Gandon added an elegant little entrance block based on the theme of a triumphal arch. All this has since been changed: the Round Room (Rotunda) became a cinema (now closed) and the Supper Room the Gate Theatre. The Pillar Room, underneath the theatre, is still used occasionally for concerts.[7]

The Gate Theatre. This theatre company opened in October 1928 as the Dublin Gate Theatre Studio, having as its objective 'the production of modern and progressive plays unfettered by theatrical convention'. Hilton Edwards and Micheál MacLiammóir ran the theatre in partnership, aided by two other directors, Madame Bannard Cogley and Gearóid O'Lochlainn. The Gate moved from the Peacock, adjoining the Abbey Theatre, to its present location in 1929. At the theatre's first production (of *Faust*) in its new premises on 17 February 1930, the heating failed, but the frozen audience were nonetheless enthusiastic. Finance was a perennial problem and the theatre only kept afloat with vital assistance provided by Lord Longford – he later became a director – who, as late as the 1950s, could be seen on the pavement outside with his collection box. Thanks to an intervention by Charles Haughey, then Minister for Finance, essential renovations were undertaken between 1969 and 1971 and, since then, the theatre has been aided by the Arts Council. A host of famous actors gained early experience in the Gate, including Orson Welles, who had to pass a gauntlet of pickets in 1951 when crowds heckled him for being a communist subversive. The theatre continues to flourish and enjoys an enviable reputation for the quality of its productions.

42 Upper O'Connell Street. This is the only building still extant from the time of Gardiner's Mall. It was built in 1752 to a design by Richard Castle (architect of the Rotunda Hospital). The typically plain façade conceals a finely detailed interior, with stucco-work ceilings and an exceptionally good carved wooden staircase. Of the sixteen houses that were built on this side of the mall while Luke Gardiner was still alive (he died in 1755) no fewer than eight were subsequently acquired by members of Parliament. Nathaniel Clements – Gardiner's partner in developing Henrietta Street – built two houses on the far side and others were built by individual speculative builders such as George Steward, a carpenter, and Alexander Thompson, a plumber. The master-builder George Darley was responsible for completing most of the remaining sites and, by the time of his last development in the early 1770s, the mall was firmly established as one of the most prestigious places of aristocratic residence in the city. The Dublin Directories of the mid-1780s, for example, record ten peers and thirteen MPs with addresses in Sackville Street.[8]

The city left to us by the Gardiners is almost entirely eighteenth-century in layout. The more important buildings are generally classical; the GPO, the Pro-Cathedral, the Church of St Francis Xavier are obvious examples. More full-blooded Victorian buildings are the exception, especially in O'Connell Street where 1916 and the Civil War wrought such a heavy toll of destruction. The relative scarcity of good Victorian buildings underlines the tragedy of permitting their demolition. One of the greatest losses was the Gilbey Building,

Men's toilets – Upper O'Connell Street.

46 and 47 Upper O'Connell Street, which was demolished in 1973. This was built in the mid-1860s to a design by William George Murray in the Venetian style which Thomas Newenham Deane and Benjamin Woodward had made popular in their Dublin buildings of only a decade earlier. Ruskin himself might have appreciated its wealth of stone carving, mouldings and fine ironwork, though perhaps not the plastering over of its original polychrome materials. It featured a marvellous porch where the owners, the wine merchants W. and A. Gilbey, had inset busts of Palmerston and Gladstone to commemorate their having reduced the tax on wine. However, now the building has gone, along with numbers 48 and 49, to be replaced by the Dublin County Council offices. O'Connell Street has certainly lost out in the exchange.[9]

Cinemas. Just south of the Gresham Hotel (1925, by Robert Atkinson) is the Savoy Cinema which was built in 1929 as the biggest 'picture house' in Ireland. It was designed by a London architectural practice, Messrs Mitchell, and could accommodate up to 3,000 people. The decor was a delightful Hollywood concoction – a vaguely Moorish streetscape set out in plaster on the auditorium walls met, in a wonderful flight of the imagination, at a proscenium arch based on the Rialto bridge. Sadly, all this went in the 1960s when the auditorium was divided into several smaller cinemas. The Carlton, directly across from the Savoy, dates from 1937. Despite the Catholic hierarchy's distrust of 'the motion picture' – one of Ireland's first acts of censorship was the Censorship of Films Act of 1923 – Dubliners flocked to the cinema. By the 1930s the Irish public, as

Metropole Cinema, 1922 (demolished 1973), architect Aubrey V. O'Rourke.

elsewhere in the English-speaking world, was addicted to the celluloid dramas emanating from Hollywood. Dublin had the largest seating capacity per head of population of any city in Europe, and on Friday and Saturday nights long queues formed outside the Savoy and the Carlton and, further down O'Connell Street, outside the Metropole and Capital (both were demolished in the 1970s to make way for the British Home Stores building, now Penney's).

The Millennium Fountain. The fountain, by Sean Mulcahy and Eamonn O'Doherty, was donated by the Smurfit business family to celebrate the very successful, though entirely bogus, Dublin 'millennium' in 1988: Dublin's history as an urban settlement goes back further than a thousand years. What happened in 989 (not even 988) was that the High King Máel Sechnaill captured the city for a second time and on this occasion he exacted tribute on the basis of the number of household units. One could call it a protection racket – or dignify it as a local tax – but in either case it certainly makes an unusual choice as a basis for a commemoration. The reclining figure in the fountain ostensibly immortalises Anna Livia Pluribel, but has been popularly dubbed 'the floosie in the jacuzzi', which, according to one commentator, is 'an epithet that might hold good for the aspirations of modern Dubliners too'.[10]

Nelson Pillar. Midway along O'Connell Street, at the junction of Henry Street and North Earl Street, stood the Nelson Pillar, a 134-foot-high doric column with a statue of the famous admiral on top. It was erected in 1808 to a design by the London architect William Wilkins, with Francis Johnston acting as site architect. The pillar closed the vista from north, south, east and west and gave O'Connell

The Nelson Pillar in the days of the horse-drawn tram.

Street a dignity which has now almost gone. It marked the centre of the city, its name on all the buses as their central destination and its image shown on endless postcards, so much so that it became almost the city's symbol. And that perhaps was its downfall, for the Dublin that commemorated Nelson has gone forever and his memorial had became an anachronism, an unwelcome reminder of the city's old political status. Various personages were suggested in place of the forlorn Nelson; some favoured John F. Kennedy, others the Virgin Mary, but for want of a suitable replacement the admiral remained until blown up by the ever-reliable 'persons unknown' in March 1966. Some patriotic sensibilities may have been assuaged but Britain was hardly worried about Dublin's loss and O'Connell Street is infinitely the poorer as a result.

The suggestion that the pillar might be rebuilt by the short-lived Dublin Metropolitan Streets Commission was said to be one of the reasons for the new Fianna Fáil Government abolishing that body in 1987. The commission had been established by the previous Coalition Government in 1986 to transform the area running from O'Connell Street to Grafton Street 'into a showpiece of architectural sensitivity and environmental awareness'.[11] This was to be done with a budget of £10 million in the space of three years. However, the change of government was to result in the commission's sudden demise and so its legacy was but another report on how Dublin might have been.

The General Post Office. The GPO is the most historic and distinguished building in O'Connell Street, though all that remains of the original building (1814-18) by Francis Johnston is the classical façade. The statues over the portico, Fidelity, Hibernia and Mercury, are by Thomas Kirk. The rebuilt interior is disappointing, though the public office contains a fine memorial to the 1916 Rising – a bronze statue by Oliver Sheppard of the dying Cuchulainn (which was, in fact, made in 1911). The choice was apt, for when Pádraig Pearse stood at the entrance to the GPO on Easter Monday 1916 and proclaimed an Irish republic to a few astonished bypassers, he and the other six signatories of the proclamation knew that a military victory was impossible but hoped that their heroic gesture would take on a mythological quality which would inspire others. If Pearse – as others before him – had reinvented the Cuchulainn myth in the hope of re-creating a heroic age for Ireland, it was a poetic aspiration which was transmuted by the Easter Rebellion into an active political force. It must have seemed an impossible dream, but yet, as Pearse had asked in one of his best known poems, 'The Fool',

> O wise men, riddle me this: what if the dream come true?
> What if the dream come true and if millions unborn shall dwell
> In the house that I shaped in my heart, the noble house of my
> heart?[12]

The nationalists whom the men and women of 1916 represented were a minority within a minority – some 160,000 Irish Volunteers were at that very time fighting for Britain in the Great War. Had sixteen of the rebel leaders not been executed, it is possible that the dampened embers of Irish nationalism might not have been so easily ignited. However, given that Britain was at the time fighting a bitter campaign in the western trenches, it was hardly surprising that the Government failed to appreciate the courage of those who had decided to defy the empire. In all, less than 700 ill-armed and poorly trained rebels took on 6,000 British troops. The toll on all sides was high, but particularly among the civilian population – 76 rebels, 132 soldiers and policemen, and some 300 civilians died – with Dublin acquiring the dubious distinction of being the first European capital to be wrecked by war in this century. The bombardment of the rebel positions in the GPO from a gunboat in the Liffey, as well as by guns stationed in Trinity College, effectively ensured the street's demolition.

If the rebellion succeeded politically, its cultural objective of creating a Gaelic Ireland was less successful. When it came to working out in practice what Pearse had envisaged, the picture was far from clear. Indeed the rebellion's literary flavour was a two-edged instrument for, in retrospect, we can see that what Pearse proclaimed was too easily assigned to a world of fantasy, deserving obsequiousness but little imaginative effort from those who were left to tackle the harsh and tortuous tasks of achieving independence and building a new state.

Clery's (1918-20, architects Ashlin and Coleman). Dublin's answer to Selfridge's sits on the site of the earlier Imperial Hotel, which, along with much of the rest of O'Connell Street, was destroyed during 1916. It was from one of the Imperial Hotel balconies that Jim Larkin made his celebrated address to the Dublin workers during the '1913 lock-out', at a meeting which ended with his arrest and with the crowd being baton-charged. William Martin Murphy, proprietor of the *Irish Independent* and a director of the tramway company with which Larkin was in dispute, was a director of the hotel. A statue of Larkin by Oisín Kelly was erected nearby in 1979.

The union at the centre of the dispute had been formed by Jim Larkin (1876-1947) in January 1909 'in a room in a tenement in Townsend Street' where, according to Seán O'Casey, 'with a candle in a bottle for a torch, and a billycan of tea, with a few buns for a banquet, the Church militant here on earth, called the Irish Transport and General Workers Union, was founded'. It was its 'church militant' quality that Murphy and other employers feared and, in particular, the use of 'the sympathetic strike'. When Murphy refused in July 1913 to employ ITGWU members and sacked 100 men who were working for the Tramway Company, Larkin retaliated by calling for a total withdrawal of labour starting

Clery's department store.

at 10.00 a.m. on Tuesday, 26 August, when the city would be crowded with visitors arriving for the opening of the Dublin Horse Show. Some 700 of the 1,700 tramway workers abandoned their trams wherever they happened to be at the stroke of ten. Tension increased over the following days and in one particularly brutal police charge at Eden quay, two workers were killed. Larkin was arrested, released on bail and rearrested after his famous appearance at the hotel balcony.

The situation deteriorated further when 404 employers issued a joint statement threatening to dismiss any worker who refused to sign a document repudiating any form of contact with the ITGWU. By the end of September the situation was desperate for the strikers and soup kitchens were set up in Liberty Hall for starving families. As the dispute dragged through October, a plan was devised to temporarily send children of the strikers to towns in England where they could be cared for (sympathetic strikes took place in Manchester, Liverpool and Birmingham). This proposal aroused the opposition of the Catholic Archbishop who warned that Catholic children might fall into the hands of non-Catholics. Violent scenes broke out as Catholic parents and priests blocked the way to the ships, and the plan was dropped. By Christmas the outlook was very bleak as the lifeline of food ships from England could not be depended on.

Faced with the failure of the British Trade Union leaders to declare a general strike, the ITGWU leadership advised their members on 18 January 1914 to return to work. Larkin's deputy, James Connolly, wrote with bitterness: 'And so we Irish workers must go down to Hell, bow our backs to the lash ... and eat the dust of betrayal and defeat.' It was a defeat: even if the employers were afraid to relive the experience it certainly put an end to any hopes of syndicalist revolution and, for Larkin, there was a prolonged exile in America. When he returned at the end of the Civil War he was to find that the pattern of the next half century had been shaped in his absence and his efforts to remould Irish trade unionism along more radical lines resulted only in splitting his 'one big union'. Nonetheless, his legend lives on, enshrined in the folk memory of Dublin workers as the man who, when he found them on their knees, had at least left them on their feet.

Lower O'Connell Street. The rebuilding of the city centre, in particular Lower O'Connell Street, was an issue of immediate concern in the weeks following the Easter Rising. If the *Irish Builder* saw 'a unique and unexpected opportunity ... to give Dublin a piece of architecture worthy of this beautiful and historic street', and the RIAI (the Royal Institute of the Architects of Ireland) envisaged controls which would ensure a uniform street frontage on the lines of Baron Haussmann's Parisian boulevards, the property owners were alarmed at the prospect and argued that 'the cost of mere beautification should be borne by the state or municipality'. With the Corporation arguing for stronger powers, and the

Lower O'Connell Street and the O'Connell Monument.

property owners against it, the Dublin Reconstruction (Emergency Provisions) Bill did not have an easy passage at Westminster. One of the seminal figures in British planning, Raymond Unwin, was dispatched to Dublin to bring about a consensus. The upshot was that the property owners had to deposit their plans with the Corporation and if the city architect considered any scheme to be 'injurious to the amenity of the street' he could 'require the plans, sections and elevations to be altered accordingly'. An expert committee, set up by the Corporation, recommended the adoption of a neoclassical style.[13]

The rebuilding of Lower O'Connell Street was not yet completed when the Civil War broke out in 1922 and destroyed the north-eastern end of the street. Unimpressed by the existing reconstruction work in Lower O'Connell Street, the city architect, Horace O'Rourke, waged a determined campaign to ensure stricter uniformity in the rebuilding of Upper O'Connell Street. The result is that the eastern side of Upper O'Connell Street is certainly more uniform but also more bland than the post 1916 reconstruction work that can be seen at 1-11 Lower O'Connell Street. Despite their individuality, these buildings work very well together, sharing a common cornice and string courses and embellished by some very fine sculptural work by Charles Harrison and Sons; see the Ulster Bank (numbers 3 and 4), the Bank of Ireland (numbers 6 and 8), as well as Clery's.

The O'Connell Monument (by John Henry Foley, 1818-74). The base, which depicts 'Eire casting off her fetters' and has four winged figures – Patriotism, Fidelity, Eloquence and Courage – was finished in 1882 by Thomas Brock, Foley's assistant. Daniel O'Connell (1775-1847) was, as the statue suggests, a larger-than-life figure, who dominates any account of the development of Irish public life in the first half of the nineteenth century. He was known as 'the Liberator' for having at last wrestled full political rights for Catholics from a reluctant Government in 1829. He did so through his mastery of mass politics, using constitutional means as never before to put pressure on the Government to accede to the will of the people. However, though British political leaders conceded emancipation, they rebuffed his second great campaign to repeal the Act of Union. In failing health, and disillusioned both by his failure to achieve repeal as well as by the outbreak of the Great Famine (1845-47), he died at Genoa on his way to Rome in May 1847. His funeral, which wound its way along Sackville Street towards Glasnevin cemetery, marked the beginning of the era of great funeral processions for which Victorian and Edwardian Dublin was renowned.

Reminders of the 'Great Dan' are all about. Just a short distance further up O'Connell Street is a memorial – by Sir John Farrell – to William Smith O'Brien (1803-64), a leader of the Young Irelanders who disagreed with O'Connell's constitutional methods and, inspired by revolutionary events elsewhere in

Europe, decided to have their own revolution at home. It was an inglorious affair, little more than a skirmish with a group of policemen in the soon-famous cabbage garden of the widow McCormack in Ballingarry, County Limerick. Upstream from the bridge, is number 11 Bachelor's Walk, the residence of Captain John d'Esterre who was fatally wounded by O'Connell in a duel. As a member of the Corporation, d'Esterre had taken umbrage at O'Connell's ridiculing of the 'beggarly Corporation of Dublin'. Striken by remorse, O'Connell vowed never to duel again and settled a pension on the widow. If O'Connell was, as John Mitchell described him, 'a royal yet vulgar soul', he was a leader beyond compare to the Catholic masses. However, at a time when popular politics and Catholicism were regarded with disdain by the Protestant authorities, such adulation and success was seen as little better than the fruits of demagoguery. That the same Catholic masses could so enthusiastically rally to O'Connell's call for repeal of the Union only fueled the worst Protestant fears of Popish domination and so the unfortunate equation of Irish nationalism with Irish Catholicism put down its roots. When in later years the Corporation attempted to rename the bridge in honour of O'Connell, there were violent objections and the matter was taken to the courts in 1885 where a permanent injunction forbidding a change of name was granted. Similarly there were objections to renaming Sackville Street and it only officially became O'Connell Street in May 1924.[14]

O'Connell Bridge. The bridge is of a scale and amplitude that does justice to O'Connell; it acquired its present width when rebuilt in 1880. The earlier bridge (called Carlisle Bridge) was much narrower though not lacking in grandeur, having a low-strung profile with a double set of obelisks at each approach. The design for this was by James Gandon and the bridge, paid for by the Revenue Board, opened to carriage traffic in 1795. Initially, Gandon had proposed a bridge with a triumphal arch in the centre, linked to either bank by colonnades. There were also reports that on the south bank of the river there was to be a semi-circular crescent on the lines of the Place Royale in Bordeaux.

Westmoreland Street and D'Olier Street. The plans for the approaches linking Sackville Street to the Parliament in College Green were the cause of much discussion and the Wide Streets Commissioners considered various proposals for Westmoreland Street and D'Olier Street: that the two new streets be flanked by covered colonnades or alternatively by buildings combining both shops and residential accommodation behind unified palatial façades. The members of the Kildare Street Club proposed 'a splendid and magnificent building' for the triangular site between the two streets, as did the Bank of Ireland who commissioned plans by John Soane for a new headquarters there. The commissioners' eventual choice, for two streets, 90-foot wide, flanked by shops set into plain uniform elevations, was less grandiose but deliberately so, for these austere elevations were to act as a foil to Soane's building (which never materialised as the bank had no need for it when they bought the old Parliament after the Act of Union). The elevations of the new street were not without significance, however, for designed shopping streets did not appear in the rival capital, London, for another fifteen years.

While the commissioners were jealously aware of contemporary developments in London – ordering copies of elevations and buying up maps to keep themselves abreast of the latest trends – their sights ranged further afield, and the stark neoclassical elevations by Henry Aaron Baker which were selected for Westmoreland Street and D'Olier Street indicate a familiarity with Parisian prototypes; certainly the use of large expanses of glass at shop level was daringly advanced for the period.[15]

Eden Quay. In 1782 the departing Chief Secretary, William Eden, suggested to John Beresford that 'if our great plans should ever go into execution for the improvement of Dublin, I beg that you will contrive to edge my name into some street, or into some square, opening to a bridge ...'[16] Their great plans did go ahead and Beresford remembered both Eden and Lord Lieutenant Carlisle, though it is only his 'contriving' on behalf of Eden that has endured. 1782 was a momentous year in the history of the Wide Streets Commissioners for it was in that year that their membership was revamped, their powers extended (to make or widen streets at their discretion, including the major approaches to the city) and their funds supplemented by the proceeds of a local coal tax. If the commissioners had been timid in their endeavours up to this point, the new members were full-blooded enthusiasts of civic improvement. Also, John Beresford, who was a key political figure in the Irish administration and had just been appointed Chief Commissioner of Revenue, was an advocate of easterly development. It was he who engineered the building of the new Custom House and who as a Wide Streets Commissioner and a 'loyal supporter of Government' (in effect Pitt's principal Irish adviser) ensured continuing support for an ambitious policy of civic improvement over the next two decades, a policy which London seems to have accepted as part of the cost of wooing aristocratic support back to the side of 'good government'.

After the Act of Union, such wooing was no longer necessary and the Wide Streets Commissioners found the Treasury in London far less accommodating. Though their work continued, it did so at a much less ambitious pace. In 1806 Henry Aaron Baker was paid for elevations for Eden Quay; these were similar to the unified symmetrical façades by Thomas Sherrard which the commissioners had already adopted for Lower Sackville Street. By 1811, with money short and building developers in even scarcer supply, the commissioners abandoned

A protester – with Eden Quay in the background

their ambitions for unified façades in both Eden Quay and Abbey Street. Though the houses were still to be built of red brick and were to correspond in style with their neighbours, the shopfront or street level was left to the owner's discretion and the buildings, total height could be four or five storeys. In 1826 their annual grant was discontinued but, though the writing was on the wall, the commissioners lingered on until their functions were finally subsumed into the reformed Dublin Corporation on 1 January 1851.

Butt Bridge. The downstream view of the Custom House, one of the most important set-pieces of late eighteenth-century architecture, has been irreparably impaired by the insertion of the Loop Line Bridge. It was built in 1891 to provide a rail connection between Westland Row (Pearse Station) and Amiens Street (Connolly Station). The road bridge alongside it was erected as a swivel bridge in 1892 but was rebuilt in its present form in 1932, the year of the Eucharistic Congress, hence its official name, Congress Bridge. Everyone, however, still uses the original name, Butt Bridge, which commemorates Isaac Butt (1813-79) the founder of the Irish Home Rule Party. Even though the Eucharistic Congress has left no physical vestiges to remind us of its importance (virtually no one is aware that Butt Bridge was officially renamed Congress Bridge) at the time it generated an enormous enthusiasm, and the arrival of church dignitaries from over forty countries in June 1932 was hailed with great excitement. According to an *Irish Independent* headline, the Papal Legate was given 'the greatest welcome in Irish history'. A week of religious ceremonies had its climax in the Phoenix Park, where a crowd of over a million attended a mass at which Count John McCormack sang. It was an extraordinary expression of popular piety in which veterans of the Civil War came together to celebrate, almost in triumph, the Catholic ethos of the new state.

Liberty Hall (1964, by Rea O'Kelly). This monument to Irish trade unionism assertively stakes a claim on the Dublin skyline as few buildings had done before and, thankfully, as few have done since. It is a far cry from the old Northumberland Buildings (1820s) which the Irish Transport and General Workers Union bought in 1912 as their headquarters and renamed Liberty Hall. It was in that historic building that the workers were organised during the 1913 lock-out. It was there as well that the Proclamation of the Irish Republic was printed on Easter Sunday 1916, and it was from here that Pádraig Pearse and James Connolly set out with a column of the Irish Volunteers and the Irish Citizen Army to take possession of the General Post Office on Easter Monday. Though the building was shelled by the gun boat *Helga* later that week, it remained intact. It was demolished in the late 1950s to make way for the new Liberty Hall.

The Custom House (1781-91). This is amongst the most imposing of the great eighteenth-century public buildings in these islands; a reflection of its impor-

Butt Bridge and Liberty Hall, from under the Loopline Bridge.

tance to the state at a time when there was virtually no income tax and the main sources of revenue were taxes on consumption, especially customs and excise. Certainly this was a temple to taxation, with a rich iconography to drive the message home. But there was more to the building than this, for in both its magnificence and its location it announced to all and sundry that the centre of gravity in the Irish capital had definitively shifted eastwards, towards pastures new in the developing aristocratic suburbs downstream of the old city. Those with property interests in the new suburbs stood to gain but there were many who did not and, encouraged by the hostility of the Corporation, mobs broke down fences and attempted to pull up the piles on the Custom House site (it was built on reclaimed slobland). The architect James Gandon described his first days in Dublin as 'a kind of imprisonment' and felt obliged to carry his 'good cane sword' when visiting the site.

James Gandon (1742-1823) was enticed to Dublin by John Beresford who had sought him out at the advice of Lord Carlow. Gandon was born in London (his paternal grandfather was a French Huguenot who had emigrated to England following the revocation of the Edict of Nantes). He was a pupil of William Chambers, the leading English architect of the period. Despite such architectural credentials, Gandon's early years were not very successful – he was placed second in the Dublin Royal Exchange competition of 1769 – and by the time he arrived in Dublin he was no longer a young man. However, his Irish work allowed him at last to give proof of his brilliance, for though 'his full maturing – intellectual and formal – as an architect, was late and sudden' it most happily coincided 'with his arrival, aged 39, in Dublin'.[17]

The plan of the Custom House was in the form of an H, with the crossing of the H being the axis which linked the north and south fronts. Low ranges on both the east and west turned the H into a rectangle. While the two principal fronts end in corner pavilions, the design is controlled by the central block which, on the river front, rises elegantly under a delightful dome. The overall effect is of a building which is long and low, powerfully illustrating Chambers' dictum that 'with regard to elevations, if the breadth be predominant, we are struck with ideas of majesty and strength'.[18] The drum and dome add a baroque note to an otherwise chaste neoclassical elevation and provide a magnificent focal point, especially when seen in raking views from along the quays. Unfortunately, when restored in 1926 (the building was set on fire by the Dublin Brigade of the Irish Republican Army in May 1921) the drum was rebuilt in Ardbraccan limestone instead of the gleaming white stone which Gandon had shipped from Portland Bill in Dorset. The sculptural decoration was a major innovation. No previous Dublin building had such an ambitious and unified sculptural programme where the sculpture played an integral role in the architecture. The theme, as one might expect, concerns the maritime trade of Ireland, a theme which was politically charged at the time, given that the right for Irish merchants to trade unhindered with the colonies had only been conceded as recently as 1779. Since it was a government building it was inconceivable that it would harbour any suspect symbolism, especially in view of the degree of commitment which the Government had been obliged to give the project.

Beresford and the other Revenue Commissioners had advocated the move to a new downstream site as early as 1773 and, despite the strong mercantile opposition, pushed their case on the basis that in its new location the Custom House (estimated as costing £40,000) would easily bring in more money (an extra £10,000 a year) and, therefore, quickly pay for itself. While the Dublin Castle administration supported the scheme, London prevaricated, worried about the mercantile opposition – there was a flood of petitions against the relocation – and sensitive to the criticism of those aristocratic landowners who feared they would lose out from a downstream development. As political events worsened in Ireland, Beresford decided to go to London to press his case in early 1780. He spent nearly a year there before he got the necessary support from the Cabinet and George III. While in London he renewed his contact with a group of artists and aristocrats connected to Paul Sandby and was introduced to James Gandon. On 22 December 1780 Beresford returned to Dublin with Gandon's plans and the following day he was sworn in as the Chief Commissioner of the Revenue Commissioners. Gandon was 'smuggled' over to Dublin in April and the foundation stone of the new Custom House laid by Beresford on 8 August 1781.

The vehemence of the scheme's opponents was not abated by this *fait accompli*. Napper Tandy, a member of the Corporation, led a mob who tried to pull up the piles on the water-logged site. Such was the opposition that even at this late stage Lord North, the Prime Minister, was willing to consider dropping the whole project. William Eden, the Irish Chief Secretary, assured North that the new Custom House had its supporters and, more importantly, that even 'if the measure had originally been wrong, it would now be very prejudicial to all steady government to revoke it'.[19] The Government, whether it liked it or not, was wedded to the project and not to go ahead would involve a dangerous loss of face. Go ahead they did, though the cost came to an incredible £201,500 (by the time the ancillary docks and warehouses were completed the total was £300,000). This was too much for the Patriot opposition in the Irish Parliament and Henry Grattan derided the result as 'a building which is more proof of prodigality in the directors than of taste in the architect – of sixth-rate rank in architecture, but of first-rate in extravagance; a building which stands as a blemish in the eye of the island and a scale to show the monstrous disproportion between our trade and our revenue'.[20]

Against this background the Revenue Commissioners, not surprisingly, opted for a sculptural programme which played up the positive aspects of government policy and of the benefits which would accrue from loyal support to the Crown. The pediment on the river front optimistically depicts Britannia and Hibernia embracing in a sea chariot while Neptune banishes Famine and Despair; the ships in the background are carrying the imports and exports on which trade depends. The design for this was by Agostino Carlini, whom Gandon had sought out in London. It was executed, however by Edward Smyth (1749-1812), who so impressed Gandon that he left most of the remaining sculptural programme in his hands.[21] Smyth was a pupil of Simon Vierpyl's (who had come from Rome to work for Lord Charlemont) and started his career as an ornament carver for Henry Darley, the contractor for the stone-cutting at the Custom House. The four figures which stood above the pediment were by both Smyth and Carlini, whereas those still standing on the northern front – Europe, Asia, Africa and America – are by Thomas Banks. The colossal statue of Commerce which soars above the dome is also by Smyth, as are the famous keystones of the lower storey, symbolising the thirteen principal Irish rivers and the produce with which their basins and ports were associated. Another keystone represents the Atlantic which Irish ships could now cross unhindered to trade with the colonies. Each of the end pavilions carries the royal arms – again by Smyth – with the lion and unicorn upholding the Irish harp surmounted by the royal crown. Though this was quite usual in coinage it was an iconographic shift in architectural terms. The norm in a royal building up to this point had been to depict the arms of the monarch – as opposed to the Irish harp – beneath the crown. Either the Revenue Commissioners were stressing their own institutional heritage, with its long numismatic tradition, or, more likely, playing along with the rhetoric of the times, showing that Grattan and his supporters had no monopoly on patriotism and that Beresford and the Dublin Castle administration could happily accept the thesis that Ireland was an independent nation but, of course, united to Britain by their shared loyalty to the crown.

The Talbot Memorial Bridge (opened 1978).[22] After all the heady symbolism of the Custom House, the Matt Talbot Memorial Bridge seems uninviting, like a wintery blast of easterly wind. Its sparse and skeletal outline make it an appropriate memorial for the Dublin labourer whom it commemorates. Matt Talbot (1856-1925) worked for a period as a messenger with the Port and Docks Board and seemed destined for little more than a life of alcoholism until he took a pledge of total abstinence in 1884. From then on he began to lead a life of increasing religious devotion and when he died on his way to early mass on 7 June 1925 it was discovered that he wore chains and cords as a means of mortification. His life of self denial and acceptance of poverty have made Talbot

The Financial Services Centre and the Talbot Memorial Bridge.

an ambiguous figure, especially for the Irish Church, for if his pursuit of the 'interior' life was for him a spiritual liberation, its message in the social and political domain was profoundly conservative. His tomb in Lourdes' Church in Sean McDermott Street lies in the heart of one of the most deprived and poverty-ridden areas of contemporary Dublin.[23] A monument to him (1990) by James Power stands on the southern side of the bridge.

Looking downstream fromTalbot bridge you can see, going from south to north: City Quay Church, or more correctly the Church of the Immaculate Heart of Mary (1863); the Gasometer, now disused as natural gas is piped direct from the Kinsale gas fields; the East Link tollbridge (1984) and the lifting-bridge on the North Wall which straddles the opening into Spencer Dock and the terminus of the Royal Canal.

The Financial Services Centre. The centre is located in the old Custom House Docks, a complex of bonded warehouses grouped around St George's Dock and the Inner Dock. Like the Custom House 200 years before, the Financial Services Centre is another self-conscious symbol, the physical proof of commercial faith in an Ireland whose future is seen to be intrinsically linked with the trading possibilities offered by the wider world. Influenced by dockland redevelopment projects abroad, and hoping to benefit from overspill from the burgeoning London financial markets, the Coalition Government set up a special Development Authority in 1986 to draw up a comprehensive plan for the Custom House Docks (as well as designating the site for special tax concessions) seeing it as the key which could unlock the potential of Dublin's redundant docklands. The problem of what to do with docklands, outmoded by new technology, is one faced by most maritime cities as they enter the final decades of the twentieth century. In Barcelona a replanned waterfront was part of an urban strategy for the whole of the city put in place for the 1992 Olympics; in Genoa a scheme by Renzo Piano was chosen to revitalise the port as part of the celebrations for the 500th anniversary of Columbus's transatlantic voyage; and in Dublin a public competition produced a winning scheme by the Irish-led Hardwicke Consortium, whose architects were the American Ben Thompson in collaboration with Dublin-based Burke-Kennedy-Doyle and Partners.

At one time there was a cabman's shelter just outside the site and, inevitably, it featured in *Ulysses*. It was there that Leopold Bloom expounded to Stephen Dedalus on how he would redevelop Dublin, in words which the then Taoiseach, Charles Haughey, quoted at the launching of the planning scheme for the site: 'My beloved subjects, a new era is about to dawn. I, Bloom, tell you verily it is even now at hand. Yea, on the word of a Bloom, ye shall ere long enter into the golden city which is now to be the Bloomusalem in the Nova Hibernia of the future'.[24] Apart from containing the necessary office space for the Financial Services Centre, the new 'Bloomusalem' is also to contain retail, residential and cultural facilities, the latter to be located in a former warehouse, Stack A (1815-20), which was originally designed by John Rennie. Rennie designed both Howth and Dun Laoghaire harbours and developed a considerable reputation for his innovative cast-iron structures. Stack A was primarily designed as a tobacco warehouse and its design was based on the concept of a single open space 20 feet high and subdivided by three rows of columns with a series of cellular vaults at basement level. Other warehouse stacks provided storage for bonded liquor and other exports and, though these have now gone, the most dramatic physical feature of the site still remains, namely the Inner Dock and George's Dock which are interconnected and linked to the river by a series of locks.

Busáras (completed 1953). This - with the exception of Desmond FitzGerald's Dublin Airport – was the first major modern building in the state. Its architect, Michael Scott (1905-89), was probably the most important figure in Irish architecture this century for, to a large degree, it was he who brought about popular awareness of the modern movement in Ireland. One of his first successes was a shamrock-shaped Irish pavilion for the New York World Fair in 1939 which was selected by an international jury as the best in the fair. Busáras was his first big commission (1944) and though a change of government in 1948 led to rows over its eventual function, the building was a popular success (the new government felt that it was too luxurious for a bus terminal and would be better suited as offices for the Department of Social Welfare). Its exuberance and optimism give it an air of almost youthful innocence, reminding us of a time when modernism was still fresh with the promise of a brighter and more egalitarian future.[25]

Beresford Place. This elaborate space was an integral part of the setting devised by Gandon for the Custom House. If we have now almost forgotten that the north-eastern pavilion of that palatial building contained the magnificent private apartments of the First Commissioner of Revenue – John Beresford (1738-1805) – the dynastic reference is at least retained in the name of Beresford Place. John Beresford was a second son of Marcus Beresford, Earl of Tyrone (builder of Tyrone House in Marlborough Street). He was educated at Trinity College where he graduated in 1757. In 1760 he entered Parliament; in 1756 became Privy Councillor; in 1770 a Commissioner of Revenue and in 1780 First Commissioner of Revenue. He was Pitt's principal Irish adviser and, as such, wielded immense influence. When the reforming Lord Fitzwilliam came to Dublin as Lord Lieutenant in 1795 he found that Beresford 'was filling a situation greater than that of the Lord Lieutenant himself' and that he was virtually 'King of Ireland'. Fitzwilliam lost out in the ensuing power struggle, for Beresford and politicians like him were as necessary as ever if the English Govern-

Busáras.

ment was to manage the increasingly obstreperous Irish Parliament in College Green. Despite the legislative independence achieved by Grattan and the Patriot Party in 1782, real power continued to lie with the 'hard men', such as Beresford, Fitzgibbon and Foster, who emphasised the profitability of the British connection. Beresford fought to rationalise duties and commerce in a manner that would provide real free trade, a form of economic community incorporating both islands, though the logic of where this would lead was eventual political union. The rebellion of 1798 came as a terrible shock, showing the limits of the sort of political management at which he was so able, and a frightened Beresford turned the riding school at the rear of the family house in Marlborough Street into a torturing barracks, giving rise to some gruesome graffiti on the stable gate 'mangling done here by John Beresford & Co'.[26] It was a vicious and unfortunate reaction, for it is this descent into barbarity which has lived on in popular memory and not that of the bluff and apparently congenial fixer[27] who enticed the unknown James Gandon from London to build this great Custom House on an unpromising stretch of wind-swept slobland at the mouth of the Liffey.

The curved terrace of houses which holds Beresford Place together is of no mean significance, for though simplified in execution, the elevations are by Gandon and show us how he envisaged the setting for his neoclassical masterpiece. At ground level the façade is rusticated but otherwise the design is restrained, save for an ornamental frieze above the windows at first-floor level. This terrace is now the only example of a unified housing block dating from the 1790s, the sole survivor of the many schemes for unified elevations which the Wide Streets Commissioners approved both for here and elsewhere in the city. Luckily, a speculative proposal of the 1960s to demolish the terrace and replace it with a bronze office block, by Michael Scott and Partners, never came to fruition.[28]

The Dublin Brigade Memorial. The memorial in the garden on the north front of the Custom House is by the Breton sculptor Yann Renald Goulet. The Custom House was set ablaze by the Dublin Brigade of the IRA on 25 May 1921 as part of an effort to undermine the British-run administration during the War of Independence. However, the time allowed to evacuate the building safely was enough for the Black and Tans to arrive and in the ensuing shoot-out five IRA men were killed and another eighty wounded and taken prisoner. The building burned for five days and when subsequently rebuilt certain liberties were taken, the most noticeable being the use of local Ardbraccan limestone in the dome and the non-replacement of the old chimney stacks which were such a conspicuous feature of the old building. Of the original interior little survives other than some lobbies at the centre of the two main fronts. The Custom House is now the headquarters of the Department of the Environment. It was there that the writer

Flann O'Brien worked as a civil servant (it was then called Local Government).

Gardiner Street. The street was laid out in the late 1780s as part of a Gardiner development, capitalising on the Custom House. If the first Luke Gardiner was responsible for giving Dublin its principal north-south axis (what is now O'Connell Street), his grandson, the second Luke Gardiner, gave the city a potentially more handsome thoroughfare, sweeping directly downhill from Mountjoy Square to the triumphal northern front of the Custom House. This was planning on a grand scale. The elevations on the eastern side of the new street (south of the railway bridge) are by James Gandon, the return of his terrace on Beresford Place.[29] A cornice on the upper floor of the terrace provides a visual link with the parapet of the four-storey houses on Gardiner Street.

Beyond the railway bridge (which cruelly cuts across the street just as it arrives at Beresford Place) is Gardiner Street Employment Exchange, originally the Protestant Episcopal Church and later Trinity Church. The church – by Frederick Darley – had its first service on Sunday, 12 November 1839. The doors to the right and left gave access to the gallery which ran along three sides of the building. It was subsequently joined together to make the first floor of the Employment Exchange, which opened in 1921. Now, some seventy years later, the numbers who receive employment benefit and assistance there are even greater, with over 11,000 applicants signing-on on a regular basis.[30]

Lower Abbey Street. It owes its present width and alignment to the Wide Streets Commissioners. In March 1784 Parliament approved of their 'plan for opening Lower Abbey Street and the quay on the north side of river, from Sackville Street eastward to the Custom House ... and a sum of £10,000 [was] granted towards opening said avenues'.[31] This approach to the 'avenue' is flanked by two major office developments by the Irish Life Insurance Company, perhaps the most important institutional investor in the Dublin property market. On the southern side there is an ambitious post-modernist building by A. and D. Wejchert (completed 1991) and on the opposite side the Irish Life Centre (1977-80) by Robinson Keefe and Devane The white arches, dark brick and tinted glazing of the Irish Life Centre owes much to the architects' earlier Stephen Court building in St Stephen's Green. The result is a formidable business citadel protected, as you approach it from the Custom House, by a dry moat with retractable drawbridges. With its Oisín Kelly sculpture, interior courtyards and shopping mall, this is a massive office complex, prefiguring by almost a decade the rival Custom House Docks development.

The Abbey Theatre (1966). The theatre is Lower Abbey Street's main claim to fame and, at the same time, its greatest disappointment. Instead of suggesting that here was something pleasurable, even exciting, the architecture seems determined to dampen the public's enthusiasm by presenting them with an

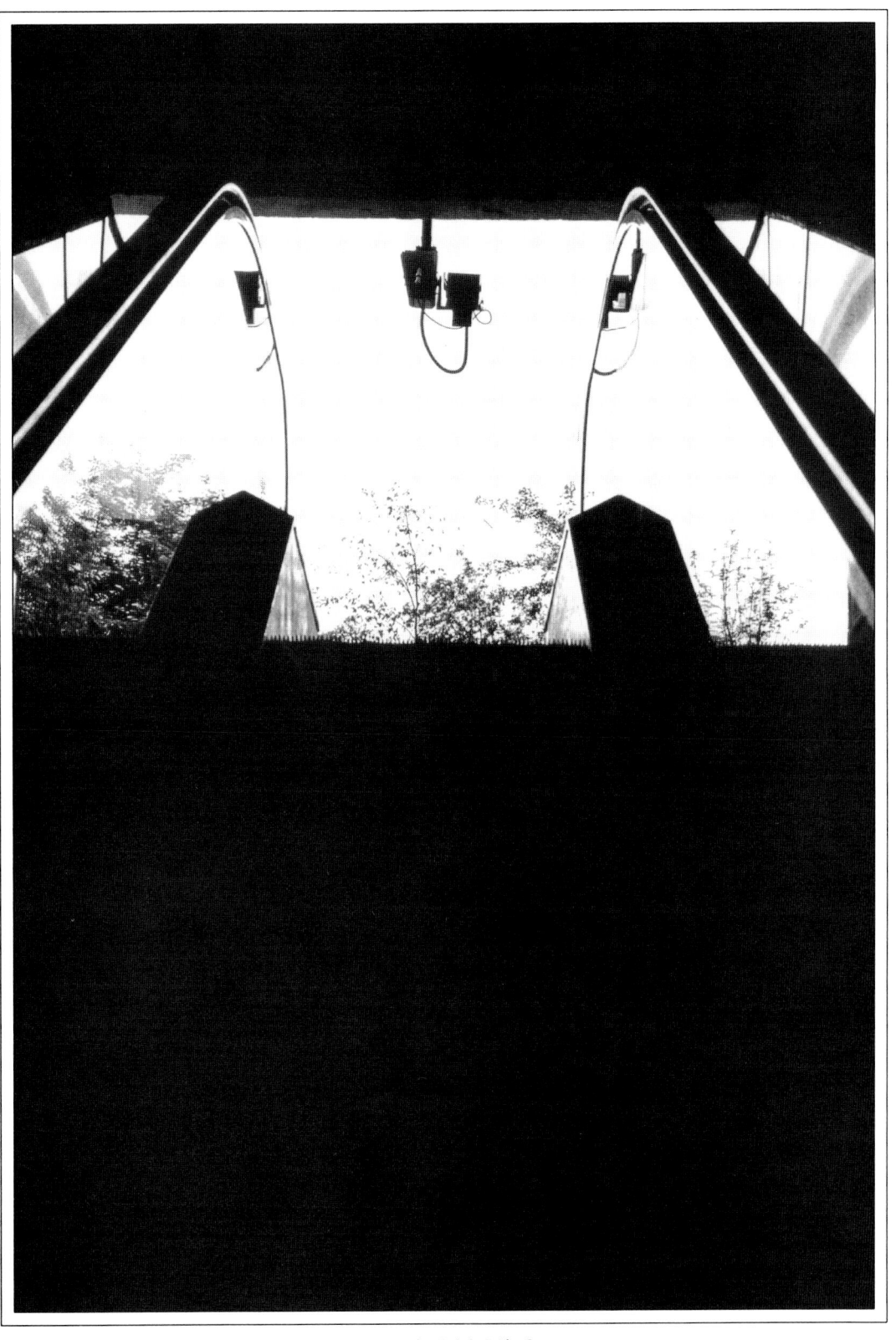

Security at the Irish Life Centre.

immense wall of forbidding grey brick. When the original Abbey Theatre opened in 1904 it was housed in a building that had variously served as a Mechanics' Institute, City Morgue and Music Hall. If the building had no great architectural value, the auditorium, apparently, had excellent acoustics and was capable of seating 500. It was badly damaged by fire on 18 July 1951 and, though there was a temptation to restore it, conservation was not in fashion. Instead, it was felt that the old lady needed a thorough shake-up and Michael Scott was asked to design a completely new building. It has two theatres, the Abbey which seats 640 and the Peacock which is used for smaller productions. Michael Scott seemed the ideal architect, given his own love and experience of theatre. In his early career he combined acting with architecture and played in the Abbey's first productions of *Juno and the Paycock* and *The Plough and the Stars*. But his building was aesthetically disappointing and from the practical point of view of those who worked in it, not very satisfactory.

If the modern movement in architecture, which the Abbey represented, was partly based on the abolition of style; the reappraisal of modernism has involved not only its rejection on the very same grounds (as being just another style) but has led to a revival of interest in designs that draw on forms inspired by the past. What is interesting in the adaptation of the entrance (1989-90, by Niall McCullagh and Valerie Mulvin) is not just the stylistic references – and their work reflects the concerns of such architectural theorists as Aldo Rossi and Leon Krier in its redefinition of spaces and its interest in re-establishing relationships which are rich in historic references (in this case to the porticos that are a feature of a number of key Dublin buildings) – but the way in which the adaptation is part of a programme linking the building to a revitalised street which, if realised, would have two free-standing columns at the river end of a pedestrianised space, in a home-grown response to the Piazzo San Marco. Sadly, however, the cars continue to have priority.

It is an ambitious architectural programme and, though not fully realised, is worthy of a theatre that has had a long and at times a very distinguished career. It was founded as The Irish Literary Theatre in 1898 by W. B. Yeats, Edward Martyn and Lady Gregory, with Miss Annie Horniman of Manchester as a crucial financial benefactor. The cultural revival with which the theatre was associated made 1916, and the political revolution which followed, possible by creating a new ideal of Ireland, though the way in which it found its theatrical expression was often controversial. Yeats's play *The Countess Cathleen* was condemned as heretical by the Catholic hierarchy and Synge's *The Shadow of the Glen* (1904), which dealt with a loveless marriage, was described by the nationalist press as 'an insult to every decent woman in Ireland'. Synge's commitment to depicting Irish peasant reality as he saw it continued to be controversial and

The ceiling of the Minister for Education's office, Tyrone House.

his *Playboy of the Western World* (1907), which showed Irish women competing for the love of an apparent parricide, provoked riots in the theatre. Seán O'Casey caused an even greater rumpus with *The Plough and the Stars* (1926) by questioning the cult of 1916, though the ostensible reason for the uproar was a scene in which the tricolour was shown in a pub frequented by prostitutes, an image of Irish womanhood which the newly independent Ireland preferred to deny.

Marlborough Street. The name probably dates from the 1720s when the Duke of Marlborough was a household name, famous for his victories in the wars of the Spanish succession. The land in the area had previously belonged to St Mary's Abbey and had later been acquired by the Piphoe family. In 1717 the property transferred to the Beresfords when Catherine Power, Baroness de LaPoer, only daughter of James Power, 3rd Earl of Tyrone, and heiress to both the LaPoer and the Piphoe fortunes, married Sir Marcus Beresford.[32]

Tyrone House (Department of Education). Around 1740 Marcus Beresford (who on account of his wife's inheritance had been created Baron Beresford and Viscount Tyrone) commissioned Richard Castle to design him a town house; built of Irish granite it was amongst the first of Dublin's great cut-stone houses. Tyrone House, as it was called, originally had a Venetian window which was centrally positioned at first-floor level. Though this and other features have since been swept away – the interior still retains some fine plasterwork by the Lafranchini brothers.[33] The Board of National Education acquired the building in 1835 and had the façade remodelled in a Greek Revival manner by Jacob

Owen of the Board of Public Works. He was also responsible for the replica building of 1835-38 which, together with Tyrone House, frames the lawned space before the Model Schools (also by Owen). The 'Pieta' by Ermegildo Luppi, was a gift from the Italian Government in appreciation of the relief supplies which had been sent to Italy during 1945-46.

The Pro-Cathedral (1815-25). This was among the first of an exceptionally fine group of neoclassical churches built by the Catholic community in Dublin in the years after Waterloo. Together they constitute the most important group of neoclassical churches in these islands and give an indication of the increasing wealth and influence of the Catholic middle-classes even before emancipation was formally acceded to in 1829. Nonetheless, anti-Catholic prejudices were still very real and so the initial idea of building it in O'Connell Street (where the GPO was later built) was abandoned due to fear of official opposition. Instead, this substitute for a full cathedral (Dublin's two cathedrals became Anglican following the Reformation) stands in a much narrower street where it is less easy to appreciate; but, appreciated it should be, for this great temple raised on a podium is one of the earliest Irish monuments of the Greek Revival. The side façade is particularly impressive with its two stark pavilions. The 'primitive'

Mass at the Pro-Cathedral.

unfluted columns used in the pavilions were not continued in either the front or side porticos (now filled in), which were added later – though as part of the original design– by Joseph B. Keane.

Despite the succession of architects who are known to have supervised the construction work – John Taylor, Richard Morrison (helped by his son William Vitruvius) and John Keane – the architectural origins of the Pro-Cathedral are unclear. The committee in charge chose a design marked 'P' in 1814 which they had received from 'an Irishman then resident in Paris'. This is presumed to be John Sweetman, a United Irishman who had gone into exile after 1798. The plans may be his, or more probably those of a French architect; certainly their advanced design implied a sophisticated familiarity with Parisian churches which would not have been possible for someone resident in Ireland or England as they had been cut off from France by war since 1793. A model of the building was made in 1816 and constantly referred to throughout the construction; it is one of the largest architectural models (with a scale of one inch to a foot) ever made in these islands and miraculously still survives.[34] The church has a splendid neoclassical interior with a stern array of doric columns supporting an uninterrupted entablature with a barrel vault overhead. The incongruous insertion of a dome was a departure from the model and confuses the design. More recently, the marble high altar by the Belfast-born Peter Turnerilli was dismantled and rearranged in the name of liturgical reform, though thankfully a notable series of neoclassical funerary monuments by John Hogan and the free-standing figures of Archbishop Murray and Cardinal Cullen by Sir Thomas Farrell are still *in situ*.

Monto. The street corner beyond the church marked the most westerly point of 'Monto', the red light district of the early 1900s which features in the writings of both James Joyce and Oliver St John Gogarty. The Pro-Cathedral also played a role in its history for Monto's existence was first acknowledged publicly at a Jesuit mission during Lent 1925, probably to put pressure on the local 'madams'; they were involved in discussions with Frank Duff of the Legion of Mary (a Catholic lay organisation) who was trying to negotiate the outright closure of the brothels. At the instigation of Duff, a massive police raid was made on the area on 12 March 1925, just as the Jesuit mission came to a close. Soon afterwards a procession of a *praesidium* of Legion girls made its way through the area, with each former brothel being blessed individually and a holy picture pinned to the door. For Duff it was the end of a campaign that he had waged over the previous two to three years and on the whole it was well received, for many of the prostitutes were diseased and demoralised; needless to say, prostitution continued but its semi-institutionalised existence had come to an end.

The area had got its name from one of its main streets which was called after

Elizabeth Montgomery, the wife of Luke Gardiner; the area was also variously known as 'the kips', 'the digs' and 'the village'. How it developed into a red light district is not very clear; one explanation is that the large number of troops brought to Dublin following Emmet's rebellion of 1803 was too much for the local barracks to accommodate and that the overflow was lodged in Mecklenburg Street; another is that the camp followers of British regiments quartered in Dublin after the Crimean War were lodged there. Certainly, Mecklenburg Street's reputation was sufficiently seedy by 1887 for the Corporation to change its name to Tyrone Street, hoping that this might bring about some transformation. However, given the poverty and the large number of soldiers stationed in the city – not to mind the demands of its own citizens – the Corporation's efforts failed. Brothel madams made a point of studying troop movements and sent their cards to the officers' mess as soon as a new regiment arrived in town.

By 1910 the 'flash houses', which catered for the top end of the market, were in decline, only to be saved by the outbreak of war. With the passing of the Defence of the Realm Acts, the attractions of Monto increased, for apart from the 'girls', it now provided the opportunity for after-hours drinking when the rest of the city's pubs were closed. However, after independence, the new Government was anxious to get to grips with what had effectively become a 'no go' area and so the brothel owners – faced on the one hand by a fall-off in business due to the departure of the troops and, on the other, by the moral power of Frank Duff– came to terms with the realities of life in the Irish Free State.[35]

St Thomas's Church (1758-62). This stood on what is now the junction of Cathal Brugha Street and Marlborough Street, forming the end of a half-mile vista down Sean McDermott Street. It had a façade modelled on Andrea Palladio's Il Redentore, though the Dublin variant of that Venetian masterpiece was never completed and the gable of the nave could be seen awkwardly protruding behind the unfinished pediment. The architect was John Smyth (he also designed St Catherine's in Thomas Street). St Thomas's was where the Gardiners were buried but, like so many other buildings with which they were associated, it was swept away, damaged by fire during the Civil War in 1922 and subsequently demolished so that Sean McDermott Street (then called Gloucester Street) could run directly through to O'Connell Street. Frederick George Hicks's (1870-1965) Lombardo-Romanesque church now stands on the island site created by the demolition of St Thomas's, and the Gardiner's remains have been transferred to a vault in nearby St George's which was originally built to contain bonded spirits of quite a different provenance.[36]

North Great George's Street. This is distinguished by a procession of tall brick mansions which line the street as it climbs upwards towards Belvedere House. The street's history echoes that of the Georgian movement in Ireland for,

St Thomas's Church, 1931. Architect F. G. Hicks.

apart from its architectural importance, it was here that Sir John Pentland Mahaffy lived (he was instrumental in founding the first Georgian Society in 1909), and the street is now the home of the North Great George's Street Preservation Society which has successfully managed to keep at bay the dereliction that has laid waste great swathes of the north inner city. Their campaign to preserve the street has been successful because, in addition to their commitment and tenacity, they had the resources – educational, social and financial – which demoralised and impoverished communities in neighbouring areas lacked. And yet, it has been an uphill campaign; instead of basking in the grateful appreciation of their fellow citizens for having preserved this architectural gem as a living street, there has at best been a reluctant acceptance of their efforts. Mahaffy's own efforts did not helped the preservationists for his 'deliberately reactionary celebration of Georgian style'[37] only put what was already suspect – namely, anything associated with the former ascendancy – into greater disrepute. But then, Mahaffy's judgement was often dubious; he contemptuously dismissed 'that man Pearse' (principal signatory of the 1916 Proclamation and a celebrated educationalist) and bracketed Joyce and George Moore as ne'er-do-wells, thanking God that they had 'cleared out of Dublin' though 'not before they had squirted stink upon all the decent people like a pair of skunks'. Yeats might claim that the minority for whom these houses were built was 'no petty people', that indeed it was 'one of the great stocks of Europe', but for others it was an elite who had 'nothing but an insidious bonhomie' or, as the Ulster poet Louis MacNeice so succinctly put it, 'an obsolete bravado, and a way with horses'. Nonetheless, that society – and particularly the array of builders and artisans on whom it depended – deserves to be celebrated for its cultural achievements, for these were as real and significant as were its obvious failings in so many other spheres.

North Great George's Street follows the line originally laid out as the main approach to Mount Eccles House, a long-vanished house which stood at the rear of what is now the Loreto Convent; numbers 41 to 46. The square crenellated tower, which stands in a playground in nearby Hill Street, was built in 1714 by Sir John Eccles as part of the former Chapel of St George. A later owner of Mount Eccles House, Nicholas Archdale, started selling off building sites along the avenue from the mid-eighteenth century onwards. The houses were built between 1770 and 1800 and many have plasterwork by some of the greatest craftsmen in what was the finest period of Irish architecture. Michael Stapleton, Charles Thorp and Francis Ryan, amongst others, decorated the interiors in a variety of styles from rococo to Adamesque.

Among the houses to be noted as you go up the street are: number 35 where, to disprove Joyce's accusation that such brown brick houses were the very incarnation of cultural paralysis, a James Joyce Cultural Centre has been opened; on the opposite side of the street the original houses were razed in the 1960s, one of them was the home of Major Swann who helped Major Sirr in the capture of Lord Edward FitzGerald, another was used by the Daughters of Erin (a revolutionary group founded by Maud Gonne MacBride); number 20 was the home of Sir Samuel Ferguson, poet and antiquarian; number 38 the home of Sir John Pentland Mahaffy (1839-1918) Provost of Trinity and erstwhile tutor and friend of Oscar Wilde, who shamefully abandoned Wilde when he was imprisoned for his homosexuality, saying 'we no longer speak of Mr Wilde at Trinity' (the tables have turned and few now speak of Mahaffy, at Trinity or elsewhere); number 45, the home of the builder and stuccodore Charles Thorp and number 2 was the Dublin residence of John Dillon (1851-1927), the leader of the anti-Parnellite group of the Irish Nationalist Party after the party split following the O'Shea divorce scandal in 1891.

Belvedere House. This great five-bay mansion, which faces down North Great George's Street, is one of the showpieces of the Georgian city, celebrated both for its architecture and as the Jesuit school which numbered James Joyce amongst its alumni. It was built in the mid-1770s for George Rochfort, the second Lord Belvedere. The architect was Michael Stapleton and the house contains some of his finest plasterwork. Ascending the grand staircase, with its bronze medallions of Apollo in the handrails, the visitor passes by walls of exquisite, vividly coloured plasterwork. On the first floor – the principal floor in an eighteenth-century townhouse – are Belvedere's three most beautiful rooms, named after Apollo, Diana and Venus, though the centrepiece of the Venus room ceiling was removed when the building became a Jesuit school in 1841. In Joyce's time these rooms were used as classrooms, the settings in which he studied Charles Lamb's *Adventures of Ulysses,* submitted an essay on Ulysses entitled 'My Favourite Hero', and became so fascinated with Belvedere's associations with carnal love that he planned to write a book about them: Lady Belvedere, second wife of the first Earl, was suspected by her husband of having had an adulterous relationship with his brother. In 1744 he had her locked up in his second country seat in Gaulstown, County Westmeath, where she remained until her death in 1774. His brother fled abroad but, when he eventually returned, hoping that his brother's temper had improved, Lord Belvedere had him thrown in prison and, to make his feelings absolutely clear, built the still-standing 'jealous wall' at his principal seat, Belvedere (also in Westmeath), to cut off the view of his brother's neighbouring mansion.[38]

Mountjoy Square (1792-1820). Mountjoy Square marks, in a very literal sense, the high-point of the Gardiner achievement, straddling a plateau on the estate and serving as the geographical and architectural focus of a series of great avenues, most notably Gardiner Street (*c*.1787) which has a magnificent down-hill vista of the Custom House set against the outline of the Dublin mountains. Tradition has it that this was the site where Brian Boru pitched the tent in which he was killed after the Battle of Clontarf on 23 April 1014.

The square was laid out by the second Luke Gardiner (1745-98). His initial intention was that the houses on at least one side would share a common façade whose design was to be far more grandiose than anything that Dublin had experienced to date. However, this pomp was never realised, largely because Gardiner, like many other ground landlords, did not finance building construction as such, but instead controlled development through building leases (these obliged tenants to build within a specified period and to follow certain proto-types). The actual construction was usually undertaken by a small number of families who had a long involvement in the building trade and they in general only undertook speculative schemes of three or four houses at a time. Despite Luke Gardiner's membership of the Wide Streets Commissioners, his Mountjoy Square project was not undertaken under their aegis. Unless he was prepared to invest substantial sums in the project, therefore, the smaller speculative developers would have shied away from such an expensive project. Gardiner evidently gave way in the face of these local realities and the project went ahead in the traditional manner, most of the square being completed by 1798 and the remaining east side by 1820. Some of it was speculative housing which would have been let to county families who could not afford a town house of their own and, consequently these buildings had relatively plain interiors; other houses (such as numbers 39-44 by Michael Stapleton) more than compensated, how-ever, and had the elaborate plaster decoration which we associate with Dublin interiors of the period.

The second Luke Gardiner was certainly imaginative in his plans for the development of the family property, though a financially burdened inheritance tempered his ambitions. He himself was a prominent politician (MP for County Dublin from the 1770s), a member of the Wide Streets Commissioners, a spokes-man for the Dublin Circular Road Trustees and he also had an involvement in the Grand Canal Company. He was a supporter of Catholic relief and introduced measures into the Irish House of Commons in 1778 and 1782 which were partially carried. His enthusiasm for the liberalisation of the property laws affecting Catholics may not have been totally disinterested, for the participation of wealthy Catholic merchants was crucial to the development of his north-side estate.[39] It was no disadvantage either that he was related to John Beresford, they were married to sisters, two of the 'Three Graces' painted by Sir Joshua Reynolds. The relocation of the Custom House opened up glorious opportuni-ties for a huge development, running three-quarters of a mile up Gardiner Street

Mountjoy Square West.

to Mountjoy Square and following the curve of the city almost as far again to a proposed 'royal circus' where the Mater Hospital now stands. The circus never got off the ground, for Luke Gardiner was killed while leading the County of Dublin Militia against the insurgents at the battle of New Ross in 1798. The rebellion marked not alone the death of Luke Gardiner but also of the society for which his great schemes had been envisaged; his heirs entered into a different century in which Dublin was no longer a capital but a provincial British city.

It is the dereliction in Mountjoy Square and its neighbourhood which is now so striking. Throughout the nineteenth century the centre city experienced a gradual filtration of the middle classes to the more fashionable suburban townships where, apart from any other attractions, they enjoyed the advantage of lower domestic rates (local taxes). The burden of maintaining services in what was already an impoverished and congested city was left therefore with those who could least afford it. The confessional affiliations which so affected Irish political life exacerbated this trend, for from the mid-century, Dublin city was under Catholic-nationalist control, whereas in the suburbs the independent townships were increasingly seen as beleaguered, if affluent, outposts of the old ascendancy.[40] As the Gardiner estate slid down the social scale, eventually becoming one of the most tenemented areas of the city, the discrepancy between Mountjoy Square and its immediate neighbourhood became more and more marked. This outpost of the upper middle classes could still count its illustrious residents, numbering, amongst others, the Earl of Annesley in number 61 and the Catholic Archbishop Dr Murray in number 44. If its sleepy gentility was not interrupted by the arrival of the tram lines its decline was nonetheless inexorable. In 1914 it could boast of a knight and several clergymen, but along with these and the inevitable solicitors were two private hospitals and 'The Distressed Irish Ladies Home'; by 1920 Seán O'Casey had arrived, installed for a few months in a tenement in number 35 (since demolished) which became the setting for *The Shadow of a Gunman*. All that now survives of the original square are the north and east sides; the west side has seen grave dereliction and the south side has been almost entirely demolished to be replaced by pastiche office buildings.

The Free Church, Great Charles Street. The church, which is located off Mountjoy Square, was erected by the Methodists when the street itself was being built in 1800 (the church was taken over by the Church of Ireland in 1828). The authorship of the building is uncertain, but it may be by an architect called Robins. It was called the Free Church because parishioners didn't have to pay for a pew, hence its popularity with domestic servants from the once-great Georgian houses in the vicinity. The church was acquired from the Church of

Doorway detail, Mountjoy Square South.

Ireland in 1989 by the Dublin Travellers' Education and Development Group, who saw in it the potential to create a resource centre for the travelling community. The architects McCullough and Mulvin, who were also responsible for the new portico at the Abbey Theatre, were commissioned to convert the church into a resource centre. They came up with the concept of creating 'a house within a house'; in effect, a large shed, which stands on stilts in the space between the galleries. This new upper structure, with its red corrugated roof, was inspired by the design of a coal-bagging plant in Carlow. One of the ideas behind the conversion was that if the building should ever again be required as a church, the new structure could simply be removed. It was a solution which has a certain appropriateness, given that 'the concept of a "temporary dwelling" is also well known to the travellers'.[41]

St Francis Xavier's Church (1829-32). Only ten weeks after the Act of Emancipation had received royal consent, the foundation of this church was laid on 2 July 1829. The architect was John B. Keane who had worked on the Pro-Cathedral. Here, however, there was no Greek Revival austerity, but rather a rich, almost romantic, classicism, suitable for a religious order who had been the first in Europe to use lavish decoration to drive home their message. The visitor was to be overwhelmed by the beauty of God's house. The façade echoes that of the contemporary Parisian church Notre-Dame-de-Lorette (1823-36), one of the most highly thought of at the time, whereas the interior was inspired by the great sixteenth-century Jesuit church in Rome, the Gesu, with its exuberant decoration leading dramatically to the church's focal point – the high altar. The altar was brought from Rome by Fr Bartholomew Esmonde, who worked closely with Keane on the design of the building. It was here that James Joyce's family were parishioners and where he recalled – in the *Dubliners* story 'Grace' – 'the light of the lamps [falling] on dark mottled pillars of green marble and on lugubrious canvases '.

Hardwicke Place. This was laid out around 1806 as the centrepiece of another Gardiner scheme with three streets all leading to St George's Church (the church had originally been intended for Mountjoy Square but was put to infinitely greater effect in being relocated as the focal point of this development). It was Eccles Street, which stretches north from here, that was to lead to the jewel in the Gardiner crown, the royal circus; and though it never materialised the circus kept obstinately appearing in plans for the city well into the nineteenth century.[42] The municipal flats now facing St George's Church follow the line of the original crescent which was demolished in 1954.

St George's Church. The church was designed by Francis Johnston and consecrated in 1814. Johnston (1760-1824), who lived in Eccles Street, was one of the most prolific architects of the early nineteenth century; he designed the GPO,

A sign of the times – St George's Church, Hardwicke Place.

The Mater Hospital.

the Chapel Royal at Dublin Castle, and adapted the old Parliament House for its new use as headquarters of the Bank of Ireland. He was a keen bell-ringer and had a five-storey bell-tower built in his back garden. However, the neighbours were less than enthusiastic about his hobby and, bowing to pressure, he presented the bells to St George's on condition that they be rung in his honour at certain times in perpetuity.

The church is certainly a gem, with a 200-foot spire modelled on London's Saint Martin-in-the-Fields. Internally, the building is wider than it is long, with galleries running U-wise round the walls. However, it was built for a congregation which has now practically disappeared; by the late 1980s not much more than thirty could be expected for a Sunday service. What has happened to St George's has happened to Church of Ireland parishes all over central Dublin. Between independence and 1950, more than three-quarters of the Church of Ireland congregation left the city, much of this being migration to the suburbs. Since then sixteen churches including St George's have closed, all of them of either architectural or historical importance and while some have found alternative uses, others, such as St Barnabas's where Sean O'Casey went to church as a boy, have been demolished.[43]

Eccles Street. The building which has determined the evolution of this important street is the hospital which stands at its northern end, for both it and nearby St Joseph's Church were built on ground which had been envisaged for the elliptical royal circus to which the street was to lead. (The hospital did not acquire the site until 1853.) This is one of the few architectural set-pieces in

Dublin, with the portico and spire of St George's in centre stage as you look down the length of Eccles Street from the Mater Hospital; it is all the sadder therefore, that the hospital, which so carefully maintained that vista when it came into being, should have so wilfully participated in its destruction in this century. The Mater Private Hospital (1984-86, by Architects Tyndall Hogan Hurley/Keppie Henderson) now sits at the eastern end of the street.[44] Eccles Street, of course, is now famous for having featured in *Ulysses* where number 7 – now almost completely destroyed – is the fictional home of Leopold and Molly Bloom. Francis Johnston (1761-1829) lived at number 64, which he enlarged and adorned with plaques emblematic of the arts. Cardinal Paul Cullen lived at number 59.

The Mater Misericordiae Hospital. (By John Burke, completed by John L. Robinson). The hospital was opened by the Sisters of Mercy in 1861. It was built in three stages, beginning with the 100-bed central section which is fronted by the city's last great classical façade; the east and west wings followed in 1872 and 1874.[45] Both here and in St Vincent's (opened by the Sisters of Charity in 1834) the nuns provided not only hospitals which had a Catholic ethos but also institutions where Catholic doctors could be trained. For long into the nineteenth century Irish hospitals had been dominated by Protestant practitioners and it was St Vincent's and the Mater which were the first to undermine this domination. In fact, the city was already well provided with public hospitals but then, as the surgeon and writer Oliver St John Gogarty was to say, 'disease in Dublin is a "modus vivendi" and it therefore assumes a religious aspect. There are Protestant, Catholic and Presbyterian diseases in Dublin'.[46]

St Joseph's Church (1880, belfry 1890). This church was built to accommodate the increasing number of Catholic families moving into the area in the latter decades of the nineteenth century. The architects were O'Neill and Byrne. The foundation-stone was laid in 1874 by Cardinal Paul Cullen (1803-78) who, in more senses than one, was the architect of modern Irish Catholicism. His period in Rome as Rector of the Irish College had left him very much a 'Roman' Catholic and on his return to Ireland he oversaw not only the building of numerous churches but more significantly the rebuilding of Irish Catholicism to Roman specifications. He championed the poor, restricted the clergy's political activities and in his opposition to political violence, as well as his refusal to attend receptions at Dublin Castle, succeeded in becoming unpopular with Fenian and Unionist opinion alike. He was to remain at the centre of the various controversies swirling round the church during his long tenure as Archbishop of Dublin from 1852 to 1878.

Mountjoy Street. As with Gardiner Street, Blessington Street, and Great Charles Street, Mountjoy Street commemorates with its name the speculative

St Joseph's Church, Berkeley Road.

proclivities of the Gardiners. If little is known of the origins of the first Luke
Gardiner, the founder of the family fortunes, he certainly did well – becoming
both a successful banker and politician – and married well. His son Charles, who
succeeded in 1755, inherited not only his father's fortune, but also in 1769 the
estates of his maternal grandfather, William Viscount Mountjoy, Earl of Blessington, though he did not enjoy them for long as he died himself in the same
year. It was his son Luke (b.1745) who succeeded in annexing the aristocratic
lineage of his maternal ancestors, being elevated to the peerage as Baron
Mountjoy in 1779 and becoming Viscount in 1795. If Luke the banker was
parvenu, Luke the grandson had certainly arrived. With all this grandeur trailing
in their wake, the Gardiners certainly saw no cause for coyness when it came to
naming their speculative developments. Appropriately perhaps, it is by these
names that they are now remembered for they have endured, unlike the family
that they commemorate. Luke the grandson – who had introduced measures of
Catholic relief in the Irish House of Commons – was killed while leading his
men against the rebels at the Battle of New Ross in June 1798, and Charles John
(b.1782), the son who succeeded, died with no heirs in 1829.

The Black Church. More correctly known as St Mary's Chapel of Ease (1830),
this building gets its popular name from the black colour which the stonework
assumes when it is wet, a not infrequent occurrence in a city where, according
to Stephen Dedalus, the skies are 'as uncertain as a child's bottom'. The architect
John Semple (*c*.1801-*c*.1873) was city architect from 1829 to 1842 and the designer
of over a dozen churches which were built in a rush of building activity before
the abolition of the Board of First Fruits in 1834. The board gave grants for the
building of Church of Ireland churches. Semple 'was a rationalist architect'[47]
and his typical church had narrow lancet windows set between closely spaced
buttresses which sometimes terminated in pinnacles. While the Black Church is
representative of the 'genre', with its striking fortress-like exterior, it is the
interior which is the surprise for it effectively has neither walls nor ceiling, but
both together, in the form of a great curving vault. This method of building in
the 'parabolic style' – each course of stones overlapping the one beneath – used
very little timber and was fire-resistant. Despite its startling effect – or because
of it – the style never caught on and the Black Church remains an exception to
the generality of Irish church architecture. The poet Austin Clarke (1896- 1974)
who grew up in the locality, called his autobiography *Twice Around the Black
Church*; local legend has it that if you run twice round the church at midnight,
the devil will appear.

Dorset Street (originally Drumcondra Lane). This former country road,
which was partly developed by the Gardiners in the mid-eighteenth century,
linked the northern approaches to the capital with Capel Street. Until the 1790s

The 'Black Church', Granby Row.

Capel Street was the most important of Dublin's streets as it was the furthest downstream that one could bridge the Liffey. Dorset Street still has some houses from the 1740s but, like in the neighbouring streets, it is the palpable poverty which is now most evident. The corporation flats date from the sixties and unfortunately, as architecture, do little for the street. They completely disrupt the street-line and the green spaces are wasted, of profit neither to the residents nor to the passers-by.

12 Dorset Street (directly across from the former fire station). This was the birthplace of Richard Brinsley Sheridan (1751-1816). In 1771 the family settled in Bath from where the young Sheridan eloped with Elizabeth Linley, the most famous singer of the day. The plays for which he is known – *The Rivals* (1775) and *The School for Scandal* (1777) – were written to support them in their extravagant lifestyle. Indeed, despite buying and managing the Drury Lane Theatre, he devoted most of his life to politics and held a seat in the Commons for thirty-two years where he was famous for his oratory. His private life, however, was calamitous; his second wife was as extravagant as himself and he died in poverty with the bailiffs in possession of his house. It was a suitably theatrical departure having, as its finale, a magnificently staged funeral in Westminster Abbey.

Henrietta Street. This is the most memorable of Dublin streets epitomising, in one short but splendid stretch of streetscape the magnificence and destitution that can be Georgian Dublin. It is the destitution that has for long been most evident and it can be difficult to imagine that this was once the most prestigious of Dublin addresses. It was laid out in the 1720s by Luke Gardiner, and called after his daughter. He himself lived in number 10 (now, along with numbers 8 and 9, belonging to the 'French Sisters', the Daughters of Charity). Behind the austere façades were palatial interiors with spacious halls and magnificent stairways leading to equally splendid reception rooms. The designs were by the best architects of the period, including Sir Edward Lovett Pearce (numbers 9 and 10, *c.*1730), who had just finished work on the Houses of Parliament in College Green.

If the exteriors are characteristic in their plainness, they are equally characteristic in their respect for proportions. The Palladian objective was to achieve an architectural synthesis of proportionally related ratios and, in the case of the façade, if you didn't quite end up with a Roman temple, you should at least be able to infer the vital elements, suggesting where the columns, cornice and pediment might be. Ideally, a façade should have been one-and-a-half times as high as it was wide (i.e., three storeys in height) but site costs dictated otherwise and so the typical Georgian front is more generally four stories in height. The standard for windows was that the ground and first floor have openings of a similar height (ideally double-square in size), with those on the second floor having a 2:3 proportion and those on the third, or attic level, being square. This sort of window arrangement can be seen in Henrietta Street. More fashionable still are those early eighteenth-century façades which reflect the Italian practice of having windows which are narrower than the area of wall that divides them from each other; useful for excluding the sun but hardly the most practical of Palladian practices given the Irish climate.

The deterioration of the once prosperous north city is nowhere better illustrated than in Henrietta Street. Just before the Act of Union in 1800, almost half of the houses were occupied by members of the aristocracy. And, no doubt, their 'drawing-rooms echoed to the kind of gilded bitchiness that the contemporary playwright Brinsley Sheridan, born only one street away, reproduced in his *School for Scandal*'. However, as Brendan Lehane (to whom I owe the quote) goes on to say 'things are different now'.[48] The Georgian Society Records chronicle the transformation:[49] by 1821 the aristocrats were on the way out with seven of the fifteen houses occupied by lawyers; by 1841 the legal profession in various guises was to be found in no less than thirteen houses and, by the beginning of this century the street had reached its nadir, epitomised in the activities of Alderman Joseph Meade, who stripped numerous houses of their valuable fittings before turning them into slum tenements. At the auction after Meade's death, his nine tenement houses in Henrietta Street were advertised as having a gross rental of £1500 per annum. (Yet, nothing is ever quite as it seems, for Meade was also noted for his active involvement in philanthropic housing schemes and was among the founders of the Association for the Housing of the Very Poor.)[50] In some of the larger Henrietta Street houses there were up to twenty single-room flats accommodating as many families in appalling conditions. This is the Dublin which provides the backdrop for the plays of Seán O'Casey. Though the tenements have now gone – as have most of O'Casey's Dubliners (to housing estates on the city's fringes) – Henrietta Street's downward trajectory has continued and despite the brave efforts of a few lone conservationists, it has survived for much of this century as a depressing reminder of the city's indifference to what should have been the showpiece of Georgian Dublin.

The King's Inns by James Gandon closes off the street at a surprising angle; its curious alignment dictated by the fact that there was already a passageway across the site. The curved triumphal arch was added later (*c*. 1820, by Francis Johnston). To the left of the arch is the Registry of Deeds and below it the King's Inns Library (1827, by Frederick Darley), which replaced three of the street's earliest houses, one belonging to the Church of Ireland Primate, hence the references to 'Primate's Hill'. Two of the early eighteenth-century primates, archbishops Boulter and Stone, exercised considerable political power and lived in great splendour. One contemporary commented that nothing he had seen in England 'could rival the Polish magnificence of Primate Stone'. At his dinner parties 'the rake took the place of the archbishop', though it was at these 'pontifical repasts' that affairs of state were settled and government policy decided.[51]

The Bolton Street College of Technology. The College stands on the site of Gasson's Hotel. It was from here that the Royal Mail coaches departed for the north. Both Gasson's and the neighbouring European Hotel were demolished to make way for the College of Technology which opened in 1913. The building is by former city architect C. J. McCarthy (1858-1947). While its restrained Queen Anne façade is not particularly distinguished, it is a representative enough example of the sort of classicism which was then favoured for libraries and other educational buildings. The School of Architecture enjoys the view from the top-floor double-height windows which can be seen along King's Inns Street. This 1987 extension is by the architects Gilroy McMahon.

Bolton Street. The street was named in 1724 after the Lord Lieutenant, Charles Powlett, Earl of Bolton, now remembered for having once recommended that all unregistered priests should be castrated. This proposal – which was rejected by the English House of Lords – represented the legislative climax of the anti-Catholic penal code which was enacted in the period following the Battle of the Boyne (1690) until the end of the reign of Queen Anne, the years in which Jacobitism was most feared as a force in British and Irish politics. Their purpose was to consolidate an economic and political monopoly in the hands of a narrow caste who differed from the overwhelming majority of the population by origin and religious affiliation; many were the descendants of recent English settlers and almost all were members of the Anglican Church of Ireland. Other Protestant denominations also suffered under the penal legislation.

The code consisted of both civil and religious restrictions, undermining Catholic land-ownership (down to 14 percent by 1703), denying political representation, excluding Catholics from education and banishing their bishops and regular clergy. Ireland became a colonial society where religion played the role of colour: Lord Chesterfield (Lord Lieutenant 1745-6) was to remark, 'the poor people of Ireland are used worse than the negroes.'[52] As the Protestant succession became increasingly secure, particularly after the failure of the 1745 rebellion, the code began to be ignored and was eventually abolished in a series of piecemeal repeals starting in 1778 and ending with the Catholic Emancipation Act of 1829. By that stage, however, the division had run too deep to be easily healed. Though those lives are very distant from us now, it is vital to try and comprehend the demoralisation involved for, perhaps, only it can explain why Catholics in the following century put so much effort and sacrifice into constructing the church buildings that now stand proudly all over the city, the visible proof that Catholicism had not alone survived but that it too was determined to prove itself as capable as Protestant Ireland. These buildings were more than mere testimonials of a Catholic presence, they were the assertion in brick and stone of an alternative world of social and cultural institutions which was capable of embodying the aspirations of an exclusively Catholic and increasingly nationalist Ireland.

St Saviour's Church, Dominick Street. The church (1861) is by the Dublin-born James Joseph McCarthy (1817-82). McCarthy was Ireland's most important advocate of Gothic revival architecture and a founding member of the Irish Ecclesiological Society (1849) which had firm views on church planning and architecture. The society also was a source of useful contacts; in the case of Dominick Street, the prior from whom McCarthy received his commission was chaplain to the society. McCarthy was responsible for the design of an enormous number of religious institutions, having the good luck to be a Catholic – with nationalist leanings – and the good fortune to launch his career in the post-emancipation era when the Catholic Church was building enthusiastically on all fronts. As his friend Charles Gavan Duffy said of him, he 'built more celtic churches than any man of Irish birth since the Goban Saor taught our ancestors to construct the Round Towers'.[53]

In fact there is little that is downright Hibernoesque in the bulk of McCarthy's work. He strenuously proselytised on the importance of returning to medieval principles, arguing, on the lines of Augustus Pugin (1812-52), that the choice of style should be dictated by the available materials, the size of the building and the dictates of the site. In rural locations a simpler style was preferable while in cities an ornate and decorative approach was called for in order to make an impact against the surrounding buildings. In St Saviour's, the most important of McCarthy's city churches, the street front is appropriately ornate, and though the carving was never finished (nor a projected tower and spire), there is no shortage of pinnacles and other decorative features. It certainly contrasts with the plain brick façades of its Georgian neighbours. Inside there are clustered columns which divide the nave from the aisles and exceptionally large windows with delicate tracery to let in plenty of light. As with other Catholic buildings of the mid-nineteenth century, St Saviour's reflected the increasing tendency to draw on French models. Regrettably, the impact of ecclesiastical models in this century has not been so benign, and the fine marble high altar and reredos have been destroyed in the cause of post Vatican II liturgical reform.

Dominican Priory (1885). The priory adjoining St Saviour's is by John Loftus Robinson (1848-94), another Catholic architect who was active in municipal politics, being a member of both Dublin Corporation and Kingstown Urban

Council. He died from typhoid fever at the relatively early age of forty-six.[54]
Amongst his other known works are Dun Laoghaire (then Kingstown) Town
Hall and the spire of St Michael's, now the only remaining portion of the old
Dun Laoghaire parish church.

Lower Dominick Street. Like Henrietta Street, this street has seen better days.
It owes its name to the Dominick family who developed their property in the
area from the 1750s on. Number 20 was among the first houses to be built and

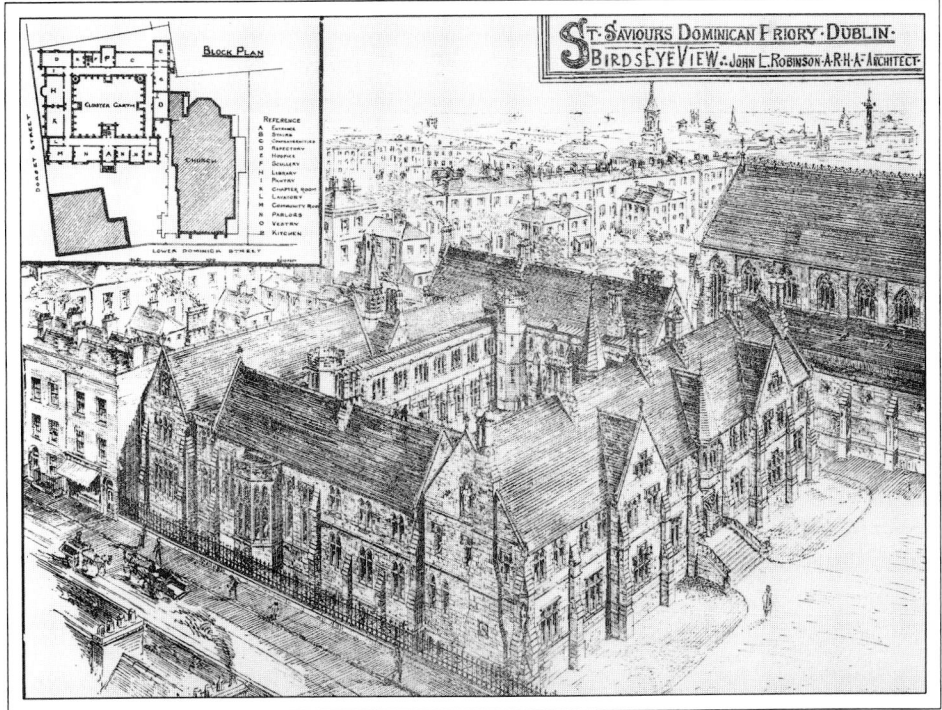

Bird's eye view of St Saviour's Dominican Priory, the Irish Builder, *15 February 1890.*

is now one of the few to remain. Robert West (d.1790), master-builder and
stuccodore, built it for himself in 1755. The interior has a stunning display of his
plasterwork, with a riotous use of swirling foliage and beautifully modelled
birds in high relief which emerge from the walls as if about to fly away. The
entrance hall represents the work at its most extravagant while the more sedate
salon indicates a strong French influence (from the use of engravings by
Boucher). In all, it represents the most remarkable example of native Irish stucco
work. The building now belongs to St Saviour's Orphanage.

Entrance hall and staircase, number 20, Lower Dominick Street.

Thanks to Lady Sydney Morgan (1783-1859), we have a description of the decor of a more conventional Dominick Street drawing-room of the late eighteenth century, though the proprietor herself seems to have been out of the ordinary. As a young woman – years before she became a patron of Dublin's literary and social life – Lady Morgan accompanied Mrs Featherstone, of Bracklyn Castle in County Meath, when she came to Dublin to dispose of the contents of her mother's town house in Dominick Street. Her mother, the Dowager Lady Steele, had died in 1800; her 'almost last words' provoked by a cry of 'fresh oysters' from a fish-women passing in the street. 'That's a lie,' exclaimed the indignant Dowager, expiring at the memory of the stale fish which the same voice had fobbed off on her days before.[55]

The young Lady Steele had been a belle at Lord Chesterfield's Court (Viceroy 1745-6) but in her old age she became a recluse. 'The best drawing-room had not been entered for some years, and on opening the doors there was a rent in the tapestry of cobwebs, which was quite suffocating.' The curtains of rich crimson satin damask were heavily lined, wadded and finished at the bottom with leaden weights to regulate the rise and fall. 'The beautiful marble chimney-piece, finely sculptured, reached halfway to the ceiling, and was surmounted with a range of Etruscan vases. The ponderous chairs and settees, as the sofas were called, were regimented against the wall, and intermingled with cabinets inscrutable from the dust.' A large table stood in the middle of the room and a thick Turkish carpet covered the floor. The walls were covered with Chinese paper, the only other decoration being 'girandoles' (branched candle brackets). Everything, of course, had to be changed and Mrs Featherstone immediately ordered new furniture from the most fashionable upholsterer in Dublin 'from whose taste there was no appeal'. Out went the Chinese paper to be replaced by highly glazed lemon-coloured hangings with dark chintz borders. Out went the Etruscan vases to be replaced by Derbyshire spar. 'Pier-tables' were painted and gilded and, under the mirrors, were placed tables covered with filigree ornaments, obligingly painted by Lady Morgan, though she disapproved of the change, dismissing it all as 'the result of the frippery influence of Carlton House on the taste of the day'.[56]

As with Henrietta Street, Dominick Street's decline was gradual but inexorable. The lower east side was demolished in the 1950s and the houses opposite were pulled down in the 1960s, all being replaced by corporation flats. Houses that have gone include number 36, the birthplace of Sir William Rowan Hamilton, the mathematician, which was demolished in the late 1970s. Number 45 was the birthplace of Joseph Sheridan LeFanu (1814-73), journalist and novelist, who made his reputation as a master of the mysterious and uncanny, with books such as *The House by the Graveyard* (1863) and *In a Glass Darkly* (1872).

Parnell Square. Originally called Rutland Square it is the second oldest of Dublin's squares. It was developed around the Rotunda Gardens over a twenty-year period, beginning with the laying out of Cavendish Row (the lower end of Parnell Square east) by Luke Gardiner in the early 1750s. Most of the leases were either taken up by private individuals on their own account or by speculative developers such as John Ensor (site architect at the Lying-in Hospital) and Henry Darley (whose family owned the Ardbraccan and Golden Hill quarries). It contained some of the city's most palatial houses; number 4 belonged to the Earl of Wicklow, number 5 was the birthplace of Oliver St John Gogarty, number 6 belonged to Richard Kirwan (1733-1812), a noted County Galway scientist whose aversion to flies was so great that he paid his servants a premium to destroy them, number 9 was a joint venture by John Ensor and Frederick Darley for Bartholomew Mosse and number 11 was the Dublin residence of the Earl of Thomond.[57]

Parnell Square North. Palace Row, as it was originally known, was laid out by John Ensor in 1755 and clients sought for the sites. The centrepiece of the terrace is number 22 – Charlemont House (1762-5) – a five-bay mansion with curving screen walls which now houses the Hugh Lane Municipal Gallery of Modern Art. It was built for James Caulfield, Earl of Charlemont (1728-99) who chose as his architect one of the greatest figures in British architecture, Sir William Chambers. Charlemont had made the Grand Tour between 1746 and 1754 (including a pioneering trip to Greece, Turkey and Egypt in 1749) and on returning to Dublin became a leading figure in the city's cultural life.[58] Charlemont House was intended to be one of Dublin's finest mansions and in choosing Chambers as his architect, Charlemont showed not only the strength of his cosmopolitan connections (Chambers's extremely influential *Treatise on Civil Architecture* had been published in 1759) but also indicated his intention of becoming an unofficial arbitrator of architectural taste in the Irish capital. Charlemont devoted himself to architecture – he built the delightful Casino (again by Chambers) at his seaside demesne at Marino – to literature and to the affairs of the Royal Irish Academy (which he was instrumental in founding in 1785). He was also involved in politics as an ally of Grattan's and became Commander-in-Chief of the Volunteer movement which played a crucial role in pressurising the Government to concede legislative freedom to the Irish Parliament.

Sadly, little remains of Charlemont's townhouse; the magnificent library rooms which stood at the end of the garden were demolished by Dublin Corporation in 1929 (along with a library by Gandon which was located to the side of the long corridor which connected the library wing to the main house); the front has been marred by the 1933 doorway and all that remains of the interior is the oval staircase and some rooms on the upper floors. Nonetheless, its transformation into an art gallery would certainly have met with Charlemont's approval.

The Hugh Lane Municipal Gallery of Modern Art. The name tells all, for the nucleus of the collection consists of the pictures left to the city by Sir Hugh Lane. He drowned in the *Lusitania* in 1916 but, as the codicil to the will in which he spelt out his intentions was not witnessed, this legacy became the subject of a long and bitter wrangle between the British and Irish authorities. (Furious over the Corporation's refusal to house the collection in a specially built gallery which Lutyens had proposed for the site of the Ha'penny Bridge, Lane had bequeathed his collection to the National Gallery in London in an earlier will). Since 1959 it has been agreed to divide the collection in two parts and these are shown alternatively in Dublin and London in five-year cycles. The collection includes works by Corot, Degas, Manet, Monet, Pissarro, Renoir and other Impressionist masters. The gallery also has other important nineteenth- and twentieth-century works.

The Dublin Writers' Museum. Numbers 18 and 19 Parnell Square, where a writers' museum was opened during Dublin's tenure as European City of Culture in 1991, are amongst the most important of late eighteenth-century

Dublin houses. There is a splendid ceiling by Michael Stapleton in what is now the Gorham Library on the ground floor of number 18 and further breathtaking Adamesque ceilings in the main rooms on the first floor. In the 1890s, when it was the home of the Jamesons – owners of Bow Street distillery – a riotous frieze was added as the rooms' original decor was regarded as too plain. An ornamental colonnade was also installed to transform what had previously been two rooms into one magnificent salon. This redecoration was carried out by Alfred Darbyshire (1838-1908), a Manchester architect who, at the age of twenty-three, had designed a sugar refinery on Grand Canal Quay which was the first building in the world to have used cast iron for load-bearing purposes (it is now the Tower Design Centre). Here in Parnell Square his redecorative work was less innovatory and more in keeping with his reputation as a theatre architect; the decoration includes the stained glass windows above the staircase which features four female figures representing Art, Literature, Music and Science, as well as the painted door panels in the main reception rooms representing the quarters of the day and the months of the year. In the adjoining building, number 20, home of the Irish Writers' Centre, there is a delightful example of a stucco-work 'bird ceiling', one of the key motifs of the local rococo style which developed in Dublin during the 1760s. Other notable examples of stucco-work were to be found at Dr Mosse's house at 9 Cavendish Row – for which Robert West

The Garden of Remembrance.

received final payment in 1758 – and at number 15 Parnell Square East which was tragically destroyed in the mid-1980s.[59]

The Abbey Presbyterian Church (1864, by Andrew Heiton of Perth). This is nearly always referred to as 'Findlater's Church' after Alexander Findlater, a Scot who established a leading grocery chain in Dublin and who financed the building of the church. Inevitably, it features in *Ulysses*.

The Garden of Remembrance. This memorial was opened in 1966 as part of the 1916 celebrations of that year to commemorate those who gave their lives for Irish freedom. The garden was designed by Daithi P. Hanley of the Office of Public Works and – though it looks as if it had been dropped into the site almost by accident – it does succeed within its own frame of reference. The sculpture (1971) by Oisín Kelly depicts the legendary Children of Lir who were turned into swans: the sculptor's inspiration being Yeats's poem 'Easter 1916' and the idea that people at certain moments of history are 'transformed utterly'.[60]

The Rotunda Gardens. The Garden of Remembrance, unfortunately, relates in no way to the surroundings or to the history of the square which developed around Dr Mosse's pleasure gardens. However, the Rotunda Gardens are among the more positive aspect of the eighteenth-century city and deserve to be remembered. Roughly where the northern arm of the sunken pool is now located was where the loggia which sheltered the musicians was situated. At the northern end of the square were two delightful little temples which apparently served as rest-houses for sedan-chair carriers.[61] A tax on sedan-chairs was one of the many means of subvention used to keep the Lying-in Hospital financially afloat. Below the loggia – along what is now the main axis of the Garden of Remembrance – there was a terrace called the orchestra and from there the gardens stepped down towards a bowling green and the hospital. The remainder of the space was laid out with winding walks bounded by shrubbery and allowed for maximum promenading. For a while the gardens were embellished with sculptures by John Van Nost but these were removed by Van Nost as he only received a part payment for his work. Nonetheless, the gardens were a great success, bringing in about £400 a year from a variety of entertainments: concerts and plays, promenading and bowling with, on special occasions, fireworks and fancy illuminations. It is disappointing that the Garden of Remembrance fails to remember Dr Mosse and his pleasure grounds. However, the new garden does provide a welcome place in which to relax, and where better, remembering not only those who gave their lives for Irish freedom but also those who enjoyed themselves when it was a much less solemn spot, a pleasure ground dedicated to aiding the countless women who were giving birth – in the most fundamental sense possible – to what always will be Ireland's future.

Detail from the elevation from the east side of Sackville Street by Thomas Sherrard, 1789.

Elevation of Beresford Place by James Gandon, 1790.

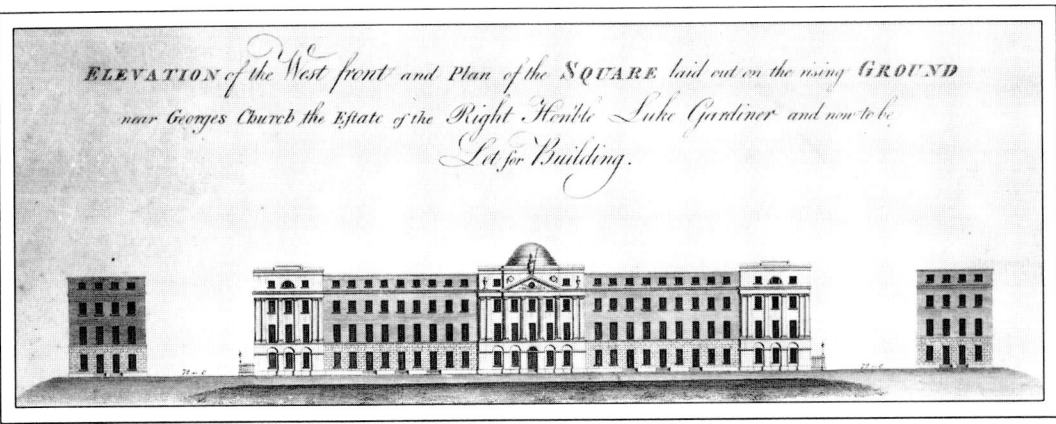

Proposed elevation of the west front Mountjoy Square by Thomas Sherrard, 1787. Though the plan for the square is by Sherrard it is unlikely that he was responsible for this elevation.

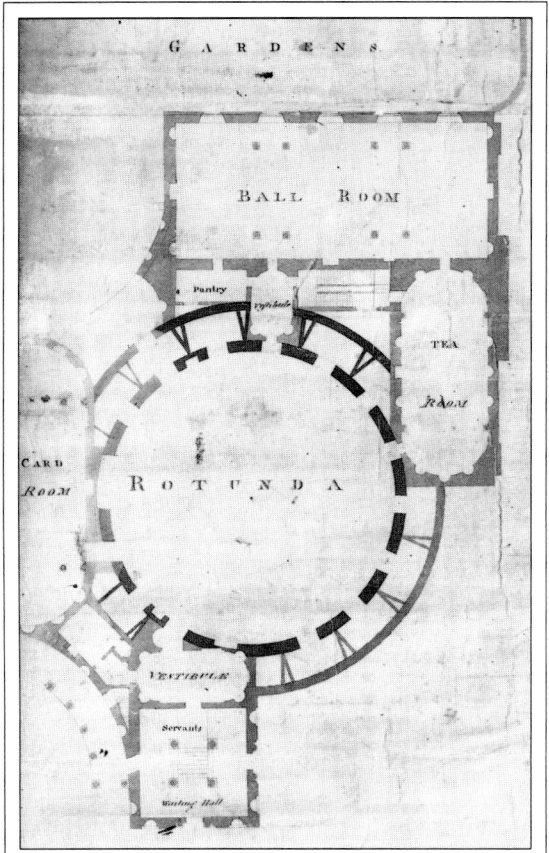

Plan of the assembly rooms at the Rotunda. Detail from a map by Thomas Sherrard, 1787.

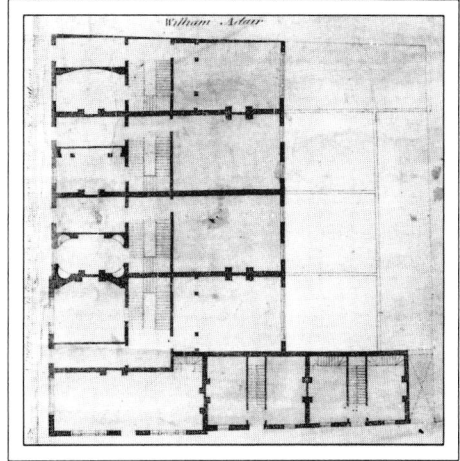

Map, elevation and plans for houses and shops at the corner of Cavendish Row and Great Brittain, now Parnell, Street. Above: Map by Thomas Sherrard, 1787. Below: The plans, probably by James Gandon, are unique among contemporary townhouses in their spatial variety.

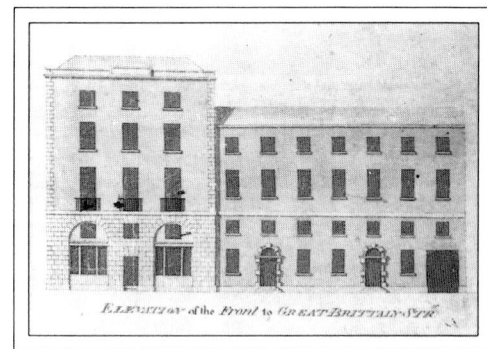

Town
&
Gown

TOWN AND GOWN

Dublin can be Heaven
With coffee at eleven
And a stroll in Stephen's Green
You don't have to worry
There's no need to hurry
You're a king and the
Lady's a queen.

SUNG BY NOEL PURCELL, C. 1940

The ground to be explored south of the Liffey is divided into three parts: the first sweeping anti-clockwise from Westmoreland Street to Kildare Street and back, the second being Trinity College and the third St Stephen's Green.

The layout of this area owes much to seventeenth-century initiatives. As elsewhere outside the old city walls, it was the potential of former monastic lands which helped determine future growth. In 1591 the former monastery of All Hallows was chosen as a location for Trinity College. In 1595 there was another important arrival when Carey's Hospital, 'a large mansion, with a gatehouse, a garden and plantation',[1] was built nearby by Sir George Carew as a place of retirement for old and maimed soldiers who had fought with him in Munster. It was never put to this use and later passed to Sir Arthur Chichester; renamed as Chichester House, it became the seat of Parliament in the early seventeenth century. Between Trinity and the old city the grounds of another former monastery – this time an Augustinian foundation – were developed by William Crow as he and his neighbours built houses with gardens stretching back to the river. The Crow, Eustace, Temple and Anglesea families have all given their names to streets in what is now known as the Temple Bar area. South of the Dame Street-College Green axis, lay property belonging to the city itself – the area around St Andrew's Church (known as 'the whole land of Tibb and Tom') and the Molesworth and Dawson estates, all of which were developed in the early eighteenth century, bridging the gap between the city and its most famous speculative development of all, the late seventeenth-century St Stephen's Green.

With Parliament and Trinity College housed at one end of the Dame Street-College Green axis and Dublin Castle at the other, it was, not surprisingly, of great interest to the Wide Streets Commissioners. Their initial brief, after all, had been to make 'a wide and convenient way ... to the Castle of Dublin', admittedly from Essex Bridge, but, with that project completed (1762), Dame Street became the inevitable, if not immediate, sequel. Various plans were mooted, including one for an entirely new street running westwards from St Andrew's Church. In the parliamentary session of 1777-8, £5000 was granted for widening the end of Dame Street near the Castle. Serious work started in 1782 when the block between Palace Street and George's Lane (South Great George's Street) was rebuilt.

The commissioners were not only concerned with the width but with the total look of the new street. Precise instructions were given as to the kind of buildings which they wished to see (the plans and elevations were by Thomas Sproule). When the windows in one house were considered to be 'a few Inches too Low' and the windows of the adjoining house 'too high by four Inches & an Half' the owners were ordered to make the necessary alterations.[2] Between 1785-1790 another block was built between George's Lane and Trinity Street and the drawings for this – by A. Baker, though derived from Sproule – were for a unified, if plain, façade with the end and middle blocks projecting slightly. This was a radical departure for Dublin architecture and equally remarkable was the fact that the design incorporated shops at the ground-floor level, with a shop window occupying the full width of every alternative arch.[3] This sort of architectural treatment was not to be realised in London until after the Napoleonic period.

By the time the eighteenth century had come to its close (and with it the Parliament which had been the focus of that society which gave us the Wide Streets Commissioners) the city's geography had been changed entirely, for Dublin had acquired an entirely different centre of gravity, defined by the axis running from Parnell Square to St Stephen's Green. It met the old medieval east-west route just outside the very door of Parliament in College Green. This new cross-river axis linked the rival late eighteenth-century suburbs which were expanding on either side of the Liffey and became the spine on which central Dublin has since developed. Up to the 1790s Essex Bridge (Grattan Bridge/Capel Street Bridge) had been the lowest crossing point on the Liffey and the streets leading to it from both north and south were consequently the principal ones in the city. By the time the commissioners achieved the laying-out of Westmoreland Street in the early 1800s, they had succeeded in shifting the city's equilibrium much further downstream. This crucial shift eastwards was no mean achievement. The laying-out of a new axis which links Parnell Square in the north with St Stephen's Green in the south involved not only the building of a new bridge (1791), where O'Connell Bridge now stands (and consequently the building of a new Custom House (1781-91) further downstream), but also the creation of numerous new streets. Without doubt it is the most significant contribution which eighteenth-century planning has made to Dublin.

Above: Portico of the Bank of Ireland, Foster Place.
Page 133: The entrance to Trinity College.

Westmoreland Street to Kildare Street

Westmoreland Street. Both Westmoreland Street (*c*.1800) and Lower O'Connell Street (1782-84) were planned on an ambitious scale. The commissioners considered various proposals for the new Westmoreland Street. Given our climate, it is to be regretted that they abandoned one suggestion for a sixty-foot-wide carriageway flanked by covered colonnades. The plan which was chosen was for a wider street of ninety feet flanked by buildings with uniform façades and incorporating shops at ground level. Unfortunately the original Westmoreland Street elevations (by Henry Aaron Baker) are now almost impossible to make out.

The creation of this new axis involved a major re-orientation in the way the city was organised. One of the most splendid examples of what this led to is the eastern portico of the former Houses of Parliament (now the Bank of Ireland). This is a relatively late addition (1780s) to a building which had been built with no thought of Westmoreland Street in mind. The former Parliament (1730s) faces southwards on to College Green. However, the eastern portico is no mere side entrance but the entrance to the former House of Lords. Perhaps its splendour was a compensation for the fact that the Lords' chamber occupied a decidedly subordinate position in the original layout of the building. Parliament was dominated, both architecturally and politically, by the House of Commons. James Gandon (1743-1823), the architect of the new entrance, married new to old by erecting the great curving wall which links the portico to the main front in College Green. Originally this wall had no decoration other than the series of empty niches. It was Francis Johnston (1760-1829) who added the engaged columns; he had the task of reconciling Gandon's work with a different extension (*c*.1792) on the far side of the building.

The Bank of Ireland. The three-sided colonnaded front of the former Parliament is probably best seen from the traffic island on College Green where Henry Grattan now presides. This was Europe's first purpose-built bicameral legislature (1720-39). The architect, Sir Edward Lovett Pearce (1699-1733), was knighted in the building on 10 March 1731. His genealogical qualifications were certainly impeccable, his mother being the daughter of a former Lord Mayor of Dublin, his father a first cousin of Sir John Vanbrugh, the noted English architect. A doorway under the central portico originally led, via two ante-rooms, to the centrepiece of the design, the octagonal chamber of the House of Commons. It was the most elegant parliamentary chamber in Europe, with the seating rising from the centre to a backdrop of ionic columns which marked the boundary between the chamber proper and the surrounding public gallery. Overhead there was a pantheon-like dome, but this was destroyed by fire in 1792. The chamber itself was replaced by one of an inferior circular design, by Vincent Waldre. It was here that the last session of Parliament ended on 2 August 1800. Following the sale of the building to the Bank of Ireland in 1802, Waldre's House of Commons was replaced by the Bank Board Room, Governor's Office and Accountant General's Office.

The chamber of the House of Lords occupied a much less prominent position than that of the Commons, lying off to the right of the building's main axis which led directly from the entrance to the House of Commons. However, unlike the Commons, the chamber of the House of Lords survived and can be visited. Edward Smyth carved the statues of Minerva (Wisdom), Justice and Liberty over Gandon's great portico to the House of Lords. On entering from College Street you pass through a processional sequence of spaces – rectangular vestibule, rotunda and a smaller vestibule again – which led directly to the House of Lords. However, as the doorway which gave access to the chamber (to the left of the inner vestibule) is closed, continue along the corridor, turning to your left, until you come to a large rectangular hallway (with several doorways opening off it), where a polite request to a bank porter may gain you admission to the Lords' Chamber. It looks much as the architect, Sir Edward Lovett Pearce intended. The rest of the bank's interior dates from the post-1804 reconstruction by Francis Johnston (1760-1829). The House of Commons, which had been the centrepiece of Pearce's building, was subdivided into offices, though the top-lit corridor which surrounded it on three sides was unchanged. The Commons antechambers were converted into the great rectangular cash office where the bank's public business is still conducted.[4]

College Street. To the south of College Street there is the great mass of Trinity College. The magnificent railings which sweep the footpath around into College Green pass beneath one of the most distinguished Palladian frontages in these islands. From the portico of the Bank of Ireland you can enjoy to the full the play between the projections and recessions in the façade and the masterly way in which the whole exercise terminates in the powerful end-pavilions with their great Venetian windows. Both Trinity and the former Parliament House dominate the junction with an authority which brooks no competition from the less-decisive Victorian arrivals. These great palatial structures not only set standards in taste and architectural propriety in their day, they also bore witness to the fact that Ireland was intent on playing its role in the mainstream of European culture and could master the classicism in which that culture found its expression.

However, the Victorian additions are not to be ignored. At the corner of Westmoreland Street and College Green there is a notable Venetian-style office building (1875) by Thomas Newenham Deane and further east – midway along the south side of College Street – the great Corinthian columns belong to the former Provincial Bank (1862, by William G. Murray). The pediment sculpture by S. F. Lynn depicts the 'genius of banking' (a seated female figure) flanked by the 'spirit of commerce and manufacture as represented by the British merchant'. Agriculture is represented by a graceful female attended by farm labourers. Behind the merchant stoops a sturdy servant who apparently illustrates 'that portion of the country's wealth which is in the form of muscle and sinew' while the black man beside him, represents the 'raw produce'![5]

Thomas Moore (1779-1825). Moore was at one time idolised as a national poet for his popularisation of traditional songs and, though fashions change, he deserved better than the lumpen piece of bronze by Christopher Moore (1790-1863 and no relation) which stands alongside a public toilet at the junction of College Street and Westmoreland Street. It has been an object of derision ever since it was erected in 1857. One of Moore's most popular melodies was 'The Meeting of the Waters' and the inevitable occurred. Leopold Bloom, in his famous trek across Dublin on 16 June 1904, passed 'under Tommy Moore's roguish finger', unkindly considering that 'they did right to put him up over a urinal: meeting of the waters'. Even Patrick Kavanagh coldly contemplated Moore's misfortune:

> The cowardice of Ireland is in his statue,
> No poet's honoured when they wreathe this stone.

Henry Grattan (1746-1820). Only a short distance from the unfortunate statue of Thomas Moore there is a more handsome memorial (by John Henry Foley, unveiled 1876) to one of the great heroic figures of the old Irish Parliament, Henry Grattan. He stands with arm upraised, declaiming to the passing populace in College Green. Through his efforts the Irish legislature succeeded in gaining an unprecedented degree of independence from the effective seat of government in London, though it failed to become the organ of statesmanship which he had hoped for. The rebellion of 1798 was to result in the demise of 'Grattan's Parliament' for it rocked the confidence of the landed society which had made Dublin the eighteenth-century city it was. Fearful of being swamped by an emancipated Catholic majority at some future date, and reeling under the effects of unprecedented bribery, the Parliament voted itself out of existence on 7 June 1800, choosing instead to incorporate itself in a new political union, the United Kingdom of Great Britain and Ireland.

Thomas Davis (1814-45). Patriotic sculpture has had a troubled history in Dublin. In addition to Henry Grattan, College Green is also home to a memorial by Edward Delaney to Thomas Davis, a leading Young Irelander and founder of the *Nation* newspaper. The four bronze figures trumpeting into the pool represent the heralds of the provinces. Bronze reliefs in the granite tablets surrounding the fountain illustrate themes from the poetry of Davis – 'The Penal Days', 'Tone's Grave', 'The Burial', 'We Must Not Fail' and 'A Nation Once Again'. A sixth bronze depicts the Great Famine. The Thomas Davis memorial, which was unveiled by President de Valera in April 1966, stands roughly on the site of an earlier equestrian statue of William of Orange. This unfortunate memorial by Grindling Gibbons (1648-1721) had been unveiled with much ceremony on 1 July 1701. However, it soon became a focus for both loyalist parades and nationalist protests. Despite being blown up in 1836, it was sufficiently restored to survive into this century before finally succumbing to another explosion in 1929.[6]

College Green. The name is all that survives to indicate that this once formed part of Hoggen Green, a stretch of open ground where the Vikings had a mound for their assembly called the Thingmote. It survived near Suffolk Street until 1685. In the Middle Ages a great pageant was enacted here each year by the city's guilds, on the feast of Corpus Christi. After the opening of the university in 1592 the area became known as College Green and the area between there and the Castle developed as a fashionable location for Stuart housebuilders. The locality's importance was confirmed when Carey's Hospital (1595) became the seat of Parliament in the seventeenth century. (Chichester House, as it was subsequently renamed, was demolished to make way for Sir Edward Lovett Pearce's buildings). The presence of the Parliament was crucial, for one of the great projects of the Wide Streets Commissioners was to improve the route between the Castle and the Parliament on College Green.

Most of the College Green banks are Victorian. Their grandiosity owes more to public relations than to any great theorising over architectural values. As the *Dublin Builder* rather disarmingly commented in 1863, if 'a man is generally regarded as a gentleman because he has a good suit of clothes on his back, so also does a respectable show by a commercial establishment inspire confidence in the healthiness of its constitution'.[7] The confidence wasn't always merited. In the case of the former Union Bank – at the corner of Church Lane and Dame Street – the architecture proved to be more durable than the actual institution. Within a year of moving into this attractive building (Venetian palazzo underneath, Flemish townhall on top) the company collapsed and the premises were taken over by the Hibernian Bank. It now belongs to the Northern Bank. The building (1867) is by William G. Murray.

The most elaborate of the College Green banks – at least for its façade – is the Ulster Bank. If anything this Baroque edifice (*c.* 1891) is in danger of being over the top. As the Victorian era drew to a close, classical architecture grew increasingly eclectic, borrowing and mixing from an ever-widening range of sources, and this ornate façade by Sir Thomas Drew (1838-1910) is no exception.[8] The modern stone-clad extension is by architects Boyle and Delaney (1982).

The chaste, if more expansive, building to the east of the Ulster Bank was previously the head office of the National Bank (it now belongs to the Bank of Ireland). The design by Charles Geoghegan (1820-1908) for the Italianate front dates from 1862, though it wasn't built until the 1880s. With Daniel O'Connell amongst the bank's founders, it is hardly surprising that the building is crowned by a piece of patriotic sculpture. Erin is depicted with her harp, an ancient crown and an Irish wolfhound by her side, along with various emblems of trade and commerce, all perched on a pedestal bearing the inscription *Erin go brágh.* The sculpture is by Pearse and Sharp and looks across at the royal arms of the former Parliament.[9] The final building in this easterly sequence (Fox's) is by T. N. Deane and Son, 1881.

Foster Place. This also evolved under the auspices of the Wide Streets Commissioners. It was developed in the late 1780s when the House of Commons was extended westwards by the demolition of the neighbouring houses. Robert Parke was responsible for the extension to the Parliament and linked his new ionic portico to the building's main front by an open quadrant of free-standing columns set before a niched screen wall. Francis Johnston subsequently brought the screen wall forward and, in order to better balance one end of the building with the other, altered Gandon's screen wall to achieve a similar result. Johnston was also responsible for the monumental arch at the end of Foster Place; it served as a former guard room for the bank (the military trophies were carved by Thomas Kirk). The neoclassical porch on the western side of Foster Place marks the entrance to the former headquarters of the Royal Bank of Ireland (by Charles Geoghegan).[10] It is now a branch office of the Allied Irish group. The handsome Victorian banking hall with its tiled floor, rich plasterwork and horseshoe-shaped mahogany counter is still intact.

Daly's Club. Francis Johnston's brother Richard was responsible for the block stretching from Foster Place to Anglesea Street. At the centre of this development was Daly's Club. The club had its origins in the less exalted confines of Patrick Daly's Chocolate House, but such was its popularity among fashionable society that by the 1780s new premises were required. The sober granite-fronted building which we see today was, strictly speaking, all that belonged to the club, though Richard Johnston (1754-1806), was asked by the Wide Streets Commissioners to add two flanking buildings in the same style as the club (architect unknown) so 'that the whole will appear as one building'.[11] Alas, these two wings have gone so that now only the exterior of the actual clubhouse remains. Even that has been much abused; the original circular windows at attic level

have been squared-off, another storey has been added and the interior mutilated.

The interior of the new clubhouse (which opened in February 1791) was
luxuriously furnished with 'inlaid tables and marble chimney pieces' and 'chairs
and sofas, white and gold, covered with the richest Aurora Silks'.[12] According
to an English visitor it was 'the most superb gambling house in the world'.[13]
The world, of course, can be small enough. However, when one particular
member of the Dublin *haute monde* was blackballed at Daly's (the Hon. William
Burton Conyngham, Teller of the Irish Exchequer and heir to the Conyngham
estates in Donegal and Slane), he and some others decided to set up a rival club
at 6 Kildare Street. Of the two establishments only the Kildare Street Club has
survived. Daly's reputed excesses were said to be the cause of his downfall. All
told, the sins of the Daly Club seem to have been conventional enough, gambling
and drunkenness and a fondness for scandal where fiction went untrammelled
because of the mundaneness of fact. Whatever the causes, by the time it closed
in 1823, Daly's leading position had long been supplanted by its more conservative Kildare Street rival.

Temple Bar. The narrow streets running northwards from Dame Street to the
Liffey pre-date the arrival of the Wide Streets Commissioners. The earliest of
these cobbled and granite-kerbed streets and alleys were laid out in the late
seventeenth century and their plan owes much to the former layout of gardens
belonging to the Stuart mansions on Dame Street. Anglesea Street was typical,
being developed on the estate of Lord Arthur Annesley, first Earl of Anglesey.
Other landowners included the Eustaces, the Cramptons, Sir William Temple (a
provost of Trinity) and the Fownes family who, in the early eighteenth century,
established a network of streets in one of the few remaining open areas (near
the Central Bank) named after family members: Cope Street, Cecelia Street and
Fownes Street. With the notable exception of the Central Bank, the built form of
the area differs little from what it was like at the end of the last century and its
rich variety of buildings enjoy a lively mix of uses.

That the Temple Bar area has survived at all is largely thanks to Córas Iompair
Eireann (CIE, the former state transport company) which bought up property
in the area throughout the 1980s with the intention of eventually replacing it by
a massive bus station. Pending the realisation of their long-term strategy, CIE
leased out its buildings rather than having them boarded-up or demolished.
Ironically it was this responsible approach which created the Temple Bar phe-
nomenon, for the new traders on cheap leases rejuvenated the area with a mix
of restaurants, resource centres and rock music rehearsal studios. These gave
the area a new lease of life and so the campaign for its survival got underway.
During the 1987 general election campaign, which returned Fianna Fáil to

Busking in Temple Bar.

power, Charles Haughey declared that the area had 'to be preserved' as one of the most historic and attractive parts of the city. He added that he 'wouldn't let CIE near the place'. The die was cast; the Dublin Corporation planners produced an 'action plan' and finally a special development company reporting directly to the Taoiseach's Department was established to take over CIE's holdings and to help spearhead development in an area running all the way from Westmoreland Street to the Civic Offices. An architectural competition in 1991 to produce a framework plan for the area gave rise to an exciting range of options and – in the words of a Barcelona-based assessor – marked a 'revolutionary' return 'to a historical tradition of considering that the design of public spaces, streets, squares, and their sequence and proportions are a subject of cultural importance to the identity of the city'.[14] Perhaps, what was even more revolutionary was that the 1991 Finance Bill extended the type of tax incentives to the area that were available in other designated areas. More interestingly still, it tilted the balance of these incentives in favour of refurbishment of existing buildings as opposed to favouring new construction. Though limited to Temple Bar, this approach suggests a crucial change of emphasis which, if followed through, could have an important impact on urban renewal.

The Central Bank. This building (1978, by Sam Stephenson of Stephenson, Gibney and Associates) was the subject of much agonising over a period of at least ten years, chiefly due to its height, as it was quite properly held that it should not intrude on the view from College Green.[15] (It certainly intrudes on Gandon's portico at the Bank of Ireland, when viewed from College Street). Nonetheless, the building has a brazen attractiveness though it totally disregards its neighbours, muscling over them in a manner which would seem more suited to Manhattan than the banks of the Liffey. The 'plaza' is a new creation and, windswept though it may be, it at least allows us to see clearly the handsome terrace of early Georgian buildings on Fownes Street; note, in particular, the attractive stepped windows of the building which stands at the corner with Dame Street (1871). This is by Thomas Newenham Deane (1828-1899) and shows the signs of his earlier collaboration with one of Ireland's most talented Victorian architects, Benjamin Woodward (1816-1861). Keep the building in mind if you visit Woodward's masterpiece, the Museum Building in Trinity College.

The eastern edge of the Central Bank forecourt is framed by the Commercial Buildings. It originally faced on to Dame Street but Sam Stephenson effectively gave the building a 90-degree twist so that it would better fit in with the new scheme of things. When compared to the scale of the bank, the Commercial Buildings seem in danger of being damned to Lilliputian oblivion. However, the toy-town effect is less pronounced than it might have been, as the main bulk of the bank appears to float overhead on a different plane altogether from what goes on underneath. It is this floating effect which makes the Central Bank unique for, unlike most other office buildings, the floors are suspended from the top of two service towers. These towers rise up through the structure to a pagoda-like roof profile. The set of four suspension bars which drop down each front of the building are another highly visible element on the main façade. Underneath, two flights of giant stairs cascade down to the plaza where at last, the *doges* of Irish banking risk meeting the common man on his own ground. The sculpture 'Crann an Oir' (unveiled December 1991) is by Eamonn O'Doherty.

The Commercial Buildings. All that remains of the Commercial Buildings (on

The Central Bank, Dame Street.

the eastern edge of the bank forecourt) is the design of the façade, for the original cut stone was found to be unsuitable for re-use after the building was demolished in 1970. The original building by Edward Parke was opened in January 1798. It had a courtyard behind which was used as a shortcut by Dubliners on their way from Dame Street to Crown Alley. It was in the Commercial Buildings that the Ouzel Galley Society held their annual November gatherings; their plaque has been re-erected on the yellow brick wall (in Dame Street), which now abuts on to the reconstituted buildings.

The Ouzel Galley Society. This curiously named body was founded around 1705 to arbitrate in commercial disputes and to promote good fellowship amongst its 'crew'. It was called after the *Ouzel Galley* which had disappeared on a trip to the Levant in 1695. After all hope had been given up she reappeared in Dublin Bay in 1700, the crew having apparently managed to recapture the ship from Algerian pirates along with a valuable cargo of booty. By this stage the ships owners had formally relinquished all rights to the galley and its cargo in favour of the underwriters who had paid out the insurance. However, now that she had returned with quite a different cargo the question was – to whom did this unforeseen booty belong? The result was a furious dispute, the sort which only lawyers can dream of, for, then as now, litigation could be long and expensively drawn-out. The row was eventually resolved in 1705 when the question was handed over to a group of merchants for arbitration. It was decided to systematise the access to this cheaper and more acceptable form of commercial arbitration by forming the Ouzel Galley Society.

The society's membership was restricted to forty, as this corresponded to the size of the original crew. The nautical allusions offered wonderful scope given the fascination with rank and social ritual which was so characteristic of the period. It was certainly a well-officered society, having a captain, two lieutenants, a master, bursar, boatswain, gunner, carpenter, master's mate, coxwain, boatswain's mate, gunner's mate and carpenter's mate, with the ordinary members being known as the hands. After a long and convivial life – for at times the society was little more than a glorified dining club – the Ouzel Galley was finally laid to rest in 1888, its more prosaic activities having been taken over by the Dublin Chamber of Commerce in 1783.[16]

Trinity Street. The Italianate building on the corner with Dame Street (now Trinity Bank) was built for the Life Association of Scotland. Scottish companies often imported their own architects – in this case, David Bryce of Edinburgh – a practice which so annoyed the *Dublin Builder* that when it commented on the building it did not mention Bryce at all. Instead, the *Builder* informed its readers that the designs were by 'a Scotch architect', and mentioned that a local architect, Charles Geoghegan, was 'superintending the execution of the work'. The contractor was Scottish, as was the material for the facing, but, as the *Builder* rather witheringly concluded, the Caledonian company were at least 'veritably faithful to their national allegiance'.[17]

St Andrew's Church. The dimensions of Trinity and Andrew Street are much more modest than those of Dame Street and College Green, though if some members of the Wide Streets Commissioners had had their way, things might have been different. The reason for their interest was St Andrew's Church. The Victorian version of this church that we see today is by Lanyon, Lynn and Lanyon of Belfast, and replaced an earlier building which was destroyed by fire in January 1860.

The earlier St Andrew's, the one which the commissioners would have known, was greatly revamped in the 1790s, when John Hartwell effectively rebuilt the old elliptical-shaped church which had stood there since the 1670s. Hartwell's reconstruction retained the elliptical plan. In 1800 Francis Johnston replaced Hartwell as architect and was responsible for the layout of the much-admired interior. It was well lit; as well as windows in the gallery, there seems to have been a large oval lantern in the roof. The gallery, which ran around the interior, was supported by columns set close to the walls. The Egyptian revival seems to have made its mark, for the decoration of the columns was said to have been inspired by 'Mr Denon's drawings of Egyptian ruins'. (A translation of Baron Denon's *Voyage dans la Basse et la Haute Egypte* was published in Dublin in 1803.) Any allusions to the Egyptian style were, however, probably restricted to the to the decoration and proportions of the classical orders. With the pews arranged so as to converge on the pulpit – and on the organ behind it on the gallery – it 'must have been one of Johnston's most powerful interiors, where he was able to join his love of ample curves, with the excitement of top-lighting', so harnessing the drama of the rotunda 'to the solemn ends of the traditional Calvinism of the Irish liturgy'.[18]

As St Andrew's was the church used by Parliament, it was suggested in 1772 that a new street be created running westwards from the church and leading to a semi-circular public space facing a new entrance to Dublin Castle. There was also to be a circular space at the junction with George's Lane, i.e., the present South Great George's Street.[19] The intention, obviously, was to provide a processional route for ceremonial occasions such as the opening of Parliament. However, the plans for Dublin's viceregal mile were not adopted.

South William Street. This narrow thoroughfare has an attractive scattering of mid-eighteenth-century houses. The most important house of all is, of course, Powerscourt House, a tall robust granite-fronted mansion which appears almost debonair, given the casual way in which it seems to disregard its cramped location. Its imposing 130-foot-long frontage can only be seen at an angle, given

the narrowness of the street. No attempt seems to have been made to create a
suitable public space to front the building or to capitalise on the possibilities of
a more deft alignment of the site with the street. Instead Powerscourt House was
grafted on to the existing seventeenth-century street structure, the rationale
underlying its layout predating more modern notions of urban beauty, security
and hygiene.

Powerscourt Townhouse. Powerscourt House was built for the third Viscount
Powerscourt between 1771 and 1794 to a design by a Robert Mack, about whom

*A cross-section of Powerscourt House.
From* The Georgian Society
Records, *Vol I, 1909, plate XLV.*

little is known.[20] Despite having passed through a number of hands the building
was maintained in admirable condition. It was converted into a highly successful shopping complex by Power Securities of Cork, in the late 1970s. The
building is a magnificent showcase of Irish craftsmanship. Inside there is a
delightful display of rococo plasterwork which runs from the entrance hall to
the staircase hall beyond. This is by James McCullagh. An ornate mahogany
stairs (carving by Ignatius McDonagh) leads upwards to the main reception
rooms where the plasterwork is by Michael Stapleton. Powerscourt, like many

other great houses, was decorated in stages and Stapleton's work dates from a later period when fashion dictated a more restrained neoclassical style, characterised by a wealth of delicate repeating patterns and Adamesque medallions.

Looking west from the front of Powerscourt House, along Castle Street, there is the great double-arched entrance to the South City Markets (by Lockwood and Mawson of Bradford, 1878-81), a Victorian predecessor of today's shopping malls. Regardless of the intended effect, the turreted skyline of the building owes more to the mass production methods of our times than to any analogies with medieval craftsmanship. Nonetheless, it is a delightful monument to the potential of terracotta. The turreted building which straddles the southern end of South William Street is the former Mercer's Hospital. This was one of Dublin's earliest hospitals, having being founded by Mrs Mary Mercer in 1734. It was one of the institutions which benefited from the first public performance of Handel's *Messiah* in Dublin on 13 April 1742.

Civic Museum. The building immediately south of Powerscourt House is the Civic Museum. Those who look at the door plaque will see that it is also known as the City Assembly House, a reminder of the days when the Corporation used the building as a city hall. It was erected for the Society of Artists who held their first exhibition there in 1766. In 1791 they sold out to the Corporation who used the octagonal exhibition room (first floor) for their meetings until 1852. On the ground floor, there is a courtroom-like chamber where the Court of Conscience met from 1811 until 1924. This was a mayoral tribunal for settling petty debts and trade disputes. The room was also used by the outlawed Supreme Court of the Irish Republic from 1920 to 1922, seditious precedent having been set by the Trinity College Historical Society which had used the building for its debates when it was barred from the college in 1794. Today the building still belongs to the Corporation and the museum is managed by the Old Dublin Society. It has a fascinating collection of exhibits associated with the city: old lampstands, pavement coal-hole covers, original maps and a fine selection of Malton prints, which depict the architectural highlights of the eighteenth-century city. These were presented by President Seán T. O'Kelly for the opening of the museum in 1953.

Clarendon Street. The street was laid out by William Williams in 1685. While it was never very fashionable, it seems to have developed into a lively enough business area with a variety of trades, ranging from silversmiths and glass blowers to pawnbrokers and roof slaters. By the end of the eighteenth century a number of the houses had been taken over as brothels and others were subdivided into tenement lodgings.

Carmelite Friary. The Discalced Carmelites, who founded their church in Clarendon Street in 1793, avoided undue attention by leaving it hidden behind

Watching the world go by on Grafton Street.

the tenements. Though the Penal Laws had begun to be dismantled from the 1770s, the Catholic church authorities were still expected to know their place. It was not until later that the Carmelites extended their church onto Clarendon Street itself. The church has an attractive Romanesque façade dating from the nineteenth century. Inside, the principal altar contains one of the finest religious works by John Hogan (1800-58), Ireland's most talented neoclassical sculptor. Born in Tallow, County Waterford, he was trained in Cork and eventually settled in Rome, staying there until the revolution of 1848 obliged him to return

Grafton Street.

to Ireland. Hogan's 'Dead Christ' (1829) is located beneath the high altar.

Grafton Street. After the opening of the new Westmoreland Street-Sackville Street (now O'Connell Street) axis in the 1790s, Grafton Street changed from being a relatively quiet residential area to a busy commercial street. It takes its name from Henry Fitzroy, first Duke of Grafton, a son of Charles II by the Duchess of Cleveland. The street was never modified by the Wide Streets Commissioners and still winds narrowly along the route of a long-forgotten country road. There is an evocative turn-of-the-century description in *Ulysses* of how 'Grafton Street gay with housed awnings lured his senses. Muslin prints, silk, dames and dowagers, jingle of harness, hoofthuds low ringing in the baking causeway.' Grafton Street is still the city's most fashionable shopping artery.

Bewley's. While now better known for its coffee, the firm came to prominence as tea importers in the mid-nineteenth-century. The first 'Oriental Cafe' was opened in South Great George's Street in 1894. Westmoreland Street followed in 1896 and Grafton Street in 1927 (with specially commissioned windows by Harry Clarke). Over the years the firm became a much-loved institution, so much so, that when it was threatened with closure in 1986, the Taoiseach, Garret FitzGerald, felt obliged to make a personal intervention 'because Bewley's was a national asset'.[21] After much negotiation, the firm (or, more correctly, the Bewley Community to whom the family had transferred their shares in a unique experiment in worker-ownership) was acquired by Campbell Catering.

In the late eighteenth century, Samuel Whyte kept a famous boys school in the rear of what is now Bewley's. The school was noted for its interest in drama. In 1771 the tragedy of Cato was acted by the boys at Crow Street for the 'relief of confined debtors'. Amongst the pupils of 'Whyte's Academy' were such future luminaries as Richard Brinsley Sheridan the playwright, Thomas Moore whose statue we have seen in College Street, Robert Emmet who led an unsuccessful rebellion in 1803, George Petrie the famous antiquarian, and the Dublin-born Duke of Wellington, who reputedly said that 'being born in a stable doesn't mean that one is a horse' (so much for his Irish background!). The Duke's father, Lord Mornington, lived in Grafton Street until 1765 when he moved to Upper Merrion Street.

Besides Mr Whyte's Academy, Grafton Street also boasted the drawing school of the Royal Dublin Society, which had been formed around the middle years of the century when the society took over the private school of the painter Robert West. The school not only trained Irish painters and sculptors but also had an architectural section where instruction was given to the craftsmen who contributed so much to the building of the eighteenth-century city. The school was taken over by the state in 1878.

The Mansion House. Joshua Dawson, who was developing and building in

Dawson Street from about 1705, erected this house for his own use in 1710.[22] It was bought by the Corporation in 1715 as a residence for the Lord Mayor and the interior still retains much of its fine eighteenth-century decor. The exterior, however, received a facelift in the nineteenth century, when the original red-brick was covered with plaster and embellished with cast-iron work and other additions such as the pediment and balustrade. The effect is rather charming and frivolous, a sort of architectural Barbara Cartland.

To the left of the Mansion House you can see the conically-shaped roof of the

Outside Kehoe's Pub, South Anne Street.

Round Room, hurriedly built by John Semple in 1821 for a banquet and ball in honour of George IV. It has hosted many famous gatherings, most notably that of the first Dáil Eireann on 21 January 1919, which adopted Ireland's Declaration of Independence and ratified the Proclamation of the Irish Republic, which had been made during the 1916 Rising.

Academy House, 19 Dawson Street. The brick-fronted building which sits between the garden of the Mansion House and St Ann's, is the home of the Royal Irish Academy. Northland House, as it was called, was built around 1770 – probably by John Ensor – for the Knox family of Dungannon.[23] It contains some exceptionally fine plasterwork. Theobald Wolfe Tone was a frequent visitor as he was a friend of Lord Northland's son, George Knox. The house was acquired by the Royal Irish Academy in 1852. The academy – which is the country's most prestigious learned body – was founded in 1783 and its *Transactions* and other publications have included notable contributions to the various sciences, as well as to 'polite literature and antiquities'. The academy's library contains an important collection of Irish manuscripts.

St Ann's Church. The present Romanesque façade is by Thomas Newenham Deane and dates from 1868. However, if you enter the church you step back into another century, for St Ann's is, in all other respects, an eighteenth-century building. The interior is nobly proportioned – a large single-spanned chamber terminating in an apse. Square ionic columns carry the galleries and, in the apse, the three windows are flanked by 12-foot high gilt plaster drops. The wooden shelves to the left of the chancel were erected to hold bread for the poor; a few loaves are still left after Sunday and early Monday services. The benefactor who deserves to be remembered, if only for the marvellous resonance of his title, was the Right Honourable Theophilus Lord Newtown of Newtown Butler. On his death in 1723 he left £13 per annum to be distributed in bread to the poor at the rate of 5 shillings per week. Also of note is the Elizabeth Phibbs memorial in the south gallery, which is by Edward Smyth.

The parish of St Ann's dates from 1707 when monies were granted by the Irish Parliament for church building. St Ann's, though built under the 1707 Act, wasn't begun until 1720. The elaborate baroque façade, which was depicted in one of the vignettes accompanying Charles Brooking's map of 1728, has been credited to Isaac Wills. However, given the façade's evident debt to Roman models, it is possible that it emanated from the circle of aristocratic patrons to which Lord Molesworth and Joshua Dawson belonged.[24] Given the vehemently anti-Papist politics of the time, the particular choice of elevation showed a most catholic breath of vision – as least as far as architecture was concerned. Sadly, it all came to nought. The façade that was actually built had a more simplified design and, at that, was never completed. Neither, it must be said, was the 1868

The Reading Room at the Royal Irish Academy,
1852-54 by F. V. Clarendon.

front, which still lacks the spire that Deane had envisaged.

Molesworth Street Corner. If one wants examples of the banality which has blighted aspects of Dublin's more recent building history, where better than at the junction of Dawson Street and Molesworth Street. There is firstly what we have lost and more depressingly – in some cases – what we have gained. Starting with the losses, there is the Royal Hibernian Hotel. This sat on the west side of Dawson Street facing down Molesworth Street. A hotel graced this site in one form or another since 1750. It was there that General Humbert and his officers were accommodated when they were on parole after the defeat of the French invasion of the West of Ireland in 1797; their Irish co-revolutionaries were less handsomely treated. In later years the hotel was used as a Bianconi coach stop. It must be said that the building itself had little architectural distinction; the front had been completely rebuilt in the 1950s and the interior much altered over the years. Nonetheless it had charm. The hotel was a major landmark in the life of bourgeois Dublin and its demise was much mourned. It was sold by the Trust House Forte Group in February 1982, with a price tag which ensured that it

Molesworth Hall and St Ann's Parochial Schools (demolished 1978).

would no longer be a going concern as a hotel, but a development site. However, the cloud had a silver lining. The new building (1987, by architects Costello, Murray and Beaumont) looks well and the façade of white Ballybrew granite continues to act as a landmark. The fenestration gives the building a strong vertical emphasis: it was the Corporation planners who insisted on the projecting windows at second-floor level.[25] Where the city has genuinely gained is in the creation of a pedestrian link with Grafton Street where none existed before and it is from this that the development takes its name, the Royal Hibernian Way.

The brick-fronted office buildings which sit on opposing corners on the other side of Dawson Street, however, are little addition to the city. The plain rectangular block on the southern corner houses (along with the Standard Chartered Bank) the Dublin offices of both the European Parliament and the Commission of the European Communities. Their choice is unfortunate. Like many other institutions, they have ended up renting space in buildings which have been erected at the expense of much finer structures. Until 1979, the Molesworth Street section of this development contained two Victorian buildings of exceptional quality and importance: St Ann's School and Hall. Apart from their intrinsic value, the buildings were of importance in that they displayed, for the first time, the way in which the Gothic style could be used in Dublin street architecture. The school (1858), by Thomas Newenham Deane (1828-1899) and Benjamin Woodward (1816-1861), was a rectangular building with a tall hipped roof broken by gabled dormers of varying shapes and sizes. It was built from rough-cut limestone and granite, the different-coloured stonework being laid in alternate horizontal bands across the façade. Alternating layers of yellow and red brick were also used in the hall, which was added by Deane in 1867.[26]

It was in Molesworth Hall that Elizabeth Bowen attended dancing classes. 'While long dazzling shafts slanted on to us through the pointed windows ... the dust', she supposed, 'was raised by our dancing feet; where it can have come from I cannot think, for the smell of the Molesworth Hall was of scrubbed floors. It had a Protestant smell.'[27] It was in Molesworth Hall that Yeats's *The Shadowy Waters* and Synge's *The Shadow of the Glen* had their premiers and it was there too that Douglas Hyde delivered his famous paper on de-Anglicisation, which sparked off the Gaelic League. Ironically enough, they believed that the revival of a national culture would save Ireland from the worse excesses of industrial society; they hadn't bargained with the office boom of the 1960s.

The inexorable process of destruction began in 1970 when Desmond FitzGerald, a former Professor of Architecture at University College Dublin, first sought permission for an office block on the site on behalf of the owners, the Church Representative Body. After this application was refused the Church Body sold their interest to the Gallagher family who eventually succeeded – despite protests and occupations – in demolishing both hall and school (as well as two adjoining eighteenth-century houses) in 1978.[28] If Deane and Woodward's buildings were considered to be an important contribution to the street architecture of their era, the same cannot be said for the present structure by Desmond FitzGerald. The vertical window openings do not disguise the fact that the building is little better than an overgrown shoebox which has been jammed lengthways into Molesworth Street. The building has irreparably marred the gentle if informal streetscape, providing no drama or individual merit of its own that might even masquerade as a justification for its existence.[29]

As is clear from the Royal Hibernian Way, not all modern office buildings need to be so crude, though the two buildings that now flank the western end of Molesworth Street do little for the genre. The Sun Alliance building (by Tyndall, Hogan, Hurley) which fussily sits on the northern corner does have a certain curiosity value however, for if you glance inside the main entrance, you can see a replica of a delightful plasterwork ceiling from 15 Dawson Street, the original house having been demolished to make way for this development. It had been built before 1761 for John Burke, MP for Naas and later, first Earl of Mayo.[30]

Molesworth Street. The street still has a peculiar charm of its own as it leads gently towards Leinster House. The street was laid out by the third Viscount Molesworth, four houses being demolished at the junction with Dawson Street so that the two streets could meet. One can still see an occasional gable, a reminder of an almost forgotten house type which was at one time a common sight in the city. However, the gable on the south side of the street that bears the date 1755 is misleading; the building dates from earlier in the eighteenth century. Inside, it still has a traditionally patterned black-and-white squared floor in the hall and handsome wainscotting on the staircase. The gable is a Victorian addition. Number 15 and its neighbour, along with two other buildings on the far side of the porticoed Masonic Hall, are all that now remain of the twenty-three Georgian houses which once lined the northern side of Molesworth Street. If one had lived there in the eighteenth century a frequent sight in winter would have been the procession of Speaker Foster, as he made his way from his house on the south side of the street to the House of Commons, dressed in his robes of office and accompanied by the Sergeant of Arms bearing the mace. This house with three gables at parapet level, was replaced in the early nineteenth century by the present numbers 29, 30 and 31.

The Masonic Hall. High up in the tympanum of the Masonic Hall, on the north side of the street (near Kildare Street), you can see a sextant, an implement traditionally associated with the masonry trade. The first recorded meeting of

Leinster House, home of the Dáil.

the Freemasons in Ireland was in 1725. Among their members were such figures as Henry Grattan and Daniel O'Connell, the 'Liberator' of Catholic Ireland. He left after a ban, issued by Pope Clement XII in 1738, was rather belatedly put into effect in Ireland almost a century later. Another late Victorian contribution to Molesworth Street, and indeed to many other Dublin streets, is the charming shamrock motif on the lampstands. These made their first appearance with the arrival of electric street lighting in 1892. Despite the conscious Irishness of the design, the lamp standards were manufactured in England.

Originally the view up Molesworth Street terminated in a heavy rusticated gatehouse set between high walls which enclosed the forecourt of Leinster House. The railings and gateway which we see today were erected in the 1880s. From 1908 until 1948 the forecourt was dominated by a enormous statue of Queen Victoria, flanked by an unlikely combination of attendant figures representing respectively, Erin, Peace and two wounded soldiers. After having languished for a number of years in the courtyard of the Royal Hospital Kilmainham, she was subsequently consigned with an assortment of other 'undesirables' to the confines of a former boys' reformatory in Daingean, County Offaly, a sad fall indeed, from empress to borstal queen. The statue – but not the attendant figures – has since been sent to Australia.

Kildare Street. The name dates from the 1740s when the 20th Earl of Kildare, who succeeded to the title in 1744, started work on a mansion in what had been the former Molesworth Fields. Kildare House (later Leinster House) was aligned so that it was the focus of the view down Molesworth Street. The new Kildare Street – previously Coote Street – was extended southwards and a new opening made into St Stephen's Green with a space left free for Kildare Place, 'a "square" that never really prospered'.[31] Its few domestic houses are now gone and, instead, Kildare Place is overshadowed by the offices of the Department of Agriculture (1974, by Stephenson, Gibney and Associates). The statue of Archbishop Lord Plunkett is by Hamo Thorneycroft. The old Department of Industry and Commerce (the title and functions invariably change with each ministerial reshuffle) is housed in the first purpose-built office building of the new state. It was the outcome of a public competition in 1935, the winning design being by J. R. Boyd Barrett, who had earlier supervised the building of the revolutionary Church of Christ the King in Cork for the Chicago architect Barry Byrne. Its pared-down classicism is very much of its time, as are the art deco entrance and stone carvings by Gabriel Hayes.

Leinster House. This sombre granite-fronted building was begun by Richard Castle for Lord Kildare in 1745. When it was finished in 1748 it was the largest and most lavish of Dublin's townhouses, its pre-eminence reflecting the social and aristocratic position of James FitzGerald, 20th Earl of Kildare and, from

Kildare Street, near the National Museum and National Library.

1766, first Duke of Leinster. In its Dublin context the building is quite exceptional for, unlike the more typical terraced house, Leinster House stands quite apart from its neighbours. Both in its scale and in its plan this is really a country house, though one that was located on the edge of the city when it was built in the 1740s. It has a central corridor on the long north-south axis and, to either side, there are two formal fronts. Inside there are several fine reception rooms which were extensively redecorated in the late eighteenth century, with some involvement by James Wyatt. On the northern side (hidden from view) there is a projecting bow which is said to be the prototype for the bow-fronted White House in Washington. Such a lineage is quite plausible, for the architect of the

White House, Carlow-born James Hoban (1762-1832), studied architecture at the Dublin Society's School where he was awarded a prize in 1780; he won the White House competition in 1792.

The house's most famous resident was Lord Edward FitzGerald (1763-1798) the twelfth child of the first Duke of Leinster and his wife Emilia Mary, a daughter of the Duke of Richmond. Lord Edward had no great love for the house. In 1794 – around the time he joined the United Irishmen – he mentioned in a letter to his mother that 'Leinster House does not inspire the brightest ideas. By-the-by, what a melancholy house it is ... A poor housemaid I brought with me cried for two days and said she thought she was in a prison'.[32] Lord Edward, who headed a military committee of the United Irishmen, held several meetings in the house with Thomas Reynolds who, unknown to him, was an informer in the pay of the Government. An attempt was made to arrest Lord Edward there on 12 March 1798 but he was warned that there were soldiers in the mansion. The soldiers had to satisfy themselves instead with asking his wife Lady Pamela for her papers as well as those of Lord Edward. Lady Pamela moved out of Leinster House soon afterwards and it is unlikely that Lord Edward visited it again. He was captured by the notorious Major Sirr in a house in Thomas Street on 19 May and in the struggle, killed one of his attackers. He himself was shot in the arm and died of the wounds on 4 June in Newgate Gaol. His aunt Lady Louisa Connolly and his brother Lord Henry FitzGerald were at his bedside. Most surprising of all, was the presence of the notorious Earl of Clare who, apparently, stood with his face to the wall in tears. For someone who was such a bitter opponent of all that the United Irishmen stood for, this was a most unexpected indication of the very real affection which Lord Edward could inspire.

The FitzGeralds sold Leinster House to the Royal Dublin Society in 1815. As the society's headquarters it became the nucleus of a complex of cultural institutions: the National Library and National Museum in matching buildings (1885-90) on Kildare Street, and the Natural History Museum (a division of the National Museum) and the National Gallery on either side of Leinster Lawn. While these cultural institutions still remain, the RDS removed itself to new buildings on its showgrounds in Ballsbridge, for Leinster House was purchased to serve as a Parliament for the newly independent Free State in 1922. The Dáil Chamber is located in what was previously a lecture theatre built by the RDS and the Senate sits in an eighteenth-century salon on the opposite (northern) end of the building.

National Museum and National Library. The Dublin Society (it acquired its royal prefix in 1820) was the first of its type in Europe, having been founded in 1731 by fourteen Dublin gentlemen with the intention of 'improving husbandry, manufactures and other useful arts and sciences'. It was immensely influential, so much so that many of the society's activities were eventually taken over by the Government as the basis of state institutions. Two of the more important of these institutions now flank the forecourt of Leinster House, which was itself the headquarters of the society from 1815 until 1922. To the north stands the National Library and, to the south the National Museum; both by Thomas Newenham Deane and his son Thomas Manly Deane. T. N. Deane was knighted on their completion in 1890. Though their design may not have been very imaginative, both buildings are of considerable interest, now that so few of their nineteenth-century compatriots have retained their original fittings and layout.

The museum has a fascinating range of collections – some of great importance – covering such disparate subjects as memorabilia from the 1916 Rising to Captain Cook's collection from the Pacific Islands. The Natural History Division (in Merrion Street) has almost two million zoological specimens and the Arts and Industries Division over a quarter of a million items ranging from jewellery and clothing to musical instruments and horse-drawn coaches. There are also extensive folk-life collections. However, it is the antiquities collections which are probably best known, for these include such treasures as the Ardagh and Derrynaflan chalices as well as bronze-age torques and splendid brooches such as the Tara Brooch. The National Library is primarily concerned with items of Irish origin or interest, and its holdings are the most comprehensive in existence. Its manuscripts and books, newspapers, maps, photographs and much more, constitute a veritable Aladdin's cave for anyone interested in Irish studies.

Royal College of Physicians. The building is by William G. Murray and dates from the early 1860s. The college itself is much older, having been founded by the Duke of Ormond in 1667. This was the site of the first Kildare Street Club, which was founded in 1782 by William Burton Conyngham and those friends who stood by him after he was blackballed at Daly's.[33] In the mid-1850s the members decided to build an entirely new clubhouse, not only to accommodate growing numbers but in order to keep pace with the increasing size and luxury of the London clubs. The decision was fortunate for in 1860 the old clubhouse at 6 Kildare Street was destroyed by fire.

The Kildare Street Club (corner of Kildare Street and Nassau Street). This was designed by the firm of Deane, Son and Woodward. Sir Thomas Deane (1792-1871) and his son, Sir Thomas Newenham Deane (1828-99) hailed from a prominent Cork family of builders and architects. The Tullamore-born Benjamin Woodward (1816-61) joined the Deanes in the 1840s and soon came to prominence due to his mastery and understanding of the principles underlying the Gothic revival. The bustling, businesslike, jovial Deane was an admirable foil to the younger, consumptive and withdrawn Woodward, who was passionately

The Kildare Street Club as it used to be.

committed to medieval art. Together they designed Queen's College Cork, Killarney Asylum, the Museum Building in Trinity College and the Oxford Museum. The Kildare Street Club was the last complete building designed by the firm before Woodward's early death in May 1861 and it is all the more tragic, therefore, that it has been so brutally mutilated.[34]

What is there to see in what remains of the Kildare Street Club? The quality of the carving for one: look out for the monkeys playing billiards at the base of the columns dividing the ground-floor windows in Kildare Street. Another item to note is the way in which the exterior reveals how the original interior was laid out. The enormous portico served as an introduction to a monumental inner hall or court, which rose the entire height of the building to a skylight in the roof. Likewise, the asymmetrical window pattern reflected the rational manner in which the interior was arranged with the principal rooms at ground and first-floor levels and the more domestic quarters above. Hidden behind the moat – at basement level – were the servants' bedrooms and copious wine cellars.

All that remains of this distinguished and important building is the exterior and a portion of the interior. In the early 1950s the club divided the premises in two and sold the corner half to the Phoenix Assurance Company. The assurance company moved on in the early seventies and the new purchasers – Rampart Holdings Ltd, a Dublin-based subsidiary of a British development company – hacked out the palatial staircase and the inner hall. In its place they inserted the maximum amount of rentable floor space, though this could have been done by inserting mezzanines in the principal rooms and so sparing the splendid entrance hall. The result is truly awful and most evidently so since the Office of Public Works have lovingly refurbished the remainder of the building. This was purchased on behalf of the National Library in 1976 and houses the Genealogical Museum; the gutted portion of the building now belongs to the Alliance Française.

Despite the partial butchery of their former premises, the Kildare Street Club itself survives – though now in harness with the University Club – at number 17 St Stephen's Green. It was the most aristocratic of the Dublin clubs, a staunchly Unionist stronghold which had little time for members such as Edward Martyn, a Catholic West of Ireland landlord, 'who combined a passion for traditional church music and a penchant for provoking apoplexy among the upper echelons of Dublin Society'. His objections to King Edward's visit to Dublin in 1907 led to expulsion from the club, followed, after an expensive legal battle, by his reinstatement. He had his vengeance by kneeling in the bay window of the morning room, rosary beads in hand, where he offered up devotions with suitable ostentation. When asked why he persisted in remaining a member of a club that was hostile to him personally, as well as being violently opposed to his religious and political beliefs, he is said to have replied that it was 'the only place in Dublin where I can get caviare'.

Nassau Street. Originally known as St Patrick's Well Lane, this formed the southern boundary of the Priory of All Hallows. The lands were granted to the university in 1592. St Patrick's Well Lane was renamed in honour of the royal house of Nassau in the eighteenth century and its level raised up ten feet to prevent flooding; hence the difference in height between it and College Park. The railings which separate it from the playing fields were put up in 1842. The middle stretch of Nassau Street is dominated by a large office complex, the Setanta Centre, by Tyndall, Hogan, Hurley (completed 1976). The scheme does not fit in too happily with its older neighbours; its horizontal emphasis runs counter to their vertical proportions and the height of the ground-level openings is totally at odds with the other shopfronts. In compensation, perhaps, the architects created an opportunity for a number of artists to display their talents. On the west side of the open forecourt there is a large mural by Desmond Kinney based on the prose epic, the *Táin Bó Cuailnge*, the cattle raid of Cuailnge. Standing on higher ground behind is an abstract work by Gerda Fromel (1930-1975), the Czechoslovakian-born artist who studied art in Stuttgart and Munich, before coming to Ireland in the fifties.

South Frederick Street. The 'Georgian idiom' which the planning authorities insisted on for the South Frederick Street elevations of this corner site development is small consolation for the demolition of one of the few remaining terraces of mid-eighteenth-century houses in Dublin. Despite being officially listed for preservation in the City Development Plan, the Corporation – supported by An Bord Pleanála – granted permission to the New Ireland Assurance Company for their demolition in September 1983. The exceptional rococo ceilings in three of the houses were salvaged after it became clear that they were to be demolished (one of these has been re-erected in the Collis Room at the Royal College of Surgeons in St Stephen's Green). In all, seven houses on South Frederick Street (running from 13-19) and another six on Nassau Street (running from 20-26) were demolished. They have been replaced by College Park House and Frederick House (1987, by architects Morris and McCullough and Associates).[35] In 1960 New Ireland Assurance demolished another five houses further up South Frederick Street – again with valuable plasterwork ceilings – to make way for an office development. However, the 1960s-style curtain walling of that earlier block has since been replaced by a much improved stone wall-panelling system with a strong vertical emphasis (1988, by architects Campbell, Conroy, Hickey in conjunction with McCullough and Partners).[36]

Molly Malone. This sculpture (at the junction of Nassau Street and Grafton Street) was the first of a series of projected 'fun sculptures' commissioned on the initiative of Matt McNulty, while director of a committee set up to stimulate activities during Dublin's Millennium celebrations in 1988. If the millennium as such was entirely bogus it at least provided the excuse for a celebration. The statue, however, has had a mixed reception. The members of Aosdána expressed their 'universal deprecation' and declared that the work was 'entirely deficient in artistic point and merit'.[37] As far as most Dubliners were concerned the unfortunate Molly simply became 'the tart with the cart'. The sculptor, Jeanne Rynhart, gave Molly an infamous decolletage as she believed that Molly (whose baptismal certificate had allegedly come to light in nearby St Andrew's Church) was not only a prosperous trader but a freelance prostitute as well. Certainly, on the basis of her generously-cut Restoration costume, it can be inferred that selling 'cockles and mussels' may not have been Molly's only means of sustenance. Even worse, there are suggestions that Molly may not have existed at all, the argument being that she was just a representative type and a nineteenth-century one at that, as the song in its present form is thought to be no older than the last century. Nevertheless, the fact remains that Molly Malone has given Dublin its unofficial anthem, a tubercular tribute to those countless Dubliners whose lives were cut short by the city's endemic poverty.

Trinity College

The college is a city within a city; a refuge of lawn and cobble in the heart of Dublin, sheltered by an unparalleled array of collegiate architecture. Though most of it is no older than the eighteenth century, the university is, in fact, an Elizabethan foundation. The 'College of the Holy and Undivided Trinity' was incorporated by royal charter in March 1592 on the site of the former monastery of All Hallows 'near Dublin'. The lands and dilapidated buildings of the suppressed monastery were a gift of the Corporation and lay about a quarter of a mile east of the city walls. At the time it was probably expected that other colleges would be created which, between them, would constitute the University of Dublin. However, as no others materialised, the terms 'Trinity College' and 'University of Dublin' are effectively synonymous.

The West Front. This is 'the surly front', which was seen by James Joyce (a student at the rival National University) as 'a dull grey stone set in the ring of the city's ignorance'. Certainly, the ravages of pollution had dulled the stone (now cleaned) but, that apart, this is one of the most distinguished Palladian façades in these islands. Both it and the former Parliament dominate College Green with an assuredness and confidence which tells us not of the city's

A section of Trinity's west front at College Green.

ignorance, but rather of its ability to accommodate and assimilate buildings which were to underpin its claim to be – in architectural terms at least – a capital of European stature. The palatial entrance front dates from the 1750s and has been attributed to an English amateur architect called Theodore Jacobsen.[38] Jacobsen's expansive façade is held in check by two pavilions at either end. It had been intended to crown them with cupolas and to give the central block a dome, but architectural fashion dictated otherwise. 'A gentleman who had lately taken the Tour of Europe and is allowed to have made very Judicious observations in the Architectonic way' objected to the cupolas and dome as such features were 'no where to be met with in Italy in such buildings'.[39] However, the massive vaulting remains at ground level though the cupola that it was to have supported was never built. The space over the entrance was used instead to house a large reception room known as the Regent House.

Standing on the lawned space on either side of the entrance are two statues by John Henry Foley (1818-74): on the left Edmund Burke (1729-97) – perhaps still reflecting on the French Revolution – and on the right Oliver Goldsmith (1728-74). Burke was a founder of the debating club which was the forerunner of the College Historical Society. Goldsmith, the son of an impoverished clergyman from County Roscommon, composed ballads to make ends meet. The students of the period had an unruly reputation. Goldsmith was involved in the 'Black Dog' riot of 1747 when the students rescued one of their compatriots from gaol, killing several people in the process. Violence was not uncommon and the students enthusiastically supported the Liberty Boys, Protestant weavers from the Liberties, in their running feud with the Catholic butchers of Ormond Market, on the north of the river. Goldsmith's tutor, the notorious Dr Wilder, was once passing by when a bailiff was being ducked at a pump in the college. Feigning the best of intentions, he called out, 'Gentlemen, gentlemen, for the love of God don't be so cruel as to nail his ears to the pump'.[40] The result, of course, was that he was left bleeding and shrieking in pain, pinned to the pump by a tenpenny nail. Fortunately, it is safer to enter the college grounds today.

Parliament Square. The lawned area inside the front gate (then a separate square) was called Parliament Square, as Parliament gave generous grants for the rebuilding of the entrance front and of the two associated wings on either side. Trinity enjoyed close links with Parliament where it was represented by two members. It was the custom for students to attend the debates in the House of Commons, for anyone in a college gown had the right of entry to the visitors' gallery, a privilege which was lost in 1795 when Speaker Foster had the students thrown out for unruly behaviour (evidently their reaction to a speech by Henry Grattan had been unduly enthusiastic).

The great expanse which stretches from the entrance to the Campanile and beyond is largely a nineteenth-century creation. Until the late eighteenth century, a visitor entering college would have seen something quite different, for a line of buildings effectively filled the open space which now lies between the two protruding porticos. The idea of enlarging Parliament Square germinated in a plan of 1775 by Sir William Chambers. His intention was not merely that this older array of buildings should be removed (they were in the 1790s) but that the visitor's eye should be led on towards a new line of monumental buildings, which was to be placed further back, where we now see the Campanile. The projecting porticos, which mirror each other to both north and south, were conceived as part of this plan, for not only does their positioning assert their importance (one is the Chapel and the other the Examination Hall or Public Theatre) but it also contracts the range of vision and, therefore, would have focused attention on the proposed centrepiece of the new building line, a tall tower and steeple. Though not completed as proposed, Chambers's intention has not been lost. When a redbrick terrace which ran across where the Campanile now stands was demolished in 1837 it was replaced, not by a monumental line of new buildings, but (on the suggestion of Decimus Burton) by an alternative point of focus, the Campanile (1852) by Charles Lanyon.

The Public Theatre. More usually known as the Examination Hall, this building was intended primarily for public meetings of the university. In plan it is similar to the Chapel, each essentially consisting of a large single chamber ending in an apse and covered by a low-slung vaulted ceiling. Both have plasterwork by Michael Stapleton. The architect in charge was Christopher Myers, Chambers having resigned from the project in 1778. Work on the Theatre began in 1777 and by the mid-1780s it was completed. The organ case in the gallery came from the former Chapel. It is thought to have been built in Dublin in 1684 by Lancelot Pease. He also worked in King's College Cambridge but this is the only known surviving example of his work. It is the oldest existing Irish-made organ case and one of the most important in Britain or Ireland.[41] Other notable contents are the chandelier of gilt wood, from the former House of Commons in College Green, and the elaborate monument to the memory of Provost Baldwin. Baldwin, who held the provostship from 1717 to 1758, was a firm believer in discipline and did his best to inoculate college from the boisterousness and disorder which characterised Anglo-Irish society at the time. He is depicted here on the point of death, languidly fondling the will in which he left vast sums to the college. A sorrowful muse lends a supporting hand while an angel rather pointedly draws attention to the crown composed of a branch of olive and a palm branch, the heavenly dividends on his departing investment. One can only presume that after all this he had a most favourable reception at the pearly gates, his departure having been well commemorated with the

The Public Theatre (Exam Hall) Trinity College.

erection of this memorial in 1784, the first neoclassical monument in Ireland. It is by Christopher Hewetson (*c.* 1739-98) an Irish-born sculptor who left for Rome in his early twenties and whose work is consequently little known in Ireland.[42]

The Chapel. Work on the Chapel started in 1787, after the Examination Hall was completed, and continued until the end of the century. It is the more elaborate of the two buildings, having a superb concave gallery which reflects the curve of the apse. It also retains its original pews. However, the floor tiles date from the last century, as do the painted windows which commemorate Archbishop James Ussher, Bishop George Berkeley and Richard Graves.

The Campanile. It was apparently here that the high altar of the old Priory of All Hallows was located. The priory had been founded in 1166 by Dermot McMurrough, King of Leinster, who is better known for having invited the Normans to Ireland. All Hallows was suppressed at the beginning of the Reformation and presented to the city in 1539 by Henry VIII. The Corporation, in turn, presented the site to the new university. As none of the buildings could be utilised they were pulled down, with the exception of the steeple which served as a landmark for ships coming up the river. This steeple was apparently situated only a short distance away, rising over a hall and chapel which stood end-to-end, running roughly from the Campanile back as far as the lawned area inside the front gate. These buildings were altered in subsequent years and were finally demolished in the 1790s. In looking at today's great expanse of lawn and cobble it is best to keep in mind, therefore, that for the greater part of the eighteenth century it was in effect divided into four distinct units: two small squares (where there are now cobbles) which lay to either side of the old dining hall and chapel, and two larger squares, Parliament Square (the lawned area inside the main entrance) and Library Square (the lawned area alongside the Campanile).

The Rubrics. The oldest surviving buildings in the college are the Rubrics, the redbrick terrace to the east of the Campanile. This dates from around 1700, though the Dutch-looking gables were added only in the 1890s. It was in his rooms at number 25 that Edward Ford, one of the Fellows, was murdered in 1734. He was apparently 'an obstinate and ill-judged man' and unpopular with the students. At that time a passage led through the building into a small walled area behind, and Wood's window looked out on this. One night he was woken by some students throwing stones at the window and, in a fury, he took out a gun and fired at them. The students ran back to their rooms where they had firearms (though these were forbidden). They returned to find Ford still at his window in his nightshirt, an easy target for their fatal shots. Five students were expelled as a result but being 'gentlemen' they had considerable sympathy from the upper classes in the city. When the college tried to prosecute them 'the ladies

Wedding party at the Trinity College Chapel.

Detail of the Campanile, Trinity College.

especially were astonished at the barbarity of the undertaking: so cruel a persecution against the sons of gentlemen, suspected only of a frolick, in which they intended no more than breaking a man's window, tho' it chanced indeed to end in his death.'[43] It has been claimed that Ford's ghost, dressed in wig, gown and knee-breeches, emerges from number 25 at night and that he wanders towards Botany Bay (behind the northern range of buildings).

Two other redbrick terraces, similar to the Rubrics, ran round the other sides of the lawned area to the east of the Campanile, but these have been replaced, to the north by the Graduates' Memorial Building (1899-1902) by Thomas Drew and, on the west, by the Campanile (1852) by Charles Lanyon. The south side of this square consists of the Library.

The Dining Hall. The old seventeenth-century Dining Hall evidently left much to be desired – one contemporary believed it to be 'the coldest room in Europe' – and in the 1740s Richard Castle drew up plans for a new building on this site. However, Castle's partially erected structure had to be taken down, due to a series of disasters, including the collapse on two separate occasions of the vaults. The actual Dining Hall which we see was erected by Hugh Darley in the 1760s. Though severely damaged by a disastrous fire in July 1984 it was magnificently restored over the following year under the direction of the architects, de Blacam and Meagher in association with the college architect Ian

Roberts.[44] Upstairs, over the main entrance hall, is the Senior Common Room. Nearby, de Blacam and Meagher provided an unexpected addition to the restoration work – a complete reproduction down to the last detail of the American Bar in Vienna's Kartner Strasse designed in 1907 by Adolf Loos, one of the great figures of the Modern Movement. To the west of the building they also created a new four-storey atrium by hollowing out the eighteenth-century kitchen block which adjoins the Dining Hall.

The niceties of social distinction were well delineated in the original Dining Hall where Fellows and students each had their separate dining arrangements. The students who enjoyed the privilege of dining with the Fellows were known as Fellow Commoners. Unlike the rest of the undergraduates, they sported sleeves and velvet collars on their gowns; noblemen could have gold and silver tassels as well. The bulk of the undergraduates were known as Pensioners. They dined by themselves and had gowns with hanging sleeves. Finally, at the end of the pecking order came the 'Sizars', poor students who paid no fees and were not charged for their keep. Amongst other jobs they served at the Fellows' Table, dining afterwards on the leftovers. They got their name from the fact that originally they only paid for 'sizings', the additional supplies from the kitchen. These were sold below market prices to members of the college in the days when Trinity still had tenants who paid their rents in kind. The Sizars wore gowns of coarse black material without sleeves. In the 1770s they numbered thirty, out of a student body of four hundred. It was in the Dining Hall that a three-day 'Visitation' was held in April 1798 to weed out any treasonable activities amongst the students. The chief interrogator was the Vice Chancellor of the university and Lord Chancellor of Ireland, the notoriously anti-Catholic John Fitzgibbon, first Earl of Clare. Fitzgibbon's 'Visitation' resulted in the discovery of four committees of United Irishmen in the college, Robert Emmet being the Secretary of one. Nineteen students were expelled as a result.

Botany Bay. The narrow opening to the east of the Dining Hall leads to a small barrack-like space which is largely taken up by tennis courts. It is known as Botany Bay not – as might be expected – because of its forbidding appearance but rather because it had once been the kitchen herb garden. The oldest buildings date from the 1790s and are to be found in the northern and eastern ranges.

The 1937 Reading Room. The front portion of the building, by Thomas M. Deane, was erected in the 1920s as a Hall of Honour in memory of the members of the college who died in the Great War of 1914-18; their names are engraved on the walls inside. The 1937 Reading Room behind contains a memorial tablet to Fr Michael Moore, who had been appointed 'Head of the College' during James II's brief sojourn in Ireland. He and another priest, Fr Teigue MacCarthy, saved the library and its contents from substantial damage after the Fellows and

Botany Bay, student quarters at Trinity College.

students were evicted and the college occupied by the Jacobite army in the months preceding the Battle of the Boyne of July 1689.

The Library (1712-32). This was the first major eighteenth-century building in the college. Indeed, both it and Pearce's Parliament House (1728-39) in College Green, were the two most significant buildings that Dublin was to see built during the first half of the century. The Library was designed by Colonel Thomas Burgh (1670-1730), Chief Engineer and Surveyor General of Fortifications in Ireland. To protect the books from damp, the ground floor originally consisted of two open arcades with a dividing wall running the length of the building. These arcades were enclosed in 1892 to give further space for book storage but, a century later, were transformed into an exhibition area by Arthur Gibney and Partners. The two upper stories have also changed. The original sandstone facing weathered badly and was replaced in the nineteenth century by granite. The dramatic interior is largely a creation of the 1860s when substantial alterations were made by Deane and Woodward. Thomas Burgh's original chamber was a much more Augustan affair. It had the same lower bookstacks that we can see but, above them, all was clear, creating a wide space under a broad flat ceiling. Deane and Woodword continued the bookstacks upwards which gave the room a narrower appearance, as well as emphasising its vertical proportions. But their crowning achievement was the insertion of the magnificent barrel vault, for this was the key to the metamorphosis by which the Library's chief chamber was transformed into a great nave, a worthy *cathedra* for such treasures as the Books of Armagh, Durrow and Kells.

New Square. Until the 1830s the Rubrics backed onto College Park. New Square came into being with the erection of the two unassuming granite terraces on the north and east by Frederick Darley, the college architect. His qualifications for the job 'were genealogically rather than architecturally convincing'.[45] Various Darleys had worked either as masons and stonecutters – on Burgh's Library and Cassel's Printing House – as supervisors (for the erection of the west front in the 1750s) or, indeed, as suppliers of stone from the family's quarries at Golden Hill (granite) and Ardbraccan (limestone) where, in the mid-eighteenth century, up to a hundred men were kept employed on the preparation of stone for Trinity.

As an undergraduate (1923-27) Samuel Beckett lived in rooms at number 39 New Square and he occupied number 40 when he returned to Trinity in 1930 as lecturer in modern languages after having spent two years at the Ecole Normale Superieure in Paris. However, university life did not appeal to him and only a year later, after receiving his Master of Arts degree, he resigned his academic post. This was followed by a number of years divided between Paris, Dublin, London and Germany before Beckett finally settled in France.

The Long Room of the Library at Trinity College.

The Berkeley Library. While its title commemorates the famous Bishop George Berkeley (1687-1753), its architecture unashamedly belongs to this century. Yet, despite the enormous difference in style, the scale and mass of the Berkeley Library (1967, by Paul Koralek of Ahrends Burton and Koralek) is appropriate to the site. Le Corbusier's belief that freshly poured concrete should reflect the roughness of the material into which it is poured, can be seen in the board-marked framework on the lower levels of the building. The building pays careful attention to its location, stepping back to create a new public space between the Library and the Museum Building and placing its entrance in careful alignment with the diminutive Printing House on the northern side of New Square. The podium which occupies this space at the junction of the Berkeley Library and its neighbours creates a sense of occasion and provides a handsome setting for Arnaldo Pomodoro's 'Sphere with Sphere' (1982-83). Inside, the Berkeley Library 'is full of secluded cells picturesquely disposed, naturally lighted and conducive, it is hoped, to study'.[46]

The Printing House. This delightful building is by Richard Castle though, with its true free-standing portico, it is unlike the rest of his work. For this and other reasons – including the existence of a drawing for a similar building by Edward Lovett Pearce – it could possibly be in part a work by Pearce, built in the year following his death.[47] The building was started in 1734 and by 1738 was already in use, when an edition of Plato's *Dialogues* – the first Irish publication entirely in Greek – was published there.

Museum Building. This Venetian Gothic masterpiece (which forms the south side of New Square) is the most important and most delightful building of its type in Ireland. It was built to the design of Sir Thomas Deane and Benjamin Woodward between 1853 and 1857, to accommodate the School of Engineering as well as the departments of geology and geography. Woodward was the more talented partner and the museum has been long recognised as his masterpiece. It is a building which is imbued with the ideas and principles which John Ruskin – foremost theoretician of the Gothic revival – had only recently published in his two enormously influential works, *The Seven Lamps of Architecture* (1849) and *The Stones of Venice* (1851 and 1853).

Unlike earlier Gothic revival buildings which played on a picturesque massing of contrasting forms, the museum has a clear and solid profile and, from a distance, its compact shape can be seen at once. This followed Ruskin's dictum that a 'noble building' should reveal its magnitude with a simple bounding line from top to bottom and from end to end. However, there is something else surprising about Woodward's design, namely that at first glance it does not look like a Gothic revival building at all. This is because at Trinity Woodward was to try to mediate between two traditions, 'designing a medieval building for a

'Sphere with Sphere', by Arnaldo Pomodoro, outside the Berkeley Library, Trinity College.

The Museum Building and College Park, Trinity College.

A resident of the Museum Building, Trinity College.

classical environment'.[48] He found the style he needed in an appendix on 'Renaissance Ornaments' in the first volume of *The Stones of Venice* where Ruskin explains 'that the transition towards the Renaissance began with a Byzantine revival in which architects replaced their Gothic pointed arches with seemingly more archaic rounded ones.' Woodward used other sources as well, most notably the round-arched garden façade of Charles Barry's Travellers' Club in London. These and other ideas were skilfully filtered and reconstructed in a building which at one level is almost classical but, in its attitude towards materials and details, is everything that Ruskin could have desired. Ornamental work was used solely to reveal and emphasise the basic structural elements, with the carvers given a large measure of freedom in carrying out their work. A contemporary critic noted that 'the architects are seeking to carry out views lately advocated (by Ruskin) by leaving the design of the ornament to the workmen themselves, in order to obtain variety, the only assistance being verbal instructions from the architects as to the arrangement by geometrical forms, etc'.[49] This was the first building where the famous O'Shea brothers from Ballyhooly, County Cork are recorded as working. The man in charge was a Mr Roe of Lambeth but he was assisted by James and John O'Shea and their nephew Edward Whelan.[50]

The building is not generally open to the public but, if you can arrange to get a discreet peep inside, it is a memorable experience for you pass from a relatively stark arcaded vestibule into a large and magnificently lit central hallway, which is dominated by a great divided staircase. Overhead there is a high double-domed sky-lit ceiling which is constructed from a richly patterned series of blue, red and yellow enamelled bricks. Not surprisingly Woodward became a fa-voured architect of the Pre-Raphaelites. William Allingham described the un-finished building to Rossetti in May 1855 as being 'after Ruskin's heart. Style, early Venetian (I suppose), with numerous capitals delicately carved over with holly-leaves, shamrocks, various flowers, birds, and so on ... Ruskin has written to the Architect, a young man, expressing his high approval of the plans, and so by-and-by all you cogniscenti [sic] will be rushing over to examine the Stones of Dublin'.[51]

College Park. This is the park which Provost John Hely-Hutchinson closed off from the city in 1775, as it 'had become a Publick Walk, and frequently for Company of the lowest and worst kind'. However, the provost in question was hardly an example of outstanding propriety. His appointment (1774-94) was the result of political jobbery and came as a shock to the college, for Hely-Hutchin-son was married (and therefore ineligible for the post), a busy lawyer, a Parlia-mentarian and had almost no academic experience. The prospect was grim indeed. 'The college walks and gardens ... hitherto sacred to the exercise and

The Luce Hall recreation centre, Trinity College.

contemplation of the sober academick' were now 'infested by himself [Hely-Hutchinson] and military officers mounted on prancing horses; his wife and adult daughters with their train of female companions; and his infant children; their nurses and go-carts; who by their pomp and clamour have banished the muses and may probably be the authors of greater and more serious evils'.[52] The worldly ways of this 'harlequin genius' had their advantages however. Anxious that Trinity should produce gentlemen as well as scholars, Hely-Hutchinson broadened the curriculum, encouraged the teaching of modern languages and urged that senior and junior common rooms 'be established', supplied with newspapers, tea and coffee. They were; and the park which he wished to protect from 'company of the lowest and worst kind' has once again become 'a publick walk' and a delight to all Dubliners, student and non-student alike.

On the eastern end of College Park you have, running from south to north, the Moyne Institute of Preventive Medicine (designed by Desmond FitzGerald and opened in 1953), the Pavilion (by Thomas Drew, opened in 1885 and added to in later years) and two derivatives of Deane and Woodward's Museum building; the Chemistry Building (completed 1885) by McCurdy and Mitchell and the Zoology Building (completed 1876) by John McCurdy. The Physics Building (1904), at the edge of the rugby pitch, is by W. C. Marshall of London.

More controversial is the Luce Hall to the north east. This sports hall, by Scott Tallon and Walker, opened in 1981. To accommodate its arrival, an opening was ripped in the side of Pearse Street and the new building dropped skew-ways into the site with no regard whatsoever for the street line, the hall being aligned instead on a grid with Front Square. Doubtless the seagulls are appreciative. A later and more popular project by the same architects sits out of sight on Westland Row – the O'Reilly Institute for Communications and Technology. Just alongside the Luce Hall, at the corner of the playing field, is the three-storey engineering laboratory, an entirely 'architect-free' scheme. Finally, to the north of the rugby pitch – facing on to Pearse Street – there is another series of new buildings, including a new theatre named in honour of Samuel Beckett by the architects de Blacam and Meagher. These have been built as part of the college's celebrations for its 400th anniversary.

The Arts and Social Sciences Building (1980, by Ahrends Burton & Koralek).[53] Unlike the Berkeley Library, which is muscular and emphatic in appearance, the Arts and Social Sciences Building is a reticent structure which seems to step back out of deference to the old library. The north side of the building is almost as much landscape garden as architecture. Trinity's version of Babylon relies on the assumption that each stepped level can be treated as garden, given the apparent impermeability of damp-proof membranes and the strength of rein-forced concrete. In any event the result is a refreshing and inventive solution to the problem of erecting a north-facing building, while at the same time allowing the maximum amount of light into Fellows Square. Once again the firm of Ahrends Burton and Koralek has given something new to the college for, if their Berkeley Library introduced Dublin to brutalism, this later complex introduced Trinity to yet another architectural fashion, that of the landscaped building. As if to reinforce the landscape theme, the black steel sculpture on the lawn outside, by the American artist Alexander Calder, is entitled 'Cactus'.

The building serves a number of different functions. The top three floors contain various departments and underneath there are lecture theatres, the Lecky Library and the Douglas Hyde Gallery. On the Nassau Street side the building presents a tall façade of Wicklow granite, which is broken up into different segments by window openings which are angled to the street. The outline is generated by the plan of the lecture halls, whereas the plan to the north is arranged so as to give every office on the top three storeys a direct view of either Fellows Square or an internal garden court. For the students and the casual visitor there is a generous multi-level concourse which provides a place to indulge in the best of all Irish past-times, sitting and talking as the world goes by.

The Douglas Hyde Gallery. The entrance to the gallery is at the western end of the Arts and Social Sciences Building (off the passageway leading to Nassau Street).[54] The gallery is called after Douglas Hyde (1860-1949), the son of a Church of Ireland rector, a founder of the Gaelic League and a fervent propagandist for 'the necessity of de-Anglicising Ireland'. A graduate of Trinity, Hyde was to become the first Professor of Modern Irish at University College Dublin in 1909 and the first President of Ireland following the creation of that office under the Constitution of 1937. It is fitting that one of the last names we meet is Hyde's, for with him there is a coming together of that particular strain of Anglo-Irish culture with which Trinity was traditionally associated and the more politically resilient version of popular nationalism to which Hyde himself had so greatly contributed. It was an uneasy mix; Trinity's image as a bastion of the former ascendancy was powerfully underlined during the 1916 Rising when the grounds of the college were used as a base by the British reinforcements who bombarded the GPO – and toasts to the King continued for long after 1921. Indeed, for the Protestant community that Trinity represented, the new state – irrespective of Hyde being its President – seemed dangerously close at times to realising their worst fears of 'Home Rule' being tantamount to 'Rome Rule'. During the thirty-one-year primacy of Dr John Charles McQuaid, who became Catholic Archbishop of Dublin in 1942, it was a 'mortal sin' for Catholics within his diocese to attend Trinity without special permission. (For its part Trinity has allowed Catholics to attend and take degrees since 1793 and all religious tests, except for those connected with the Divinity School, have been abolished since 1873.) This ban was finally removed by the Catholic hierarchy in 1970 and today the idea of Trinity as some lingering bastion of the former ascendancy is entirely erroneous, though not surprising given the burgeoning power of the heritage industry – certainly an industry which has a fondness for the sort of imagery which is fuelled by the more arcane rituals of Trinity Week.

The Nassau Street Entrance to the college is a delight in itself with the old granite wall and railings gently curving to meet the new building. The whole composition was carefully aligned in order to maintain a tree which has now become the principal feature of the entrance, perhaps an appropriated symbol for those who hope to find in Trinity a sanctuary which offers, if only momentarily, 'an escape from everyday things'.[55] Glancing through the railings to the west of the tree one can see an arched opening which runs under the pavement of Nassau Street. This leads to St Patrick's Well where, according to tradition, the 'old Primates of Armagh' took a drink of water on St Patrick's Day.

The Provost's House. Behind the large rusticated gateway which opens on to the lower end of Grafton Street shelters the private residence of the Provost of Trinity College, a magnificent townhouse built by Provost Andrews in the 1760s. Andrews entered Trinity in 1732, became a Fellow in 1740 and Provost in 1758.

He was a member of Parliament and, as the house indicates, had ambitions and tastes which ranged well beyond academia. The house has all the pretensions of a great nobleman's residence, with a splendid series of ceremonial antechambers leading, via a dramatic octagonal stairway, to a magnificent saloon which runs the entire length of the first floor. Little is known of the origins of this remarkable interior, save that it may be by the English architect Henry Keene.[56] Unfortunately, all that we can whet our appetite on is the exterior, but it is of no mean significance. The façade of the centre block was copied from the garden-front of a London house (1723) by the Earl of Burlington (a descendant of the famous Earl of Cork) which he in turn had taken directly from an elevation by Palladio: an appropriate return to original sources for the house of a leading academic and a fitting tribute to an architect who had such an important and enduring influence on the development of Irish architecture.[57]

St Stephen's Green

St Stephen's Green is the earliest of Dublin's great squares dating back to the 1660s when the Restoration city at last pushed decisively beyond its medieval confines. By the end of Charles II's reign (1660-85) the population had doubled to over 40000, making Dublin the second city in the British dominions and much the largest in Ireland. The expansion was such that more of the city now lay outside the walls than within. The new lines of quays on both sides of the river was one response to this revolutionary new growth; another – and one which was quite remarkable given that Ireland was still in many respects a medieval society – was St Stephen's Green. Nothing like this had previously been experienced in Ireland and, indeed, nothing on this scale was ever again repeated. At over thirty English acres, St Stephen's Green is one of the largest squares in Europe.

The inspiration for such ambition and, in particular, for the awakening of a new-found civic pride in Dublin as Irish capital has been attributed to James Butler, the first Duke of Ormond and Viceroy to the newly restored Charles II. The Duke had returned to Dublin in 1662 with ideas and ambitions fuelled by his long sojourn in Paris with the exiled Stuarts. It was under his impetus that Dublin began at last to take on the air of a capital, instead of being merely a convenient town where Parliament might sit, though even that had not always been certain as the 'Confederation Parliament' of 1649 had opted for Kilkenny, and Drogheda had previously been a favoured location.

However, the immediate impetus was decidedly pragmatic if the Corporation's records are anything to go by. As ever, the Corporation was short of money – due, we are told, to 'the late rebellion and long continued troubles of this Kingdom' – and so it was decided that 'the outskirts of St Stephen's Green and other waste lands about the city that now addeth nothing at all to pleasure or profit may be set for 99 years, or to fee farm, and a considerable rent secured'.[58] The 'waste lands' in question had up to then been a marshy commonage, a haunt of snipe and other birds, where the mayor grazed his cattle and the poor foraged for firewood. Public executions were carried out there from time to time, one of the more noted being that of the unfortunate John Atherton, a Protestant Bishop of Waterford who had fallen foul of the politics of the time and was executed there on grounds of bestiality in 1640. The Green took its name from the nearby Hospital of St Stephen, a medieval institution which cared for lepers and which survived until 1698. (It was situated where Mercer's Hospital was later built, at the western end of South King Street).

In 1664 the central portion of the old commonage was marked out as a park and lots were drawn for the building land around the perimeter. The Corporation was anxious that minimum standards be met. It was stipulated that any lot-holders who wished to build 'be engaged to build of brick, stone and timber', that the buildings should have at least two floors and that they be covered with tiles or slates.[59] (Two years later, after the Great Fire of London, the Corporation prohibited thatched roofs within the city.) Building progressed in a desultory fashion. The north and west sides were the first to be developed, but of these early houses there is nothing now to be seen. Architectural standards seem to have varied. John Wesley complained, in 1747, that 'the houses round about it (besides that some are low and bad) are quite irregular and unlike each other'.[60] If by 1756 the park had acquired a centrepiece, in the form of an equestrian statue of George II (by John Van Nost, the younger), the overall result was nonetheless in quite a different tradition from such inventions as the Place Royale which were to be found in seventeenth-century France. In these, the monumental buildings which defined the Place were as crucial to the overall design as the statue of the monarch which justified such ostentation. St Stephen's Green was in the tradition of spaces such as the Lincoln's Inn Fields in London, except bigger. There was no attempt to enforce any particular design, nor any insistence on grandiose elevations, still less any proposals for buildings with unified monumental façades, though by placing the statue of George II on an inordinately high pedestal, there seems to have been a conscious attempt to at least make it the focal point of axial vistas along Dawson Street and York Street.[61]

The Park. The swampy meadow which was the centrepiece of the new square was levelled and a deep ditch dug around the perimeter to carry off the water, though, if an early nineteenth-century visitor is to be believed, the 'dirty ditch' also served as 'the receptacle of dead cats and dogs'.[62] On either side of the ditch, walks were laid out; the inner ones were of grass lined with hawthorn hedges, the outer ones of gravel lined with lime trees, with a low stone wall separating them from the roadway. Before long the square became a fashionable place of promenade. 'Why don't you walk in the Green of St Stephen?' asked Dean Swift of Stella and Mrs Delaney in 1710, 'the walks there are finer gravelled than the Mall.'[63]

Promenading along such gravelled walks was an important social ritual in the eighteenth century, with the various ranks of society from nobleman to prosperous merchant parading to and fro, perhaps for the air but certainly for the spectacle – identifying and being identified as members of 'polite society'. The west side was known as French Walk because of the number of Huguenots who had property in the area, while the east and south sides were known respectively as Monck's Walk and Leeson Walk; both of these families owned land in the neighbourhood. However, the most fashionable parade was Beau Walk on the northern fringe of the park. It was evidently an asset in advertising housing; a house in Merrion Row, for instance, was described as being only 'three doors from the Beau Walk of St Stephen's Green'.[64] Other fashionable promenades would have been Gardiner's Mall (now O'Connell Street) and, towards the end of the century, carriage parading on the North Circular Road became the vogue.

Due to the bad drainage, the Green returned to its former swampy state in winter, though this had its benefits for those who enjoyed snipe shooting. Mindful of the danger to the neighbouring residents, the Lord Mayor prohibited the shooting of snipe there in 1752, with the result that the park became a sanctuary for wild fowl. However, as more houses went up around the square the central common was improved. In 1746 the limes were replanted and in 1749 the square temporarily embellished with a Temple of Peace, the centrepiece of a fireworks display in celebration of the peace concluded at Aix-la-Chapelle. Enclosed by a balustrade of lighted obelisks, pillars and rockets 'this was Dublin's own version of the festival architecture of Rome'.[65] A more permanent centrepiece was erected in 1756, the brass equestrian statue of George II by John Van Nost, the younger. It survived for almost two centuries until it was blown-up in May 1937 to coincide with the coronation of his descendant, George VI.

The park that we enjoy today is a Victorian creation which bears little relation to the symetrically laid out grounds of the late eighteenth century. By the early 1800s the Green was in a bad way. Knowing that improvements would be costly and that revenue was scarce, 'privatisation' seemed the only solution. The Corporation closed the park to the public and rented it instead to the surrounding residents. They had the drainage ditch filled in and replaced the old formal avenues with winding walks and gardens, designed in accordance with the principles of the 'picturesque'. It was Sir Arthur Guinness, later Lord Ardilaun, who generously provided the funds which enabled the park to be reopened to

St Stephen's Green – preparing for the show.

the public in 1880. He had the grounds redesigned at his own expense, with a new ornamental lake fed from the Grand Canal. Thousands now enjoy its contours, curving, according to George Moore, 'like a piece of calligraphy'. The grounds are now admirably maintained by the Office of Public Works. In the summer the lawns are festooned with office workers and the formal flower beds a riot of regimented colour. Couples relax there, as Samuel Beckett describes in *Eh, Joe*: 'when we sat watching the ducks ... holding hands, exchanging vows'. The main changes to the park since Sir Arthur's time are the memorials, ranging from Henry Moore's work, irreverently known as the 'Potato Crisp', in honour of William Butler Yeats (1865-1939) to such androgynous pieces as the bust of James Clarence Mangan (1803-49) and Countess Markievicz (Constance Gore-Booth, 1868-1927). One of the best sculptures bequeathed to Dublin by the 1988 Millennium extravaganza – Grace Weir's 'Truce' – stands just outside the park, in front of the Bank of Ireland at the north-eastern corner of the Green.

Wolfe Tone. If the shape and pattern of contemporary Dublin owes much to the late eighteenth-century oligarchy who made it their showpiece capital, our political environment owes even more to another figure from that period, Theobald Wolfe Tone (1763-1798). A larger-than-life size statue of him (by Edward Delaney) dominates the north-eastern entrance to the Green. Tone was a spirited and romantic figure whose evident charm even captivated his opponents. According to Arthur Wellesley, the MP for Trim (1791-95) who later became better known as the Duke of Wellington, 'Wolfe Tone was a most extraordinary man, and his history the most curious of those times.' The times were those of the American and French revolutions, the first bolstering the successful claims for legislative independence by the Irish Parliament, the second inspiring radicals such as Tone, who sought to rectify the inequities of that very Parliament by forging an alliance with revolutionary France.

Unlike others of the period, we know much about Tone for, before 'embarking on a business' – as he disarmingly described it – with the French in 1796, he sat down in Paris and wrote his life story. The 'business' did not work out quite as he had hoped – a French expedition under Admiral Hoche was scattered by storms in December 1796 – and, when the rebellion for which he had worked so hard finally broke out in May-June 1798 it lacked coordination (most of the leaders had been arrested) and was widespread only in the south-east where it took on a sectarian character. He himself was captured, along with a small fleet of twelve French ships, off Lough Swilly in October of the same year and brought to Dublin where he was sentenced to be hanged. He took his own life instead. It was his writings which were to be his most important legacy, for Wolfe Tone more than any other leader, is central to the philosophy of 1798 and the successful grafting of the republican aspects of French revolutionary ideology onto more traditional Irish movements of popular protest. The result would not necessarily have been to his liking, for the goal of creating a new non-confessional society along the lines of the French Republic faded quickly and Irish republicanism became in time not an ideal to be achieved for its own sake – as Tone wished – but rather a means towards a nationalistic end.

The Shelbourne Hotel. Perhaps not surprisingly, Wolfe Tone seems to gaze pointedly away from any sight of the Shelbourne Hotel lest it remind him of Kerry House, which had an inglorious claim to fame as a torturing barracks during 1798. The house had been rented to the Government as a billet for troops sent to Dublin to put down the rebellion and, as often happens in such instances, the troops stayed longer than envisaged; in fact for another twenty years until one of them unwittingly burnt the place down. The mansion had originally belonged to the Fitzmaurices, Earls of Kerry and subsequently Earls of Shelbourne. On its site were erected four new houses, three of which were leased for use as a hotel in the early 1820s.[66] These, plus two adjoining houses, were demolished to make way for the present Victorian building which opened its doors in January 1867.

From the outset the Shelbourne was the haunt of fashionable society. It was particularly associated with the Dublin season – which lasted from February to March – when many of the gentry who could not afford or feigned disinterest in the London season, opted for the Dublin alternative. This revolved around the Viceregal Court at Dublin Castle, starting with the 'Levée' and the first of two 'Drawing Room' sessions for the presentation of debutante daughters – and ending with St Patrick's Ball. Of the five or six hundred who received invitations to the various functions only a hundred or so would have had the true-blue credentials which went with land and a suitable lineage. However, apart from these 'county families' there was always the possibility of the occasional aristocratic catch in the Viceregal establishment and the various regiments stationed in and about the city could be depended upon to supply a requisite number of suitable English officers. The Shelbourne provides a setting for George Moore's *Drama in Muslin* in which he describes the stratagems of the Irish matrons who shepherded their daughters up from the country in the hope of making a suitable match. This was a social minefield where the Dublin matrons would have had to tread warily, for if bourgeois Dublin was renowned for its snobbery, so too were the matrons who made the Shelbourne a temporary base of operations for the Dublin season, and in these subtle matrimonial campaigns, bourgeois Dublin would have been easily outgunned by the superior social status of the landed families.

St Stephen's Green Clubs. If the Shelbourne was the operational headquarters where ambitious mothers plotted out their moves on the matrimonial front, the

The lobby of the Shelbourne Hotel.

nearby clubs provided a refuge for their menfolk. There is quite a number of them on the north side of the Green, all resolutely male; their popularity amongst married men suggesting that perhaps all was not bliss in the sanctity of the Victorian home. By and large these were professional men's clubs and, despite the actual genealogy of one or two, were quite different in spirit from the political and gambling clubs of eighteenth-century Dublin. Just as the boisterousness of establishments such as Daly's in Dame Street was characteristic of Georgian Ireland, the institutionalisation of these clubs was equally representative of the Victorian period. While housed in eighteenth-century surroundings, the principles behind their organisation reflect the values of a later era. There was a greater subdivision of specialised public rooms, with a library and a dining-room (indeed, at times separate dining-rooms for members and guests), smoking rooms and card rooms, rooms for conversation and formal meetings – in all, a degree of organisation which only the very rich could have afforded to implement in their own homes.[67]

16-24 St Stephen's Green North. Numbers 23 and 24 (on the corner with Kildare Street) are both by Ronnie Tallon of Scott Tallon and Walker. Scale and proportion are used to harmonise with the older buildings nearby. Initially there was only one building in this rigorously modern idiom (number 24, completed 1973) and it worked very well, but now that there are two, and both in the same colour, the effect has been weakened. Number 22, with its elaborate wrought-iron balcony at first-floor level, dates from the 1790s. Since 1910 it has been the headquarters of 'the Friendly Brothers of St Patrick', a club which traces its origins back to a society founded in the seventeenth century with the aim of suppressing duelling. The large brown Stephen Court (by Andrew Devane) was completed in 1971 for the Irish Life Assurance Company. Four years later it was highly commended in the European Architectural Heritage Year awards as an example of how infill building could sit happily in a Georgian context. Number 17, now the home of the Kildare and University Club, was originally built in, or around, 1776 for Joseph Leeson, the newly created Earl of Miltown (1763). His father's house and brewery were situated on the far side of the Green. The house was bought by the University Club in 1850 (it amalgamated with the Kildare Street Club in 1976). The interior, with its period furniture and plasterwork by Michael Stapleton, still retains the atmosphere of an aristocratic townhouse, though it was certainly one of the more opulent, having such refinements as architraves and chair-rails chased with fillets of silvered tin. Number 16, which now contains Electricity Supply Board (ESB) offices, was built around 1776 for Gustavus Hume. It later became the palace of the Protestant Archbishops of Dublin. It too contains fine ceilings and other plasterwork by Michael Stapleton.

8 and 9, St Stephen's Green North. Two further clubs are located in the short

Number 17, Stephen's Green, now the Kildare and University Club.

range of buildings which run from the top of Dawson Street to the top of Grafton Street. The St Stephen's Green Club, at number 9, has all the appearance of a nineteenth-century building. The impression is misleading, for despite the extensive alterations, the house dates from around 1756. It still retains its magnificent rococo plasterwork which has been attributed to the Lafranchini brothers. The ceiling in the large dining-room depicts a 'triumph of Bacchus' with drunk and riotous putti setting an example for the members. Next door (number 8), behind the curved double sweep of steps and balustrades, the Hibernian United Services Club occupies the house built in the 1770s for Samuel Hutchinson, Bishop of Killala. It too contains fine examples of late eighteenth-century plasterwork. The club was founded for young officers stationed in Dublin, but its membership no longer retains any special military connection. Sir Walter Scott stayed there in 1825 as his son, who was in the army, was serving in Ireland at the time.

The St Stephen's Green Centre (completed 1978). George Moore was horrified in the early years of this century 'at the sight of a shop that had been run up at the corner of the Green' – one wonders what he would have made of this.[68] In both scale and spirit this enormous shopping mall is indeed a cathedral of our age with a nave worthy of that ambition. However, from the outside, a different mix of metaphors is conjured up. If this is a great flag-ship of commerce, moored at the southern end of the city's central shopping district, the section which faces the Green is suggestive of a beached Mississippi paddle-steamer. The gleaming white iron-work is certainly more reminiscent of New Orleans than any hoped-for analogies with the Crystal Palace. On South King Street it was the neighbouring Gaiety Theatre which evidently provided the inspiration. Unfortunately, the design is little more than expensive wallpapering; there is too much of it and the break between the upper and lower levels is far too abrupt. It is the interior which is genuinely spectacular, with three tiers of shopping space ranged along the length of a great atrium. It is disappointing that at ground level this sense of space and scale is lost. There is no central route which does justice to what should be a great vista and instead of being enticed to go further, you get shoved to left and right by a squabbling assortment of free-standing shopping units.

The four-acre site used to be occupied by a varied collection of mainly Georgian buildings, over sixty in all, including one cinema and two well-known pubs, Sinnot's and Rice's. The saga of the site accumulation is worthy of a soap-opera, beginning in 1963 with the Slazengers (owners of Powerscourt demesne in County Wicklow) and featuring Patrick Gallagher, one of Dublin's more noted property developers who went bankrupt not long later, his liquidator selling out to Robin Power, the Cork dentist-turned-property-developer. The scheme as finished was designed by a team led by Jim Twomey, chief architect

The Royal College of Surgeons.

of Power Securities who built the complex in a joint venture with British Land.[69]

The Fusiliers' Arch (1907). This triumphal arch was built as a memorial to the officers and men of the Royal Dublin Fusiliers who lost their lives in the Boer War of 1899-1900: their names are inscribed in the panels of the arch over the gate.

Robert Emmet (1778-1803). A statue of Emmet by the Irish-American sculptor, Jerome Connor (1876-1943), stands a short distance south of the Fusiliers' Arch (inside the park railings). Emmet's birthplace, 124 St Stephen's Green, stood opposite, but has been demolished. The young Emmet became one of the leaders of the United Irishmen at Trinity College, but after the Lord Chancellor's famous visitation in April 1798, he left the university, eventually going to the Continent where he discussed the prospects of Irish independence with Napoleon and Talleyrand. He returned to Dublin in 1802 to organise a rebellion and did so with a greater degree of professionalism than is often realised. However, when he eventually set forth in his uniform of green coat, white breeches and cocked hat to attack Dublin Castle on 23 July 1803, he was supported by only a hundred or so undisciplined followers. The result was an abysmal failure with nothing achieved, other than the murder of the Lord Chief Justice and his nephew whose bad luck it was to be passing in their coach. Emmet fled to the Dublin mountains but was captured on returning to the city to join his fiancée Sarah Curran. He was hanged at Thomas Street on 20 September 1803. Victorian Ireland took the tragic lover of Sarah Curran to its heart, treasuring in particular the stirring declaration which concluded his famous speech from the dock: 'When my country takes her place among the nations of the earth, then and not till then, let my epitaph be written.' If, as has been suggested,[70] Emmet's actual declaration was not quite like this it is not important; indeed, that Emmet's rising was little more than the last splutter of the 1798 rebellion is perhaps immaterial. What mattered to later separatists was that Emmet's failure was a heroic one, a noble and sacrificial gesture which they hoped might inspire later generations to take their turn and strike a blow for Irish freedom. The reality of what had happened in 1803 was shoved aside in favour of its potent symbolism and so transformed, Emmet entered the pantheon of Irish nationalism.

The Royal College of Surgeons. This would seem to be an unlikely link with nationalist Ireland and the many currents which it contained; yet it was here during the 1916 Rising that a small contingent of the Citizen Army under Michael Mallin (1850-1916) and Countess Markievicz (Constance Gore-Booth, 1868-1927) did their bit to rekindle what had seemed to be the dying embers of radical nationalism. If the real-life ambitions of such eighteenth-century revolutionaries as Tone – and perhaps even Emmet – were retrospectively transformed so that they became little more than symbolic gestures, it was a reductionist process which went into reverse in 1916. When a small group of radical nationalists took to the Dublin streets that Easter Monday it was the gesture that came first and their hope was that the real-life revolution might follow in its wake. Their vision was prophetic. For 1916 can be seen as agit-prop theatre taken to its extreme, and for once life did indeed follow art and, in the words of Yeats, 'a terrible beauty was born'.

Of the seven signatories of the 1916 Proclamation, four were writers and three were poets. Only one, James Connolly, was a socialist. A question that is often asked is what the Citizen Army – a socialist militia group set-up by Connolly to defend workers during the bitter lock-out of 1913 – had to do with all this. There has never been a satisfactory answer, and while the Citizen Army fought bravely in 1916, in the longterm it gave neither them nor their ideals any real leeway in determining the nature of the state that came into being a few years later. Socialism, even at its mildest, was suspect and was never incorporated into the subsequent Easter Week cult.

During the week-long rebellion, Mallin, with Countess Markievicz as his second in command, attempted to hold St Stephen's Green. At the outset they wasted valuable time digging trenches in the park, seemingly oblivious to the fact that it was overlooked by buildings on all sides. The tallest of these was the Shelbourne Hotel and it was speedily occupied by troops who consequently dominated the rebel position. They, nonetheless, remedied their position in time by retreating to the College of Surgeons where they held out to the end. Doubtless the Park Superintendent was glad to see them go. In his report to the commissioners of Public Works he added that, apart from the more evident deaths and damage he was 'sorry to say six of our wildfowl were killed or shot'. He meant it, for, as the commissioners noted, he had in full oblivion of the carnage 'fed the birds in the Green daily under considerable risk of being shot'.[71]

The Dublin-born Mallin was one of the sixteen leaders executed after the Rising, but the Countess's death sentence was commuted to penal servitude for life. After being released under general amnesty in 1917 she was returned as the MP for St Patrick's division in Dublin in the 1918 general election. As a result she became the first woman to be elected to Westminster though, in accordance with Sinn Féin policy, she refused to take her seat. She was a member of the first Dáil and Minister for Labour. On the run, like other ministers, she spent two more periods in jail, in Mountjoy and in Cork. The Countess opposed the Anglo-Irish Treaty of 1921 and continued to advocate republican views until her death in Dublin on 15 July 1927.

The college itself survived the rebellion without any great damage and is now one of the few buildings on the western side of the Green to have survived the more destructive development clearances of recent years. It was built in 1806 to a design by Edward Parke but, in 1827, was extended northwards and recentred in the process. If you look at the window openings you will see that the new front is at odds with the older plan for some of the window embrasures open slant-wise into the rooms behind. The statues above the pediment, Aesculapius, Minerva and Hygieia, are by John Smyth, eldest son of the renowned Edward Smyth who executed the famous riverine heads on the Custom House.

Lord Ardilaun. The seated figure inside the railings (almost across from the Royal College of Surgeons) is Arthur Guinness, Lord Ardilaun, the man who opened the park to the public in 1880 and who had it laid out at his own expense. The statue, by Thomas Farrell, was paid for by public subscription.

119 and 120, St Stephen's Green West. Richard Castle (*c.* 1690-1751) had already laid the foundation for this handsome pair of houses when he died at Carton in February 1751 while writing to a carpenter employed at Leinster House. It was property which he was developing himself and the site along with plans were sold by his executors to a Richard Thwaites who completed the project as Castle envisaged. Castle (or Cassels) was born in Germany of a Huguenot family around 1690 and came to Ireland either at the behest of Sir Edward Lovett Pearce, the most notable Irish architect of the period, or else at the request of Sir Gustavus Hume for whom he built a house on the shore of Lough Erne. He worked with Pearce and eventually inherited his practice. The greater part of his output was made up of country houses and, significantly enough, three of his most important Dublin buildings are effectively country houses in an urban setting; these are Tyrone House (now the Department of Education), Leinster House (now the Dáil) and the Rotunda Hospital. He has also been credited with the temple-like Printing House in Trinity College and, closer at hand, with number 85 St Stephen's Green South. Castle, it is said, was also responsible for the introduction of the Venetian window to Ireland and, in particular, with the use of a blind centre in the middle panel, as in this case.[72] Though one building has been marred by subsequent alterations at ground level they still constitute a very handsome pair.

While numbers 119 and 120 are now amongst the oldest of Dublin's semi-detached houses they certainly were not the first. Many semi-detached houses, with the characteristic Dutch gables of the period, were built in the early decades of the eighteenth century though only a few survive, and often much remodelled. There were advantages in building in pairs – a single chimney stack could be shared and, even if not, at least the builder could live in one house and sell off the other to reduce his costs. Aesthetically, as in the case here, they could make more of an impact as a symmetrical unit. It proved to be a durable prototype, and semi-detached houses continued to be built in the nineteenth-century suburbs, though often on a much more elaborate scale. In this century the semi-detached came into its own, though the strain has certainly been well-diluted since this Palladian pair was completed in 1761.

The Unitarian Church. The church is by William Henry Lynn (1829-1915), one of the most able of Ireland's Victorian architects. At seventeen he became an assistant in the office of Charles Lanyon, the Antrim county surveyor and such was his talent that by the time he was twenty-four he had become a partner. It was his mastery of ecclesiastical architecture, in particular, which established his reputation. In 1860 the practice – now Lanyon, Lynn, Lanyon (due to the arrival of Lanyon's son John) – opened a Dublin office, so great was the volume of ecclesiastical and domestic business. The Unitarian Church (1861-62) dates from this period as does St Andrew's Church (1860-62) in Suffolk Street. The partnership was dissolved in 1872 and in his final years he concentrated on public buildings, winning, as late as 1910 – when he was eighty-two – an anonymous competition for the extension of Queen's College Belfast.

The South-west Corner of the Green. This does little credit to either God or mammon, represented in this instance by the Corporation and property developers who, between them, have wrought havoc on this part of the Green.[73] The Corporation's road-widening plans have fallen like a curse on whole sections of the city condemning them to a lingering death, for it can take years to acquire the necessary sites. In the process properties decay, but worse, whole communities are demoralised and destroyed long before the final death rattle comes with the crunch of the bulldozer. In this case a property development company in the shape of MEPC (Ireland) saw the potential of allying itself with the Corporation, and between their private acquisitions and the Corporation's compulsory purchases, a two-acre site was cleared. What went had not only a strong residential element – in upper-floor flats – but a truly urban mix of activities which no office development could ever replace: grocery and vegetable shops, handcrafts and antiques, a tobacconist, a furrier and an optician, two restaurants and two schools, a printing works, a pipe manufacturer, a solicitor's office, a bank, two building and decorating contractors and the Winter Palace Gardens, a famous pub which had been briefly occupied by the Volunteers during Easter week. Though the pub emerged from that battle relatively unscathed it had no hope against the Corporation's street-widening campaign. Some road-widening is undoubtedly needed, but the high costs in social and architectural terms – not to mention the bill which has to be picked up by the tax payer – seems to have held little weight in the balance of Corporation priorities. In this instance Cuffe Street has been the chief victim, though Harcourt Street has not been knocked into shape without a few bruising experiences. What is doubly disappointing is that in many cases the office blocks which eventually replaced the older buildings are nothing to write home about. The

Ardilaun Centre (1982, by architects Costello, Murray and Beaumont),[74] which surrounds the Unitarian Church pays no heed to the new street line in Cuffe Street and anyone driving along the southside of the Green can now see the lines of washing hanging on the rear balconies of the Mercer House flats. It certainly adds a domestic note to the urban scene, but in one of the most important public spaces in a European capital, one might have expected better.

82-100 St Stephen's Green South. This is now the only substantial stretch of Georgian building left on the Green. Where numbers 92 to 95 are now, was originally the site of the gardens and dwelling house of Joseph Leeson, a wealthy Dublin brewer whose brewery covered a considerable amount of ground to the rear of his house. Shortly before his death in November 1740, the brewery was sold to Patrick Sweetman but it wasn't until the late 1790s that P. and J. Sweetman, porter-brewers, moved their business to Francis Street in the Liberties. Numbers 92 and 93 were built on the gardens to the east side of the old Leeson townhouse and number 95 and the Methodist Centenary Church on the site of the house itself.[75] The church (1843 by Isaac Farrell) was destroyed by fire in 1973. What remained of the building was used as the external fabric for a modern office development by the P.V. Doyle Group and is now the headquarters of the Smurfit Paribas Bank.

Numbers 92 and 93 constitute another handsome pair of semi-detached houses, though less elaborate than the mid-eighteenth-century Palladian couple (numbers 119 and 120) on St Stephen's Green West. Each house has a matching façade, front and rear, broken by a carriage arch at ground level. Both have matching doric doorcases with Greek doric columns and, inside, the standard layout of a late eighteenth-century Dublin townhouse. At ground level a narrow entrance hall leads to a staircase hall, while running alongside there was a study to the front and a dining-room to the rear. At first floor the main reception room ran the full width of the house while to the rear a smaller drawingroom for everyday family use, shared the available space with the stairwell. The floors above were used for bedrooms.[76]

The Catholic University Church. This Byzantine-like interior is hidden behind a stone-and-brick porch, distinguished, if that is the word, by a diminutive belfry which floats on a canopy overhead. The entrance is squashed into a former laneway between the two adjoining buildings and gives little hint of the beautiful church beyond. John Henry Newman, later Cardinal Newman, was responsible for its being built. 'My idea was to build a large barn and decorate it in the style of a basilica.'[77] His friend John Hungerford Pollen (1820-1902) came from England to do exactly as he wished. Choice specimens of Irish marble were used lavishly throughout. The result is one of the most delightful and surprising church interiors in Dublin.

The Catholic University. The adjoining buildings (numbers 82 to 87) formed the main buildings of the Catholic university which opened in 1856 with John Henry Newman as first rector. It was in preparation for this role that Newman wrote his celebrated, 'Discourses on the scope and nature of University Education' which he delivered at the Rotunda in 1852. Non-denominational Queen's Colleges had been established at Belfast, Cork and Galway by an Act of Parliament in 1845, but they were condemned as Godless institutions by the Catholic bishops who, instead, decided to establish a Catholic university of Ireland with neither aid nor recognition from the state. Newman hadn't an easy tenure – not all the bishops were enthusiastic about the project and others were uneasy about his Englishness.

In 1883 the university was entrusted to the Jesuits and it became an 'approved college' of the newly established Royal University of Ireland (1879-1909) which acted solely as an examining body. The Royal University had its headquarters not far away at Earlsfort Terrace. This was the period when Gerard Manley Hopkins was professor of Greek (1884-89) and James Joyce a student (1898-1902). In 1909, following the passing of yet another piece of legislation, the Catholic University was finally transformed into University College Dublin, a constituent college of the new non-denominational National University of Ireland. The college has since been relocated to a new campus built at Belfield in the southside suburbs.

Newman House, 86 St Stephen's Green South. This expansive granite-fronted house dates from the mid-1760s. It was more than likely built by Robert West who was responsible for the sumptuous rococo plasterwork. All the main reception rooms have delightful ceilings, with broadly symmetrical patterns and no shortage of scrolls, foliated curves and the birds for which West was noted. The lion who languishes nonchalantly over the front entrance is by John Van Nost, the younger. The house's owner, Richard Chapel Whaley, was a notorious priest-hunter more commonly known as 'Burn-Chapel-Whaley'. There is a certain justice therefore in the fact that his house is now known as Newman House, in honour of a man who was not only a Catholic but a priest, and a priest who had converted from Anglicanism. Burn-Chapel-Whaley would have had little time for the Oxford Movement. His son, Thomas 'Buck' Whaley (1766-1800), was a notorious rake. He inherited an income of £7000 a year along with some £60,000 in cash at the age of thirteen, but quickly went through his fortune and had to leave Paris – where he had gone with a tutor – as he had run up enormous debts. He is probably best known for accepting a wager to travel to Jerusalem and back within a year, which he did between September 1788 and June 1789. He became an under-age MP in 1785, but his most remarkable contribution came later when, according to Sir Jonah Barrington, he accepted

The bed of Gerard Manley Hopkins, Newman House.

bribes both for voting for the Union and for doing a *volte face* and voting against. As Winston Churchill was to quip many years later: 'Anyone can rat – it takes talent to re-rat!'

Clanwilliam House, 85 St Stephen's Green South. Newman House's older neighbour was built about 1740 for Captain Hugh Montgomery by Richard Castle. Though the smaller of the two houses, its importance is underlined by its pivotal position on the north-south axis of the Green. Despite the modest villa-like proportions of the exterior the house is considerably larger than it appears and contains stunning stuccowork by the Swiss brothers Paul and Philip Lafranchini. At the rear, it has an attractive Gothic extension of *c.*1780. The principal reception room at first-floor level takes up the full front of the house and, following the best Palladian principles, has the proportions of a double cube. The carved ceiling, with allegorical panels and putti swinging from garlands, is one of the richest Lafranchini works. About 1785 the house came into the possession of Viscount Clanwilliam and is still known as Clanwilliam House. Number 85 contains the Physics Theatre where Joyce read 'Drama and Life', a paper in defence of Henrik Ibsen, to the Literary and Historical Society and where the fictionalised Stephen discusses the nature of beauty with Fr Darlington.

Iveagh House. This former Guinness residence, now the Department of Foreign Affairs, incorporates two houses, numbers 80 and 81. The Portland stone façade was erected in 1866 by Sir John Benjamin Lee Guinness (1798-1868) who decided to incorporate number 81 with his own home (number 80) which he bought in 1856. Number 80 was Richard Castle's earliest known Dublin house, being built for Bishop Clayton of Killala in the 1730s. Some of the original eighteenth-century interior survives, but Sir Benjamin, as head of Ireland's greatest brewing and industrial concern, had both houses extensively remodelled so that he could entertain on a lavish country-house scale. The grandest of these additions was a vast ballroom (by William Young) which, together with the stairhall and ballroom vestibule, creates a monumental and sumptuous ensemble 'worthy of the most glittering of Oscar Wilde's final acts'.[78] It is now used for state receptions. The second Earl of Iveagh offered the house and its gardens to the nation in the late 1930s.

Office Development, St Stephen's Green South. Between Iveagh House and the corner of Earlsfort Terrace there is a disappointing array of buildings, emblematic in their way of what the office boom of the sixties and seventies meant for Dublin. Four houses were demolished to make way for the grimmest development of the lot, Desmond FitzGerald's offices for Colmstock Properties which now houses the Department of Justice. One of the demolished houses, number 76, had a plasterwork ceiling of the Four Seasons which was salvaged

Iveagh House, The Department of Foreign Affairs.

by the Office of Public Works and is now in Dublin Castle. Another, number 73, was the residence of Maud Gonne. Whatever her vision of a romantic and revolutionary Ireland may have been, it certainly wasn't this. Three houses were demolished to make way for Heinault House, completed in 1966 by Stephenson, Gibney and Associates for Heinault Investments (contemporary developers are discretion itself when it comes to identifying themselves with their works). This was Dublin's first pre-cast concrete office block. However, the sixty-four pre-cast window units did not last and had to be replaced in 1984. Finally, on the corner site, four houses were replaced by Canada House, completed in 1973 by Tyndall, Hogan, Hurley for Hardwicke's Ltd. Here again the pre-cast panelling didn't live up to expectations and within a decade, bits were falling onto the street below.[79]

Earlsfort Terrace. The connection with St Stephen's Green was made in 1839, following the demolition of a row of small gabled houses at the bottom of Leeson Street. The junction with Leeson Street is now dominated by the tall office building which runs diagonally onto Earlsfort Terrace. It was built as the headquarters of the Irish Sugar Company in 1965; the architects were Boyle and Delaney. The rest of the eastern side of the street is taken up by two related developments by architects Burke-Kennedy-Doyle and Partners – the Conrad Hilton Hotel (1990) and the Goodbody Building (1986, on the corner with Hatch Street).[80] Despite the considerable space given to the plaza, there seems to have

'A Flight of Birds' by Colm Brennan outside the Conrad Hilton Hotel, Earlsfort Terrace.

been little attempt to establish a relationship with the National Concert Hall and, while the buildings may work effectively in themselves, as far as the street is concerned the result is disjointed and disappointing.

The National Concert Hall. This is a highly successful conversion (1981 by Noel de Chenu, Michael O'Doherty and Allen Smith of the Office of Public Works) of the former main buildings of University College Dublin. The original building was completed in 1919 to a severe neoclassical design by Rudolph M. Butler (1872-1943) which had been selected following an architectural competition in 1912. Butler's long and elegant façade was derived from the splendid riverside front of Gandon's Custom House. The building occupies the site and part of the premises of the International Exhibition of 1865. These had been extended in 1888 to provide examination halls for the non-teaching Royal University of Ireland. The garden behind originally belonged to Clonmel House in Harcourt Street and was later bought by the Guinness family, as it backed on to the Guinness residence on St Stephen's Green. Lord Iveagh presented both the garden and the house to the nation in the late 1930s, but whereas the house is well known, the gardens are almost forgotten.

Hatch Street. The oldest buildings on the street date from the early nineteenth century, though the Leeson family had let sites for development to John Hatch as early as 1759 (these were on the corner with Leeson Street). Though the street was not built until much later, at least the Leesons had arranged that it link up with Pembroke Street (a Fitzwilliam family development on the far side of Leeson Street), hence the gentle curve as Hatch Street bends its way round to accommodate this most neighbourly of arrangements. University Hall, which sits on the southern curve of the street, was opened in 1913 to provide accommodation for students attending the nearby university. It was founded by the Jesuits, with the bulk of the initial funding coming from a past pupil of Clongowes College, Charles Kennedy. The University Hall Chapel has five abstract windows by the stained-glass artist Evie Hone (1894-1955) which she executed in 1947, not long before her monumental work for Eton College Chapel (1949-51) which had an important impact on contemporary artists of the period.

Lower Leeson Street. This was originally the Donnybrook Road. The former country road was renamed in the 1730s after the Leeson family who began letting out plots for development on their property on the western side of the old road. The Leesons had come to Ireland around 1680 and made a fortune in brewing and property development (they had a brewery behind their original Dublin townhouse on the south side of St Stephen's Green). Like the Gardiners, the Leesons consolidated their social position in the second generation, starting off with the title of Baron Russborough in 1756 and following with Viscount Russborough in 1760 and Earl of Miltown in 1763. The new earldom required a new townhouse – number 17 St Stephen's Green – which, perhaps not surprisingly, was located on the far side of the Green from the brewery. In the country nothing further could be required, as a vast Palladian mansion (by Richard Castle and Francis Bindon) had been completed at Russborough in County Wicklow in the early 1750s. If Russborough is theatrical – its magnificent façade makes the most of the house and the outbuildings by stretching them lengthways across the landscape – it also has depth and what lies behind is as genuine as what we perceive from the front. Sadly, all that can be said of this stretch of Leeson Street is that it is now a stage set and little more. As a solution for one or two missing buildings, pastiche may be legitimate but taken to its extreme it becomes ludicrous, everything is fake – and frequently looks it – though at least the charade was carried through to the front rooms on the south side of the street. Even here, despite all the undoubted attention given to period details by the architects Burke-Kennedy-Doyle and Partners, the interiors are entirely modern and the façades are not replicas of the originals; the proportions have been slightly altered, elements borrowed (such as the portico to 'Ossorey House', from a ruined original in number 29 Clare Street) and actual fronts transposed; the delightful Dutch Billy at number 19 is a reconstruction of a house formerly located at number 11.[81]

The Magdalen Asylum. The chapel spire of this Leeson Street institution was a local landmark until replaced by the tall Irish Sugar Company head office in the 1960s. The asylum was founded in 1766 by the 'pious and amiable Lady Arabella Denny, for unfortunate females abandoned by their seducers, and rejected by their friends, who preferred a life of penitence and virtue to one of guilt, infamy and prostitution'. The principal source of revenue was the asylum chapel, which opened in 1768 with an 'excellent sermon' which raised £150 from the fashionable congregation. Admission was initially by ticket only, children being discouraged from the charity sermons in order 'to reserve as much room as possible for the benefactors'.[82]

Lady Arabella was also concerned with the James Street Workhouse which had been reconstituted in 1730 as both a foundling hospital and workhouse. On the direction of Archbishop Boulter, the Protestant Primate, a revolving basket was placed on the gate into which unwanted children could be put anonymously. When a bell was rung the porter revolved the basket inwards and took the baby from it. Conditions were appalling. The infants died in great numbers and their bodies were allowed to accumulate in a large coffin under a stairs before being buried. Various parliamentary committees reported on the horrific and cruel regime, but Lady Arabella Denny was one of the few prominent citizens sufficiently moved to try and improve conditions. She spent over £4000 during the 1760s enlarging and improving the hospital buildings and introduced various devices to ensure that the children were properly fed. A special grandfather clock rang every twenty minutes 'to mark that as children rear'd by the spoon must have but a small quantity of food at a time, it must be offer'd frequently, for which purpose this clock strikes every twenty minutes, at which notice all ye infants that are not asleep must be discretely fed'. A kinswoman, Catherine Fitzmaurice, invented what the governors described as 'a most useful bottle resembling a human breast' and was rewarded with a gold box. Despite the improvements however, out of some 14000 children admitted during the sixteen-year period from 1756, at least 10000 had died by 1771.[83]

55-59, St Stephen's Green West. The terrace of Georgian houses that make up this development had been occupied for over a century by St Vincent's Hospital until the Sisters of Charity sold out in 1972 to the British-owned Lyon Group. Despite the fact that five of the buildings were listed for preservation, the company got permission from the Minister for Local Government to demolish the lot. Fortunately, fearing a repetition of earlier confrontations with conservationists there was a compromise: the two most important houses were restored and others faced with faithful replicas.[84] Number 56 is the most impressive, having a magnificent stairwell and rococo plasterwork by Robert West.

52 and 53, St Stephen's Green West. These two houses were built by Michael Stapleton in 1771. Number 52 – now the office of the ombudsman – was originally the residence of David La Touche, a member of the great Huguenot banking family and first Governor of the Bank of Ireland. His grandfather, also David, had first come to Ireland as an officer in the army of William of Orange. He subsequently settled in Dublin where he started a manufacture of silk, poplin and cambric, as well as founding the bank which was carried on by his descendants. The house is handsomely decorated, in a style befitting one of Dublin's most important bankers, whose clientele included not only the nobility and gentry but also, on occasion, the Government. Besides having plasterwork by Stapleton, the house also has a ceiling with a centrepiece by Angelica Kauffmann; she was a friend of La Touche and was in Ireland in the year the house was built. In the music room there are monochrome wall paintings of Apollo and similar subjects by Peter de Gree, a Flemish chiaroscuro painter who worked in Ireland in the late 1780s. Perhaps more unusual, at least for having survived this long, are the holders in the hall for sedan chair poles.

The 'Battle of Hume Street'. The group of buildings running from the Office of Public Works to Hume Street was at the epicentre of one of the most notable preservation battles of the sixties and seventies. It started off innocuously enough when in May 1966 the Corporation granted outline approval to the Green Property Company for an office block – designed by Stephenson, Gibney Associates – covering number 1 Hume Street and numbers 46-49 St Stephen's

Green. (Numbers 1 and 46 belonged at the time to the state.) This, of course, necessitated the demolition of the houses involved and it was an architecturally distinguished terrace. In addition, however, the Corporation also gave the developers an assurance that the other corner of Hume Street was not in any way affected by a preservation order. Amazingly no one appealed this decision and once the statutory three-week period for objections had passed, the Green Property Company had a *carte blanche* to go ahead. In his famous 'belted earls' speech in the Dáil some four years later, Kevin Boland rightly pointed out that this had been a disastrous error and that the preservationists had 'clearly failed in their duty to protect our national heritage at the appropriate time'. This, he informed the Dáil, 'was a decision in which no iconoclastic Fianna Fáil minister had hand, act or part. It was made by the planning authority and formally acquiesced by An Taisce, Fine Gael, Labour, the Guinness aristocracy, the Dublin City Council, Senator Sheehy Sheffington, Uncle Tom Colbey and all'.[85] If the unholy alliance so colourfully evoked by Kevin Boland had come belatedly onto the stage, at least they arrived before the drama had really got underway. 'Hume Street' as it turned out was to have a cast of thousands and the protracted saga mobilised public opinion as never before.

With a valid planning permission in their pocket, the Green Property Company quickly demolished the three houses in their possession and then set about acquiring further property in and around Hume Street. Once again plans by Sam Stephenson were put forward, though now for a scheme which covered both sides of the entrance to Hume Street. By this stage however, the Corporation had belatedly listed for preservation all of Hume Street and the eastern side of St Stephen's Green. In addition, a more active group, the Dublin Civic Group, had appeared on the scene. The Corporation refused permission for Stephenson's latest scheme but in June 1969, after a public enquiry, the Minister for Local Government – fearing a massive claim for compensation from the Green Property Company – granted full permission to go ahead. To add insult to injury, the Office of Public Works were instructed to go ahead with the sale of state property to facilitate the project. The head of steam which had been building up over the previous years at last exploded when demolition work started at number 45 St Stephen's Green. A more radical group decided to occupy the house and received enthusiastic support from a rainbow coalition covering all kinds of opinion, from the Connolly Youth Movement to the Georgian Society. Some wanted to stop speculators, others saw it as a housing protest and others were involved for heritage reasons. The sit-in lasted for months and the continuous media coverage put considerable pressure on the developers. After some heavy-handed efforts at dislodging the occupiers in June 1970, things seemed to be getting out of hand. The then Taoiseach, Jack Lynch, and his new Minister for Finance had at this stage other dramas to contend with. The republic was in the midst of the Arms Crisis and some solution to lesser irritants such as office development in Hume Street had to be found. The result was a compromise, the offices could go ahead but with façades 'in a style that will maintain as far as possible the existing quality and character of the streetscape'. In many respects it was a pyrrhic victory for the conservationists, for not only did it result in poor pastiche in Hume Street but it became the Trojan horse for unscrupulous developers elsewhere; any building could be torn down as long as the façade was replaced with a Georgian replica.

8 Ely Place. Both Hume Street and Ely Place were laid out at the same time by Gustavus Hume, a surgeon, who also speculated in building lots.[86] The first house to go up was number 8, on ground which Hume leased in 1770 to Henry, 4th Viscount Loftus of Ely (by the time it was completed in 1771 its extravagant owner had been created Earl of Ely). The builder was Michael Stapleton and the interior contains delicate plasterwork by him. More unusually, a life-sized statue of Hercules greets visitors at the foot of the main stairs. The house was originally a seven-bay house and was divided in 1811 without damaging the interior. It now belongs to the Knights of Columbanus.

6 Ely Place (now the Valuation Office). This house was built by Hume in 1771 and, after a succession of owners, was sold in 1781 to 'Black Jack' Fitzgibbon (1749-1802), the first Earl of Clare, one of the more ruthless *realpolitik* figures of the period and detested for it. Fitzgibbon's origins were humble enough. His grandfather was a Catholic farmer in Limerick. His father had been destined for the priesthood but thought better of it, opting instead for Protestantism and a lucrative career at the Bar where he was sufficiently successful to see one of his daughters marry into the powerful Beresford family. John, his second son (the elder died prematurely), was a contemporary of Henry Grattan's in Trinity College but their routes differed afterwards as he unashamedly sought out the post of Lord Chancellor, which he was to hold from 1789 to 1802.

The largely anti-Catholic Penal Laws were, in Fitzgibbon's opinion, a political necessity: the only system by which a minority could rule a hostile majority and to repeal them would therefore be an act of madness. When Catholics were given the vote in 1793 he became an enthusiast for Union with the English Parliament and coolly doled out the patronage, peerages and other bribes necessary to achieve that objective. Union was necessary, in his view, because Ireland without the Penal Laws would be 'Ireland like an unmanacled maniac'. When Fitzgibbon eventually discovered that Catholic leaders had been promised emancipation (though it didn't come for another three decades) his fury was understandable; he had fought for the Union to prevent emancipation not to bring it about. Despite his championing of flogging and house burnings during the lead-up to the 1798 rebellion, Fitzgibbon tempered his public ruthlessness with sympathy for individuals: he abandoned a dinner in his house in Ely Place to accompany Lady Louise Connolly to Lord Edward FitzGerald's deathbed. Once the rebellion was suppressed – if brutally – he sought an immediate end to severities and this at a time when ascendancy Dublin was so bloodthirsty as to astonish even the English military. Not surprisingly he was hated by the Dublin population. After he had obtained the withdrawal of Lord Fitzwilliam, a popular liberal Viceroy, a Dublin crowd rioted and went with a rope to his house in Ely Place to hang him. When he died in 1802 they pelted his coffin with dead cats.

4 Upper Ely Place. This was the townhouse of John Philpot Curran (1750-1817), a noted lawyer who first came to prominence by taking up the case of a Catholic clergyman, who had been horse-whipped by Lord Doneraile. As an MP he was an advocate of Catholic emancipation and strongly criticised government patronage and corruption. After the 1798 rebellion he defended Wolfe Tone and later was a vehement parliamentary opponent of the Act of Union. However, he is now best remembered – if remembered at all – as being the harsh father of Sarah Curran. When he discovered after the abortive rising of 1803 that his youngest daughter had been engaged to Robert Emmet he was outraged; her attachment threw suspicion on him and he was examined by the Privy Council – though cleared. In 1806 he became master of the Irish Rolls. He had behaved so harshly to his daughter, however, that she had been obliged to take refuge with friends in Cork. She did not live for long. In 1805 she married a captain by the name of Sturgeon but three years later she died in England. Her father did better, retiring from public life in 1814 with the then fabulous pension of £2700 a year. He moved to London, joining the likes of Thomas Moore (who immortalised his daughter's tragic story in his song 'She Is Far from the Land'), and died in Middlesex on 14 October 1817.

Number 4 now bears a plaque telling us not of the Currans, but of George Moore (1852-1933), who lived there from 1901 to 1911. The son of a wealthy Catholic landlord, he initially hoped to be a painter and in 1873 went to Paris with this in mind. He opted, however, for a literary career and in 1901 moved to Dublin where he was associated with the Irish literary revival. His autobiography, *Hail and Farewell* gives a candid, if egotistical, account of his ten years in Dublin, which he left due to increasing difficulties between him and his literary associates. He returned to London where he died in January 1933.

The RHA Gallagher Gallery (headquarters of the Royal Hibernian Academy). The gallery (1972-1989, by Raymond McGrath, completed by Arthur Gibney) was the brainchild of the legendary Matt Gallagher, founder of the Gallagher Group which by the 1970s had become one of the largest construction companies in the country. The gallery was intended partly as a monument to himself and partly as a gift to the RHA. However, when Gallagher died prematurely in January 1974 it transpired that he had made no provision in his will to complete the scheme and his son Patrick seemed more interested in racehorses and increasingly controversial building projects. For years the building remained a concrete shell. Its relative completion in 1989 was due to an extensive fund-raising campaign by the RHA and assistance from the state and private donors as well as handsome contributions from other members of the Gallagher family. The gallery sits on the site of Moore's former garden and the home of Oliver St John Gogarty (1878-1957), a surgeon and accomplished poet noted for his acerbic wit. Despite his many talents, Gogarty has entered history not on his own account but due to his early friendship with Joyce, who immortalised him in *Ulysses* as 'stately plump Buck Mulligan'. His sympathy with the Free State Government – he was nominated to the first Senate – led to his capture by the republicans during the Civil War. He escaped their malevolent intentions by swimming the Liffey, but his house at Renvyle in Connemara was not so fortunate for it was burned; though later rebuilt as a hotel. His flamboyant personality was out of tune with an increasingly conservative Ireland and in 1939 he departed, eventually settling in America where he died in 1957.

Merrion Row. This narrow thoroughfare is something of an anachronism, for it suddenly widens into the much broader Baggot Street a short distance further on. Baggot Street had been widened and straightened by Lord Fitzwilliam. The Wide Streets Commissioners, who had approved the Fitzwilliam plans in 1791, must have envisaged a similar exercise for Merrion Row, but if they had such ambitions they never came to fruition. Merrion Row therefore gives us the scale of Dublin streets before the Wide Streets Commissioners got under way. If narrow, it has a jostling and vibrant character of its own, with a lively range of commercial activities and an even livelier range of public houses. The best-known is O'Donoghue's which has been long associated with the ballad boom of the 1960s and, in particular, with The Dubliners group who began singing there in the days when the singing pub was still a novelty.

The Huguenot Cemetery. The cemetery, on the north side of Merrion Row, where it meets St Stephen's Green, is now one of the few reminders of late seventeenth-century Dublin and the world which gave us the Green. In 1662 – just a year before the Corporation hit on the expedient of laying out St Stephen's Green as a means of raising money – Parliament did its own bit of commercial promotion by passing 'An Act to encourage Protestant Strangers to settle in Ireland'. Of course, their religious affiliation was all-important but certainly Parliament also hoped that these 'strangers' would bring the skills and commerce for which they were reputed with them to Ireland. The most prominent group of 'Protestant strangers' were the Huguenots, French Calvinists who were fleeing religious persecution and whose numbers in Dublin were sufficiently important by 1666 for them to be granted the Lady Chapel of St Patrick's Cathedral as a place of worship. Many of these, as well as later influxes of Dutch and Flemish Protestants, settled in the Liberties where they set up workshops for working wool, silk and linen. They were particularly associated with the development of poplin (a fabric which was hand-woven from pure wool and pure silk) for which Dublin became famous. The cemetery (1693) has been restored as a quiet enclave in memory of the Huguenot diaspora who fled to all corners of Europe, following the revocation of the Edict of Nantes in 1685. The city which they came to was Protestant, not just in terms of politics and civic control but in actual household numbers, and it wasn't until the mid-eighteenth century that the city had a clear-cut Catholic majority. Demographically and otherwise Dublin is now quite a different place and even the famed 'Dutch Billies' – the distinctive late-seventeenth-century front-gabled houses which the Huguenots are credited with having introduced to Dublin – have gone. However, this cemetery remains as a testimonial to our Huguenot past and, near at hand, there is St Stephen's Green which was laid out with such ambition and hope in the years when they first found refuge on these shores.

Detail from the elevation by Henry Aaron Baker for a range of 18 houses on the south side of Dame Street, between South Great George's Street and Trinity Street, 1785. This design was adopted and built by the Wide Streets Commissioners.

Elevation of the north side of College Green from Anglesea Street to Foster Place by Richard Johnston, 1789. Johnston had been requested by the Wide Streets Commissioners to incorporate the elevation of Daly's Club (architect unknown) as the centrepiece of the overall design.

Elevation of the west front to Foster Place by Richard Johnston, 1789.

CONCLUSION

Dublin has long been one of the great European cities. As far as literature, drama and contemporary music are concerned, this is a statement which would go unchallenged. Yet, when Dublin was designated European City of Culture for 1991, at least one architectural historian was amazed by the audacity of the Government in seeking the designation; amazed, not because Dublin did not merit the title, but, to the contrary, because of the very importance of its architectural heritage which 'no European city had done more in recent years to destroy'. [1] Indeed, according to an editorial in the London *Times*, Dublin's conservation record was such that it better merited the designation 'city of European philistinism'.[2]

There are various reasons why Dublin's core appears to have been 'left to rot', not least being the lack of political vision as to the city's role in Irish life. [3] In an assessment of Dublin's year as European City of Culture, the *Irish Times* saw it as a 'missed opportunity'. As an editorial in the paper noted, 'there was never any evidence that anyone at Government level had a strong vision as to why Dublin should be City of Culture in 1991.' [4] Yet Dublin, as this book hopefully has demonstrated, is not only a centre of cultural importance, but, in architectural terms, can be counted among the great European cities. Physically – and I quote Dan Cruickshank (the architectural historian who was amazed by the city's poor conservation record) – this claim to greatness 'is derived solely from the city's inheritance of eighteenth- and early nineteenth-century architecture, and to a bold street plan that makes the most of the city's position on the gently-flowing and curving Liffey.'[5]

The direction in which Dublin developed was in large measure determined by its topography and experience; crucial factors being the expansion of the quays as the city pressed relentlessly seaward, the laying-out of urban estates on former monastic property and the ability to develop expansively given the absence of any real threat of military invasion (unlike Continental cities such as Paris and Vienna). Although the archaeologists – and some surviving street names – may remind us of the Viking and medieval city, very little remains of it to be seen. The real interest of Dublin lies in its Georgian streets and buildings. These were developed in accordance with the aspirations of its dominant classes – aristocratic and merchant – with institutions and a built environment which were intended to serve their interests and reinforce their values. There was no single grandiose scheme, but a patchwork of formal set-pieces developed by an oligarchy of landlords, including the Corporation, around a network of existing topographical and property lines. If this gave the city one of its most persistent characteristics – an evident dislike of uniformity – there was nonetheless a strong stylistic unity 'guaranteed by common attitudes to art, property and lifestyle' [6] which was reinforced by the planning strategy of the Wide Streets Commissioners.

Dublin, like other great cities, offered the possibilities of conspicuous self-indulgence and significant display. The rationale underlying buildings such as the Custom House and the former Parliament on College Green, or such projects as St Stephen's Green and Gardiner Mall, transcend the merely practical and utilitarian, as did the proliferation of elaborate plasterwork in house after house which 'gives to the city a character that must make it, even for interior work alone, one of the most important urban environments in Europe.'[7]

The city, of course, was – and is – more than a place for mere display. It is also a port, a commercial centre and, as the history of O'Connell Street so well illustrates, an arena for both the class struggle and the competing ideologies that make up the nationalist tradition. That Dublin was created and survived almost intact into this century 'as a near complete expression of a single era' has been attributed to its failure to develop in the nineteenth century, and especially its poverty. [8] Poverty is unlovely and neither the poverty with which the Georgian city became associated nor the ascendancy society who had long abandoned their 'spectral mansions' made it a place seeming worthy of conservation, still less to be celebrated and lived in.

And yet, despite the crusading reformers who since classical antiquity have contrasted 'urban vice with rural virtue' – and the fact that we now enjoy the means and the technology 'to arrange our lives in a non-urban or post-urban' fashion, there has been an alarmed response to the decay and depopulation of once flourishing cities, Dublin included. This, according to Donald J. Olsen (and it seems appropriate that I should conclude with the author to whom I owe my title) 'would suggest that we are unwilling to contemplate a world in which cities no longer exist, no longer serve as magnets for the talented and ambitious, no longer provide the concentration of ideas, objects of beauty and opportunities of sociability that they have throughout recorded history.' Buoyed, he believes, by a conviction that 'the pleasures that cities, especially capital cities provide justify their existence, irrespective of the wealth they may produce, the vice they may encourage, and the misery they often contain ... we are today searching for ways to restore life to dying cities, and turn to those cities that retain an earlier vitality for guidance and inspiration.' [9]

In the case of Dublin, we should be attentive to the urban heritage not simply because much of what we have inherited can be classified as art of a high quality: we should care because in a wider cultural sense the fabric of the city is a text which can reveal much about the values and aspirations of those who preceded us, while at the same time serving as a source 'for guidance and inspiration' where we can analyse and understand the aesthetic and other parameters which satisfy ever-present, universal needs of communal living. Above all, we should be concerned because architecture and urban form play an active part in shaping and structuring experience, in defining both our personal and public histories. We all need a tangible and enduring sense of the physical entity of which we are part, for, in the case of most of us, it is an inalienable part of our everyday life; in a very personal sense it makes Dublin part and parcel of what we are.

INTRODUCTION

1. D. J. Olsen, *The City as a Work of Art: London – Paris – Vienna*, (London, 1986).

2. M. O'Loughlin, *The Inside Story*, (Dublin, 1989), p.17.

3. A. Rossi, *The Architecture of the City*, (American edition, Cambridge, Mass., 1982), p.130.

4. Ibid., p. 32.

5. L. Mumford, *The Culture of Cities*, (New York, 1938), p.5.

6. T. Brown, *Ireland: A Social and Cultural History, 1922-85*, (London, 1985).

7. R. Kearney, *Transitions, Narratives in Modern Irish Culture*, (Dublin, 1988).

8. M. Cronin, 'Over Dubs, the art of the city', in *Graph*, issue 8, (summer 1990), p.23.

9. D. J. Olsen, op. cit., p.3.

10. L. MacMathuna, 'An Ghaeilge mar theanga phobail i mBaile Atha Cliath', in J. Kelly and U. MacGearailt, eds., *Dublin and Dubliners*, (Dublin, 1990), pp.147-173. As late as 1815, there seem to have been two Irish-speaking areas in the city, one behind the north quays bounded on the west by Stoneybatter and another in the Liberties between Whitefriar Street and Thomas Street.

11. B. Friel, *Translations*, (London, 1981), p.66.

12. D. Bolger, *Invisible Cities: The New Dubliners*, (Dublin, 1988), p.9.

THE QUAYS

1. Quoted in M. Craig, *Dublin, 1660-1860*, (Dublin, 1952), p.3. See also JRSAI, LXXIX, 93, (1949).

2. J.T. Gilbert, ed. (later Lady Gilbert), *Calendar of Ancient Records of Dublin* (1954), vol. II, p.176.

3. Anon. 'History of Amory lease gives fascinating insight into Dublin of 1675', *The Irish Times*, 13 February 1974.

4. Quoted in P. Fagan, *The Second City, Portrait of Dublin, 1700-1760*, (Dublin, 1986), pp.20, 21, 33.

5. F. O'Dwyer, *Lost Dublin*, (Dublin, 1981), p.83.

6. G. Semple, *A Treatise on Building in Water*, (Dublin, 1776), p.27.

7. Wide Streets Commission Maps, no.329.

8. 31 Geo. II, c 19.

9. J.T. Gilbert, *History of the City of Dublin*, vol. II, (Dublin, 1854), p.8.

10. Quoted in M. Fraser, 'Public building and colonial policy in Dublin, 1760-1800', *Architectural History*, vol. 28 (1985), p.104.

11. P.F. Byrne, 'Dublin's oldest shop changes hands', *Dublin Historical Record*, vol. XLII, no.4, (September 1989), p.121.

12. Quoted in M. Fraser, op. cit., p.25, p.104.

13. E. McParland, 'James Gandon and the Royal Exchange Competition, *Journal of the Royal Society of Antiquaries of Ireland*, vol. 102, (1972), p.70.

14. Quoted in J.T. Gilbert, *History of the City of Dublin*, vol. II, (Dublin, 1854), p.139.

15. Kenneth Browne in *The Architectural Review*, vol. CLVI, no. 933, (November 1974), p.271 and 298.

16. See D. Culligan, 'Road widening and the Liffey quays', in G. Cahill and L. Kealy, eds., *Dublin City Quays projects by the School of Architecture, UCD*, (Dublin, 1986).

17. J.T. Gilbert, *History of the City of Dublin*, vol. 1, (Dublin, 1854), p.388.

18. J.T. Gilbert, *History of the City of Dublin*, vol. III, (Dublin, 1854), p.385.

19. F. McDonald 'The battle for the quays', *The Irish Times*, 10 August 1989. See also, 'Usher's Chambers Dublin' in *Plan*, vol. 18, no. 1, (January 1987), pp.17-20.

20. Olive Cook in *Micheál MacLiammóir, Ireland*, (London, 1966), p.141.

21. Quoted in E. McParland, *James Gandon, Vitruvius Hibernicus*, (London, 1985), p.150. For the Four Courts, see pp.149-165.

22. Wide Streets Commission, Maps, nos.49 and 50; *Minutes* 36, pp.163-4, 166-7, 268.

23. Op. cit., Maps no. 51, Minutes, 37, pp.97-8, 108-9, 118.

24. P. Raftery 'The last of the traditionalists: Patrick Byrne 1783-1864', *Quarterly Bulletin of the Irish Georgian Society*, vol. VII, no.2-4, (April-December 1964), p.53.

25. Quoted in F. McDonald's 'Numerous changes in Civic Offices', *The Irish Times*, 21 September 1983. See also T. Farel Heffernan, *Wood Quay: the clash over Dublin's Viking past*, (Texas, 1989), and J. Bradley, ed., *Viking Dublin Exposed, The Wood Quay Saga*, (Dublin, 1984).

26. G.F. Mitchell, *Archaeology and Environment in Early Dublin*. (Medieval Dublin excavations 1962-1981, series C, vol. I, 1987.)

27. H. Clarke, 'The medieval Liffey', *Dublin Arts Festival Programme*, 1979, p.37.

28. N. Burke, 'The making of medieval Dublin', *Dublin Arts Festival Programme*, 1976, pp.17-22. See also N. Burke, 'Dublin's north-eastern city wall: early reclamation and development at the Poddle-Liffey

confluence', *Proceedings of the Royal Irish Academy*, vol.74, Section C, no. 3, (1974), pp.113-132.

29. See S. Rothery, *Ireland and the new architecture 1900-1940*, (Dublin, 1991), pp. 27-29.

30. *Irish Independent*, 28 and 29 March 1933.

31. I. Lumley, 'Loss of heart for the city', *AJ: the Architects' Journal*, (16 November 1988). See also F. McDonald, 'Potential of quay-side survives the speculators', *The Irish Times*, 21 August 1990, and J. Fagan '£25m scheme in Dublin quays', *The Irish Times*, 17 October 1991.

32. Quoted in J.V. O'Brien, *Dear Dirty Dublin, A City in Distress, 1899-1916*, (London, 1982), p.55. The controversy gave rise to Yeats's poem 'To a Wealthy Man who Promised a Second Subscription to the Dublin Municipal Gallery if it were proved the People wanted Pictures'. The wealthy man was Lord Ardilaun who, Yeats believed, should have shown the spirit of a Renaissance Prince irrespective of the views of the 'blind and ignorant town'. For an assessment of Lutyens's proposals, see S. Rothery, op. cit., pp.49-52.

33. M. McCarthy, *The Irish Revolution*, (Edinburgh and London, 1912), p.364.

34. See 'Mitchell proposes renaming quays', *The Irish Times*, 22 March 1991.

35. *The Times*, 23 March 1991. For a response from Gay Mitchell TD, see *The Times*, 6 April 1991.

GARDINER'S DUBLIN

1. D. Dickson, 'Large-scale developers and the growth of eighteenth-century Irish cities', in P. Butel and L. M. Cullen, eds., *Cities and Merchants: French and Irish Perspectives on Urban development, 1500-1900*, (Dublin, 1986) pp.115-120. For a Gardiner genealogy see the *Irish Builder*, vol. XXXV, no. 806, (15 July 1893), p.160. See also a National Council for Education Awards Publication, *Gardiner's Dublin: a history and topography of Mountjoy Square and Environs*, (Dublin, 1991).

2. See Mark Girouard, 'Parades and Promenades', *The Listener*, (13 October 1983), pp.6-8.

3. For Sackville Street and the Wide Streets Commissioners see E. McParland, 'The Wide Streets Commissioners': their importance for Dublin architecture in the late eighteenth-early nineteenth century, *Quarterly Bulletin of the Irish Georgian Society*, vol. XV, no. 1, (January-March 1972), pp.1-32; and E. McParland, *James Gandon Vitruvius Hibernicus*, (London, 1985), pp.35-37, 41-44, 74-76, 87-95.

4. G.N. Wright, *An Historical Guide to Ancient and Modern Dublin*, (London, 1821), p.8.

5. A. Clarke, *Twice Around the Black Church*, (London, 1962), p.127. For an account of the Parnell Monument see T.J. O'Keefe, 'The art and politics of the Parnell Monument', *Eire-Ireland*, vol. XIX, no. 1, (spring 1984), pp.6-25.

6. See I. Campbell Ross 'The early years of the Dublin Lying-in Hospital', and N. Casey 'Architecture and decoration', in I. Campbell Ross, ed., *Public Virtue, Public Love: The early years of the Dublin Lying-in Hospital*, (Dublin, 1986), pp.9-52 and 53-95.

7. N. Casey, op. cit., and E. MacParland (1985), op. cit., pp. 91-93.

8. The busts by S.F. Lynn are now in the National Gallery. Also removed was a magnificent eighteenth-century ceiling which, as its centrepiece, depicted a satyr playing the uilleann pipes. See *Plan*, vol. 6, no. 4, (June 1975), p.33. For a description of the new development at 46-49 Upper O'Connell Street, see *Plan*, vol. 5, no. 4, (June 1974), pp.6-11.

9. E. Walsh, 'Sackville Mall: The first one hundred years' in David Dickson, ed., *The Gorgeous Mask: Dublin 1700-1850*, (Dublin, 1987), pp.30-50. See also *The Georgian Society Records*, vol. III, (1911), pp.74-98.

10. R. Moore, 'The floosie in the jacuzzi', *Blueprint*, (September 1988), p.63.

11. See advertisement feature in *The Irish Times*, 11 February 1987. For a summary of the report see K. Meghen, 'Dublin Metropolitan Streets Commission', *Irish Architect*, no. 63, (September-October 1987), pp.20-21. One of the most interesting projects which was organised for the 1988 'Dublin Millennium' was one where proposals were invited for a replacement for Nelson's Pillar: see S. O'Toole, *The Pillar Project*, (Dublin, 1988).

12. For 'The Fool' (1915), see S. O Buachalla, *The Literary Writings of Patrick Pearse*, (Cork, 1979), pp.23-24. The standard work on Pearse is R. Dudley Edwards, *Patrick Pearse: The Triumph of Failure*, (London, 1977). See also P. Rafroide, 'Imagination and revolution: The Cuchulain myth' in O. MacDonagh, W.F. Mandle and P. Travers, eds., *Irish Culture and Nationalism, 1750-1950*, (London, 1953), pp.137-148.

13. See M. Miller, 'Raymond Unwin and the Planning of Dublin' in M. J. Bannon, ed., *The Emergence of Irish Planning*, (Dublin, 1985), pp.263-306. See also M. Shaffrey, 'Sackville Street / O'Connell Street Part 1 - Development of the first boulevard street, part II - devastation and rebuilding', *The GPA Irish Arts Review Yearbook (1988)*, pp.144-156.

14. For O'Connell see O. MacDonagh, *The Hereditary Bondsman: Daniel O'Connell, 1775-1829*, (London, 1988); and *The Emancipist: Daniel O'Connell, 1830-*

1847, (London, 1989); S. O'Faolain, *King of the Beggars*, (1938, republished Dublin, 1980); H. Potterton's, *The O'Connell Monument* (Ballycotton, 1973); and, for the dispute over renaming O'Connell Street, P. Alter, 'Symbols of Irish Nationalism', in A. O'Day, ed., *Reactions to Irish Nationalism*, (Dublin, 1987), pp.12-14.

15. E. MacParland (1985), op. cit., pp.74-76.

16. W. Beresford, ed., *The Correspondence of the Rt. Hon. J. Beresford*, vol. 1, (1854), p.233, (27 October 1782).

17. E. McParland (1985), op. cit., p.184.

18. W. Chambers, *A Treatise on Civil Architecture*, (London, 1759), p.64.

19. W. Beresford, op. cit., vol. 1, (1854), pp.166-67, (18 August 1781).

20. Quoted in M. Fraser 'Public building and colonial policy in Dublin, 1760-1800', *Architectural History*, vol. XXVIII, (1985), pp.102-23.

21. See P. Lenehan, 'Edward Smyth, Dublin's Sculptor', in *The GPA Irish Arts Review, Year book, (1989-90)*, pp.67-76.

22. See 'Talbot Memorial Bridge', *Plan*, vol. 9, no. 3, (March, 1978), pp.10-13.

23. See 'Moral issues and the Catholic Church: Matt Talbot and the theology of incarceration', in R. Sheehan, *The Heart of the City*, (Dingle, 1988), pp.149-167.

24. See 'The new Bloomusalem', in R. Sheehan, op. cit., pp.171-181. For a report on the public competition for the docks site see *Plan*, vol. 18, no. 11, (November 1987), pp.28-40.

25. For contemporary comment see the *Architectural Review*, vol. 115, no. 688, (April 1954), pp.242-257 and the *Architects Journal*, (15 April 1954), pp.453-465.

26. Quoted in J. Barrington, *Personal Sketches and Recollections of His Own Times*, (London, 1827), vol. I, p.295.

27. The Beresfords, however, did well out of the hurly-burly of eighteenth-century politics. By 1812 Edward Wakefield believed that 'one-fourth of all the places in the kingdom are filled with their dependants or connections.' E. Wakefield, *Account of Ireland, Statistical and Political*, (London, 1812), vol. II, p.202.

28. See 'Threat to Gandon's surviving crescent', *Plan*, vol. 4, no. 12, (October 1973), pp.4-5. For the original plan and elevations see Wide Streets Commissioners, *Maps* 23/1 and 2 and *Minutes* 9, pp.318, 327-8, and 334.

29. Wide Streets Commissioners, ibid.

30. C. Clancy, 'Gardiner Street Employment Exchange', *Dublin Historical Record*, vol. XL111, no. 1, (spring 1990), pp.47-51.

31. Wide Streets Commissioners, *Extracts from the Minutes of the Commissioners Appointed by Act of Parliament for making wide and convenient ways, streets and passages in the City of Dublin: containing the copy of a memorial to His Excellency the Lord Lieutenant, together with a General Statement of their Proceedings, Engagements and Funds from the commencement of the institution in 1757, to January 1802*, (Dublin, 1802), p.5.

32. M. Craig, *Dublin 1660-1860*, (Dublin, 1952), p.31.

33. *Georgian Society Records*, vol. III, (1911), pp.68-73.

34. See E. McParland, 'Who was P?' *Architectural Review*, vol. CLVII, no. 936, (February 1975), pp.71-3.

35. See R. Sheehan, op. cit., pp. 61-66; J Finnegan, *The Story of Monto*, (Cork, 1978), and L. O Broin, *Frank Duff, a Biography*, (Dublin, 1982) pp.17-26.

36. See M. Craig, op. cit., p.179, and F. O'Dwyer, *Lost Dublin*, (Dublin, 1981), p.68.

37. R.F. Foster, *Modern Ireland, 1600-1972*, (London, 1988), p.167. Mahaffy's essay 'Society in Georgian Dublin' which was published in vol. III of the *Georgian Society Records* caused great indignation; for a brief account see Desmond Guinness's 'Introduction' to the reprint of the records, (Shannon, 1969) p. viii.

38. See A.P.W. Malcomson, *The Pursuit of the Heiress: Aristocratic Marriage in Ireland, 1750-1820*, (Belfast, 1982), p.37. For a description of Belvedere House see the *Georgian Society Records*, vol. III, (1911), pp.57-67.

39. See D. Dickson, op. cit., p.119-20.

40. See B. Murnane, 'The recreation of the urban historical landscape: Mountjoy Ward Dublin, *circa* 1901', in W. J. Smyth and K. Whelan, eds., *Common Ground: Essays on the Historical Geography of Ireland*, (Cork, 1988), pp.189-207.

41. F. McDonald, 'Church conversions need not be sacrilegious', *The Irish Times*, 13 June 1990. See also 'House in a church', in J. O'Regan, ed., *New Irish Architecture, V-AAI Awards, 1990*, (Dublin, 1990), pp.40-41.

42. The foundation walls of the enclosing base were, apparently, built. See 'Memories of the past: The Royal Circus Eccles Street', *Irish Builder*, vol. XIV, no. 306, p.255, (15 September 1872).

43. See P. Thompson, 'Vanishing World of St George's', *Irish Press*, 10 February 1988, and P. McGarry, 'Pressure on Protestants', *Magill*, (February 1989), pp.30-37.

44. For a description of this building see 'Mater

Private Hospital, Dublin', *Plan*, vol. 17, no. 7, (July 1986), pp.11-17. For an indication of the degree of destruction – particularly on the north side of the street – to make way for this and other developments, see F. McDonald, 'Who can stop the ruin of Eccles Street?', *The Irish Times*, 26 February 1988.

45. *Centenary Mater Misericordiae Hospital Dublin, 1861-1961*, (Dublin, 1961), pp.23-25. The triangular park between the hospital and St Joseph's Church was paid for entirely by the Sisters of Mercy, with the work being executed under the direction of a Mr W. Hughes, see the *Irish Builder*, 'Memories of the past', vol. XIV, no. 306, (15 September 1872), p.255.

46. Quoted in P. Somerville-Large, *Dublin*, (London, 1979), p.269.

47. M. Craig, 'John Semple and his churches', *The GPA Irish Arts Review Yearbook*, (1989-90), p.146.

48. B. Lehane, *Dublin*, (Amsterdam, 1978), p.37.

49. *Georgian Society Records*, vol. II, (1910), pp.28-30.

50. M.E. Daly, 'Housing conditions and the genesis of housing reform in Dublin, 1880-1920', in M. J. Bannon, ed., *The Emergence of Irish Planning, 1880-1920*, (Dublin, 1985), p.88.

51. *Georgian Society Records*, op. cit., p.12.

52. Quoted in E.M. Johnson, *Ireland in the Eighteenth Century*, (Dublin, 1974), p.19.

53. Quoted by J. Sheehy in *J.J. McCarthy and the Gothic Revival in Ireland*, (Belfast, 1977), p.13.

54. See his obituary in the *Irish Builder*, vol. XXXVI, no. 835, (15 October 1894), p.231.

55. Lady Morgan (Sydney Owenson), *Memoirs*, vol. I, (London, 1862), p.172.

56. Ibid., pp.172-173.

57. *Georgian Society Records*, vol. III, (1911), pp.99-110.

58. See H.C.S. Ferguson, 'Lord Charlemont's travels in Greece', *Irish Arts Review*, vol. 4, no. 4, (winter 1987), pp.33-38.

59. These are illustrated in a National Gallery exhibition catalogue; J. McDonnell's, *Irish Eighteenth Century Stuccowork and its European Sources*, (Dublin, 1991).

60. See 'The Garden of Remembrance', *Oibre: Bulletin of the Commissioners of Public Works*, no. 4, (Samhain 1966), pp.17-18.

TOWN AND GOWN

1. Quoted in N. McCullough, *Dublin An Urban History*, (Dublin, 1989), p.24.

2. E. McParland, 'The Wide Streets Commissioners: Their importance for Dublin architecture in the late eighteenth-early nineteenth century', in *Quarterly Bulletin of the Irish Georgian Society*, vol. XV, no. 1, (January-March 1972), p.11.

3. Ibid, p.12.

4. For a detailed architectural account see C.P. Curran, 'The architecture of the Bank of Ireland', *Quarterly Bulletin of the Irish Georgian Society*, vol. 20, no. 1 and 2, (January-June 1977) pp.3-6, and vol. 20, no. 3 and 4, (July-December 1977), pp.40-56. For Gandon's contribution see E. McParland, *James Gandon Vitruvius Hibernicus*, (London, 1985), pp.76-87 and, for Francis Johnston's contribution see E. McParland, 'Francis Johnston, Architect, 1760-1829' *Quarterly Bulletin of the Irish Georgian Society*, vol. XII, nos. 3 and 4, (July-December 1969), pp.124-128.

5. Quoted by J. Sheehy in 'A respectable show: Victorian commercial buildings in Dublin', *Country Life*, vol. CLXVI, no. 4279, (12 July 1979), p.83.

6. F. O'Dwyer, *Lost Dublin*, (Dublin, 1981), p.27.

7. *Dublin Builder*, vol. V, no. 95, (15 December 1863), p.201.

8. *Irish Builder*, no. VXXXIII, no. 746, (15 January 1891) pp.18-19.

9. *Irish Builder*, vol. XXXI, no. 697, (1 January 1889), p.14.

10. M.J. McDermott, 'The Geoghegans' *Irish Architect*, no. 61, (April-May 1987), p.30.

11. Quoted in E. McParland, 'The Wide Streets Commissioners', op. cit., p.13.

12. R.F. Brooke, *Daly's Club and Kildare Street Club, Dublin*, (Dublin, 1930), p.8.

13. C.T. Bowden, *A Tour through Ireland*, (Dublin, 1791), p.18.

14. D. Mackay, 'From a European perspective', in J. Graeve, ed., *Temple Bar Lives! A Record of the Architectural Framework Competition*, (Dublin, 1991), p.11. See also a report completed by the Dublin City Association of An Taisce, *Dublin, The Temple Bar Area: A Policy for its Future*, (Dublin, 1985).

15. See F. McDonald, *The Destruction of Dublin*, (Dublin, 1985), pp.165-175. See also 'Central Bank Dame Street' *Plan*, vol. II, no. 1, (January 1980), pp.6-16.

16. L.M. Cullen, *Princes and Pirates: The Dublin Chamber of Commerce, 1783-1983*, (Dublin, 1983), pp.25-31.

17. *Dublin Builder*, vol. V, no. 96, (15 December 1863), p.201.

18. E. McParland, (1969), op. cit., p.112.

19. E. McParland, (1972), op. cit., pp.9-10. *Wide Streets Commissioners' Maps*, no. 90.

20. *Georgian Society Records*, vol. 1, (1909), pp.14-18.

21. T. Farmar, *The Legendary Lofty Clattery Café*, (Dub-

in, 1988), p.63. For an account of the recent remod-elling of the Grafton Street Café see 'Bewley's Grafton Street, Dublin', *Plan*, vol. 19, no. 4, (April 1988), pp.39-43.

22. *Georgian Society Records*, vol. IV (1912), pp.102-113.

23. Ibid., pp.62-66.

24. See, for example, the correspondence relating to Lord Molesworth's offer to pay for a new design for St Werburgh's Church and his efforts to have his protégé Alessandro Galilei appointed as architect in P. Judge, ed., 'The state of architecture in Ireland 1716', *Irish Arts Review*, vol. 3, no. 4, (winter 1986), pp.62-63.

25. 'Friends Provident Centre, Dublin', in *Plan*, Vol 18, no. 18, (October 1987), p.4.

26. E. Blau, *Ruskinian Gothic: The Architecture of Deane and Woodward, 1845-1861*, (Princeton, 1982), pp.147-148.

27. E. Bowen, *Seven Winters*, (London, 1943), p.33.

28. For an account of Patrick Gallagher's 'site clear-ance' tactics see F. McDonald, *The Destruction of Dub-lin*, (Dublin, 1985), pp.222-226.

29. Quite a contrary view where the architect is extolled for being 'adventurous' is given in 'Retain-ing Character', *Build*, vol. 15, no. 3, (July 1980), pp.13-18.

30. 'New life for Sun Alliance', *Build*, vol. 16, no. 6, (January 1982), pp.23-25.

31. N. McCullough, op. cit., p.53.

32. Quoted in Gilbert, *A History of the City of Dublin*, vol. 3 (1861), p.285. A description of Leinster House is given in Gilbert and in the *Georgian Society Records*.

33. R.F. Brooke, op. cit., pp.6-7.

34. E. Blau, op. cit., pp.126-132. For an account of Edward Martyn's opposition to the visit of Edward VII in 1903 see C. Deutsche-Brady, 'The King's Visit and the People's Protection Committee, 1903', *Eire-Ireland*, vol. X, no. 3, (fomhar 1975), pp.3-10.

35. 'College Park House/Frederick House, Dublin', *Plan*, vol. 18, no. 8, (August 1987), pp.3-10.

36. 'New Ireland Assurance, Dublin', *Plan*, vol. 19, no. 10, (October 1988), pp.3-7.

37. See P. Woodworth 'A barrow-load of trouble', *The Irish Times*, 30 September 1989; and 'letters' of 2, 10 and 12 October 1989.

38. For this and other information concerning Trinity College see E. McParland, 'Trinity College, Dublin' in *Country Life*, vol. CLIX, no. 4114 (6 May 1976), pp.1166-7; no. 4115 (13 May 1976), pp.1242-5; no.

4116 (20 May 1976), pp.1310-13

39. E. McParland, op. cit., (13 May 1976), p.1244.

40. C. Maxwell, *Dublin under the Georges, 1714-1830*, (Dublin, 1936, reprinted 1979), p.158.

41. I am grateful to Dr McParland for this informa-tion.

42. See B. de Breffny, 'Christopher Hewetson', *Irish Arts Review*, vol. 3, no. 3, (autumn 1986), pp.52-75.

43. C. Maxwell, op. cit., p.112.

44. See A. Rehill, 'The restoration of the Dining Hall, Trinity College, Dublin', *Irish Arts Review*, vol. 3, no. 1, (spring 1986), pp.26-37.

45. E. McParland, op. cit., (20 May 1976), p.1312.

46. E. McParland, 'The College buildings' in C.H. Holland, ed., *Trinity College Dublin and the Idea of a University*, (Dublin, 1991), p.181.

47. M. Craig, *The Architecture of Ireland from the Earli-est Times to 1880*, (London, 1982), p.168.

48. M.W. Brooks, *John Ruskin and Victorian Architec-ture*, (London, 1989), p.114.

49. Quoted in E. Blau, op. cit., p.41.

50. See J. Sheehy, 'Lively Irishmen: The Ruskinian tradition in Ireland', *Irish Arts Review*, vol. 3, no. 4, (winter 1986), pp.66-69.

51. Quoted in E. Blau, op. cit., p.31.

52. C. Maxwell (1936), op. cit., p.155.

53. See 'Building study: Arts facility building, Trin-ity College, Dublin', *AJ: The Architects' Journal*, vol. 170, no. 29, (18 July 1979), pp.121-135.

54. See G. Dawson, 'The Douglas Hyde Gallery', *Irish Arts Review*, vol. 4, no. 4, (winter 1987), pp.39-42.

55. H.V. Morton, *In Search of Ireland*, (London, 1930), p.24.

56. See E. McParland, 'An academic palazzo in Ire-land: The Provost's House, Trinity College, Dublin - I', *Country Life*, vol. CLX, no. 4137, (14 October 1976), pp.1034-7; and 'Cherishing a Palladian masterpiece: The Provost's House, Trinity College, Dublin - II', *Country Life*, vol. CLX, no. 4137, (14 October 1976), pp.1106-9.

57. D. Cruickshank, 'Tracing a Palladio elevation', *The Architectural Review*, vol. CLXXXV, no. 1045, (March 1984), pp.44-47.

58. M. Craig, *Dublin, 1660-1860*, (Dublin, 1952), p.19.

59. J.T. Gilbert, ed., *Calendar of Ancient Records of Dublin*, vol. IV, (Dublin, 1894), p.298.

60. Wesley was not alone in his poor view of the St Stephen's Green houses. In the 1790s James Malton complained about the 'many very indifferent old

brick dwellings', though neither was he impressed by 'the modern plain taste of building'. James Malton, *A Picturesque and Descriptive View of the City of Dublin*, 1799. (Reprinted Dublin, 1978.)

61. E. McParland, 'A note on George II and St Stephen's Green', *Eighteenth-Century Ireland*, vol. 2, (1987), pp.187-195.

62. Quoted in C. Maxwell, *Dublin under the Georges*, (Dublin, 1936), p.257.

63. F. Elrington Ball, ed., *The Correspondence of Jonathan Swift vol. 1*, (London, 1910), p.128.

64. Quoted in N. Burke, 'Dublin, 1600-1800: A study in Urban Morphogenesis' (Ph.D. thesis, University of Dublin, 1972), p.377.

65. N. Sheaff, *Iveagh House: An Historical Description*, (Dublin, 1978), p.11.

66. *Georgian Society Records*, vol. II (1980), pp.48-52.

67. For example when 8 St Stephen's Green was acquired by the Stephen's Green Club 'numerous alterations and additions were made in the house to render it suitable for the purposes of a club'; i.e., throwing two rooms into one to form a large coffee-room, adding two billiard rooms and more bedrooms, creating a new club dining-room and so on. See *Georgian Society Records*, vol. II (1910), p.46.

68. G. Moore, *Hail and Farewell*, vol. II, 'Salve' (London, 1912), p.206. For an assessment of the shopping centre see J. O'Reilly, 'St Stephen's Green Centre', *Irish Architect*, Nn. 69, (November-December 1988), pp.9-13.

69. F. McDonald, *The Destruction of Dublin*, (Dublin, 1985), pp.267-268, 274-276. See also A. O'Toole, 'Dublin's Hottest Property', *Business and Finance*, (22 September 1988), pp.12-15.

70. R.N.C. Vance, 'Text and tradition: Robert Emmet's speech from the Dock', *Studies*, vol. LXXI, (summer 1982), pp.185-90.

71. Quoted in *St Stephen's Green, 1880-1980: A Centenary Booklet*, (Commissioners of Public Works, Dublin, 1980), p.10.

72. M. Craig, op. cit., p.130. See also, The Knight of Glin, 'Richard Castle, architect, his biography and works', *Quarterly Bulletin of the Irish Georgian Society*, vol. VII, no. 1, (January-March 1964), pp.31-38.

73. See F. McDonald, op. cit., pp.255-261.

74. For a description see 'Ardilaun Centre, St. Stephen's Green', *Plan*, vol. 13, no. 13, (October 1982), pp.13-16.

75. K. Doyle in *Sixty Years in Residence*, (Dublin, 1981), p.13,

76. For an architectural appraisal see W. Garner, 'A pair of semi-detached houses', in *Sixty Years in Residence*, op. cit., pp.5-11.

77. F. McGrath, *Newman's University: Idea and Reality*, (Dublin, 1951), p.406. For an account of how Newman went about creating University Church see L. McRedmond, *Thrown among Strangers*, (Dublin, 1990), pp.152-161, and E. Kane, 'John Henry Newman's Catholic University Church in Dublin', *Studies*, vol. LXVI, no. 262, (summer-autumn 1977), p.105-120.

78. N. Sheaff, op. cit., p.21.

79. F. McDonald, op. cit., pp.27-29, 251-252.

80. For architectural commentaries see B. Hogan, 'The Earlsfort Centre: The Goodbody Building', *RIAI Bulletin*, no. 59, (November-December 1986), pp.29-59; and G. Mitchell, 'The Conrad', *Irish Architect*, no. 77, (March-April 1990), pp.28-33.

81. See 'Earlsfort Centre', *Irish Architect*, no.89, (March-April 1992), pp.29-33.

82. F. O'Dwyer, *Lost Dublin*, (Dublin, 1981), p.120.

83. J. Robbins, *The Lost Children: A Study of Charity Children in Ireland, 1700-1900*, (Dublin, 1980), pp.23-28.

84. F. McDonald, op. cit., pp.101-2 and 263-4.

85. *Dáil Debates*, 11 March 1970. For a detailed account of the Hume Street debacle see F. McDonald, op. cit., pp.78-100; see also D. Kelly, 'The lost battle of Hume Street', *The Irish Times*, 7 June 1990.

86. For Hume Street and Ely Place see the *Georgian Society Records*, vol. II (1910), pp.113-127.

CONCLUSION

1. Dan Cruickshank, 'Call this a City of Culture', *The Independent*, 21 November 1990.

2. *The Times*, 23 March 1991.

3. Letter from Kaija Santaholma, Chief Architect of the Finnish Ministry of the Environment, *The Irish Times*, 15 October 1991.

4. *The Irish Times*, 4 January 1992.

5. Dan Cruickshank, op. cit.

6. Niall McCullough, *Dublin, An Urban History*, (Dublin, 1989), p.6.

7. Alistair Rowan, 'The historic city' in Kevin B. Nowlan, Nicholas Robinson and Alistair Rowan, eds., *Dublin's Future: The European Challenge, A Conservation Report for An Taisce*, (Country Life, London, 1980), p.10.

8. Niall McCullough, op. cit.

9. Donald J. Olsen, *The City as a Work of Art: London – Paris – Vienna*, (London, 1986), p.x.